# Quick-Reference Table of Applications

# Merriam-Webster's
# Pocket Guide
# to
# Business
# and
# Everyday
# Math

## Brian Burrell

Merriam-Webster, Incorporated
Springfield, Massachusetts

# A GENUINE MERRIAM-WEBSTER

The name *Webster* alone is no guarantee of excellence. It is used by a number of publishers and may serve mainly to mislead an unwary buyer.

*Merriam-Webster™* is the name you should look for when you consider the purchase of dictionaries and other fine reference books. It carries the reputation of a company that has been publishing since 1831 and is your assurance of quality and authority.

Copyright © 1996 by Brian Burrell
Philippines Copyright 1996 by Brian Burrell
*Library of Congress Cataloging-in-Publication Data*

Burrell, Brian, 1955–
     Merriam-Webster's pocket guide to business and everyday
math / Brian Burrell.
          p.   cm.
     Includes index.
     ISBN 0-87779-505-3 (paper)
     1. Mathematics—Handbooks, manuals, etc.   2. Finance,
Personal—Handbooks, manuals, etc.   I. Title.
QA40.B87   1996
510—dc20
                                    96-20183
                                       CIP

Printed and bound in the United States of America

123456NFWP99989796

# Contents

# Preface

*Merriam-Webster's Pocket Guide to Business and Everyday Math* is a handy reference to the mathematical symbols, concepts, and procedures encountered in everyday life. It rather broadly interprets "mathematics" to mean anything that involves numbers. Thus its scope takes in such numerically oriented activities as shopping, paying bills, renovating a house, reading a map, investing money, paying taxes, and even gambling.

For the sake of clarity, every topic is presented as a series of numbered paragraphs, each of which covers a single concept or definition. Examples are provided in many instances; these are indented and set off with a bullet (•). Mathematical terms, when first presented and defined, appear in bold (e.g., **reciprocal**). Other technical terms are given in italics (e.g., *price/earnings ratio*) when they first appear. Both types of highlighted words appear in the index, and cross-references are also provided. To further enhance the book's utility, a list of practical applications is printed on the first three pages, providing a concise directory to the entire book.

The majority of what most readers will think of as everyday math occurs in Chapters 3, 4, and 5. These chapters, which cover household math, statistics and probability, and business applications, assume the reader is familiar with basic arithmetical procedures such as working with percents or plugging numbers into formulas. Because some readers may need to refresh their memories on some of these points, the rules of numerical computation, including decimals, percents, and fractions, are covered in Chapter 1, while Chapter 2 deals with the concepts of algebra and geometry. The use of simple electronic calculators is also addressed at length in Chapter 1, and here and there in later chapters. In particular, the book describes how a calculator can be used in carrying out complex procedures such as calculating probabilities or compound interest.

The Appendix contains an explanation of mathematical symbols as well as a comprehensive set of conversion tables. Because of the ubiquity of electronic calculators and spreadsheet software, many of the tables found in mathematical reference books are no longer necessary, and are omitted here.

This is more than a helpful reference book. It is intended to show how mathematics is woven into the fabric of everyday life, often in fascinating or unexpected ways. Yet it also has an important underlying premise—that mathematical knowledge is not only useful but essential in making sound judgments, whether in financial, medical, or practical matters.

Stephen J. Perrault assisted with the preparation of illustrations, the text was meticulously proofread by Paul F. Cappellano, and the index was prepared by Robie Grant. The author wishes to thank Mark A. Stevens for his direction of this project, and Frederick C. Mish for his support, and to acknowledge the suggestions and comments contributed by Christopher Burrell, Jon Bushey, Christopher Casale, Ed Malinowski, Jr., Jim Shields, Sean Sutton, and Ed Tornick.

# Chapter 1

# Numbers and Computation

Most everyday uses of mathematics involve numbers. This leads to the perception that anything numerical is mathematical, and vice versa. In fact, the work of theoretical mathematicians involves few if any numbers; for them, the heart of mathematics consists of concepts, rules (theorems), and logic. But for the non-mathematician, mathematical understanding begins with an understanding of quantity, size, amount, and number.

To begin with, *numbers* should be distinguished from *digits*. The ten **digits**—0, 1, 2, 3, 4, 5, 6, 7, 8, 9—are the symbols used in various combinations to represent numbers. Thus a *digit* is a *symbol*, whereas a number is an expression of actual *quantity*.

There are many types of numbers and many terms used to classify them. In this section, the classifications of numbers are defined, and examples are included to show how they are used in everyday settings.

## Number Systems

**1.** The numbers that a child first learns are the **counting numbers** or **natural numbers**: 1, 2, 3, 4, 5, . . .

**2.** The **whole numbers** or **cardinal numbers** consist of the counting numbers and zero: 0, 1, 2, 3, 4, 5, . . .

**3.** The set of **integers** refers to the whole numbers and their additive inverses (the negative counting numbers). This set can be represented as

$$. . . -3, -2, -1, 0, 1, 2, 3, . . .$$

It is often used to label a simple number line.

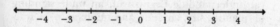

**4.** A **fraction** is a *quotient* of two integers. Fractions are often referred to as **rational numbers** because they are *ratios* of integers. (See pages 41 and 85 for the definitions of *quotient* and *ratio*).

The integer on top is called the **numerator**; the one on the bottom is the **denominator**.

**5.** There are three types of fractions: **simple fractions**, such as ½ or ¾, in which the numerator is less than the denominator; **improper fractions**, such as 11/8 or 43/5, in which the numerator is greater than the denominator; and **mixed numbers**, such as 2½, in which an improper fraction is expressed as a whole number with a simple fractional remainder.

**6.** Fractions and integers do not account for every number on the number line. Between any two fractions there can always be found an **irrational number**, a number that cannot be represented as a fraction. The most common irrational numbers are π *(pi)*, the ratio of a circle's circumference to its diameter; the square root of 2; and the number *e*, which occurs naturally in calculations involving *compound interest* (see Chapter 5).

**7.** The spectrum of numbers outlined above—integers, fractions, and irrational numbers—accounts for every possible value or place on the standard number line, or **real number line**. That is, the **real numbers** consist of the counting numbers, the negative counting numbers, zero, all fractions, and those numbers such as $\sqrt{2}$, $\sqrt{3}$, and $\pi$ that correspond to real places on the number line but cannot be expressed as fractions.

# Representations of Numbers

### DECIMALS

**1.** In **decimal representation**, a number consists of a string of one or more digits occupying place values. The place values represent powers of 10. Thus the number 256 represents 2 *hundreds* plus 5 *tens* plus 6 *ones*. The number 0.075 represents 7 *hundredths* plus 5 *thousandths*.

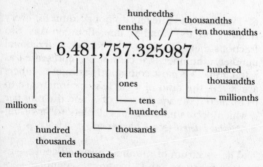

Every real number has a decimal representation. The simplest real numbers—the whole-valued numbers such as −3, −2, −1, 0, 1, 2, 3, etc.—are already in decimal form. To express a fraction as a decimal, divide the denominator into the numerator. This connection between fractions and division is suggested by the division symbol $\div$ which itself resembles a fraction. Thus ½ can be written as $\frac{1}{2}$ or as $1 \div 2$. Its decimal form is 0.5. Notice that the addition of zeros after the last digit to the right of a decimal point does not affect the value of a decimal number. So 0.5 is equivalent to 0.50 or 0.500.

**2.** Fractions can be converted to one of two types of decimals—**terminating decimals** or **repeating decimals**.

- ⅞, or $7 \div 8$, is equivalent to 0.875—a decimal which terminates.

- ⅚, or $5 \div 6$, is equivalent to the decimal number 0.833333 . . . .

The ellipsis ( . . . ) indicates the repetition of the digits. Another way to express repetition is to use a horizontal bar over the digits that repeat.

- ⅓ can be written as $0.\overline{3}$.

- 5⁄12 can be written as 0.416666 . . . , or as $0.41\overline{6}$.

- 4⁄33 can be written as 0.1212121212 . . . , or as $0.\overline{12}$.

**3. Irrational numbers** also have decimal representations, but these decimals are **nonterminating** and **nonrepeating**. This means that a number such as $\sqrt{2}$ has a decimal representation consisting of a string of digits that never repeats a pattern. For practical purposes such decimals are always *rounded off* (see page 22). A scientific calculator, for example, will express $\sqrt{2}$ as 1.41421356. It should be understood that this value is not exact even though it comes from a calculator. The machine can only display nine characters, and thus it *rounds* or *truncates* the decimal. For most computational purposes, however, the calculator's nine decimal places are more than adequate to insure reasonable accuracy.

## PERCENTS AND PERCENTAGES

The word *percent* means "out of one hundred." The percent symbol, %, like the division symbol, represents a quotient. Seventy percent means 70 out of 100, or 70/100, or 0.7. Thus a **percent** describes a portion of an amount by using a scale based on the number 100.

The amount to which a percent is applied is referred to as the **base**, and the number derived from the base is called a **percentage**. In order to find a percentage, multiply the percent times the base amount.

- 25 percent of 120 is written as 25% × 120, or as $^{25}/_{100}$ × 120, which is 30.

Any percent can be expressed as a fraction or as a decimal, and any decimal or fraction can be expressed as a percent.

**1. Finding a Percent** To find what percent one number is of another, divide the percentage by the base.

• After a year of employment, a clerk's salary of \$32,000 is increased by \$1600. \$32,000 is thus the base, and \$1600 represents some percentage of it. The percent increase is $1600 \div 32,000 = \frac{1}{20} = \frac{5}{100} = 5\%$.

**2. Converting a Percent to a Decimal** A percent can be converted to a decimal by moving the decimal point two places to the left and removing the percent sign. In the expression 5%, the implied position of the decimal point is after the 5. That is, 5 is the same as 5.0, and thus 5% is equivalent to 0.05. 86% is equivalent to 0.86. Sometimes decimals (or fractions) and percents are mixed in a single expression. To convert a percent that contains a mixed number (a whole number and a fraction) to a decimal, the mixed number must first be converted to its decimal form.

• $84\frac{1}{2}\%$ is equivalent to 84.5% or 0.845.

• An interest rate of $6\frac{3}{4}\%$ is equivalent to 6.75%, which is equivalent to 0.0675.

**3. Converting a Decimal to a Percent** The rule for converting any number in decimal form to percent form is to move the decimal point two places to the right and write a percent sign.

• 0.35 is the same as 35%.

• 1.6 is 160%.

• 0.015 is 1.5% or $1\frac{1}{2}\%$.

**4. Converting a Repeating Decimal to a Percent** Like an ordinary decimal, a repeating decimal can be converted to a percent by moving the decimal point two places to the right. But this still leaves a repeating decimal, which should not be followed by a percent sign. The repeating part of the decimal can be rounded or truncated (usually after the hundredths' place), or the repeating decimal can be expressed as a fraction. The result will be a **mixed-number percent**.

- 0.666 . . . is equivalent to ⅔. Moving the decimal two places to the right leaves 66.666 . . . , or 66⅔. Thus 0.6̄ is approximately equal to 66.67% and exactly equal to 66⅔%.

**5. Converting a Fraction to a Percent** Fractions should be converted to decimal form before being converted to percent form. Once the decimal point has been moved two places to the right, the decimal can be converted to a fractional percent.

- 1⅜ equals 1.375, which converts to 137.5%, or 137½%.

- Mortgage interest rates are listed in increments of ⅛ of a percent. 7⅜%, for example, is equivalent to 7.325%, which in decimal form is 0.07325.

If a fraction has a repeating decimal representation, the repeating portion of the decimal can be converted back to fraction form after the decimal point has been moved.

- ⅓ equals 0.33̄3̄, which rounds to 33.3%, although it can be expressed exactly as 33⅓%.

**6. Converting a Percent to a Fraction** Because *percent* means "out of 100," any percent can be converted to a fraction by placing it over 100. With a mixed-number percent, the best way to proceed is first to convert to a decimal, and then to a fraction.

- $48\% = {}^{48}\!/_{100}$
- $8\frac{1}{2}\% = 8.5\% = 0.085 = {}^{85}\!/_{1000}$

Table 1.1 lists the most common fraction-decimal-percent equivalents.

**7. Finding a Number Using a Percentage** In general, if $A$ is a percent of $B$, then $A = r \times B$, and $B = A \div r$, where $r$ is the decimal form of the percent.

- In qualifying for a mortgage, a borrower must meet income requirements that are expressed in percent form. Specifically, the monthly cost of the new home must not exceed 28% of the prospective buyer's gross monthly income. If the house would cost $900 each month (including property tax and insurance), then 28% of the borrower's gross monthly income should be at least $900. To find the qualifying gross monthly income, divide $900 by 28% (in decimal form).

$$\$900 \div 0.28 = \$3214.29$$

Multiplying by 12 gives the qualifying annual income: $38,571.43.

**Table 1.1. Common Fractions with Decimal and Percent Equivalents**

| *Fraction* | *Decimal* | *Percent* |
|---|---|---|
| ½ | 0.5 | 50% |
| ¼ | 0.25 | 25% |
| ¾ | 0.75 | 75% |
| ⅓ | $0.33\overline{3}$ | $33\frac{1}{3}\%$ |
| ⅔ | $0.66\overline{6}$ | $66\frac{2}{3}\%$ |
| ⅕ | 0.2 | 20% |
| ⅖ | 0.4 | 40% |
| ⅗ | 0.6 | 60% |
| ⅘ | 0.8 | 80% |
| ⅙ | $0.16\overline{6}$ | $16\frac{2}{3}\%$ |
| ⅚ | $0.83\overline{3}$ | $83\frac{1}{3}\%$ |
| ⅛ | 0.125 | $12\frac{1}{2}\%$ |
| ⅜ | 0.375 | $37\frac{1}{2}\%$ |
| ⅝ | 0.625 | $62\frac{1}{2}\%$ |
| ⅞ | 0.875 | $87\frac{1}{2}\%$ |
| ⅒ | 0.1 | 10% |
| 1⁄12 | $0.083\overline{3}$ | $8\frac{1}{3}\%$ |
| 1⁄16 | 0.0625 | $6\frac{1}{4}\%$ |

**8.** A **percentile** is a means of establishing a rank or position within a group. Technically, the word *percentile* refers to one subdivision of an ordered group that has been divided into 100 equal parts. But in its everyday sense, a percentile separates a large group or population that has been divided according to some criterion into two subgroups. The 95th percentile, for example, divides a set of scores or numbers into a top 5% and a bottom 95%. The term *95th percentile* is used to specify the top 5%.

- A group of 100 people is arranged in order of age from youngest to oldest. The oldest 25% (the last 25 people in the line) are referred to as the *75th percentile* because 75% of the group is younger.

**9.** The *50th percentile* divides an ordered group in half. The term used to describe the cutoff point of the 50th percentile is **median** (see page 203). In a group of scores ordered from lowest to highest, half fall above the median and half below. The 50th percentile of the group refers to the upper half.

**10.** The 75th percentile can also be referred to as the top **quartile**. In any sample of test scores—on the SAT, GRE, MCAT, or LSAT exams, for example—there are four quartiles, which divide all scores into a top 25%, bottom 25%, and two middle 25% groups, which are called the **interquartile range**.

**11.** If an ordered group is divided into fifths, each fifth is referred to as a **quintile**. A group broken into quintiles consists of five equal divisions of 20 percent each.

- "Between 1980 and 1989 federal tax rates paid by the bottom three quintiles of the income distribution rose, while tax rates declined for those in the top two quintiles." Notice that this statement divides the taxpaying population into the bottom ⅗ and the top ⅖, which together constitute the entire population. The statement says nothing about actual amounts; instead it refers to relative amounts: ⅗ (or 60%) of the whole group versus ⅖ (or 40%) of the group.

**12.** Beyond quartiles and quintiles, the most commonly used division of ordered scores or numerical data is the **decile**, which refers to one of 10 equal divisions of 10%.

## APPLICATIONS OF DECIMALS AND PERCENTS

In mathematics, the word "of" almost always means multiplication. Consequently, 50% of $100 is $50, because 50% is equivalent to ½, and ½ of 100 is 50. A "percent of" some number or amount is called a **percentage**.

• In pari-mutuel betting, a racetrack takes 15% of all the money wagered on a particular race, and distributes the rest as winnings. If $18,000 is bet on a particular race, the track's percentage is 0.15 × 18,000, or $2700.

**1. Points and Basis Points** In financial markets, percentages are referred to in terms of **points**. For home mortgages, a **point** is prepaid interest in the amount of 1% of the amount borrowed. In the stock and bond markets, a **basis point** refers to

¹⁄₁₀₀ of 1% of the yield (or interest rate of earnings) of an investment. 100 basis points equals 1%; thus one basis point equals ¹⁄₁₀₀ of 1%.

- If the yield of a 30-year treasury bond climbs 25 basis points in one day's trading, then the interest rate rose ²⁵⁄₁₀₀ percent, which is ¼ of a percent.

**2. Majority and Plurality** The terms *majority* and *plurality* arise most often in connection with political elections and polls, or with demographic studies. The **majority** of a group is any subgroup that constitutes more than 50% (or half) of the group. In a vote or study in which people divide into two unequal groups, the larger group is the majority. However, if a population is divided into more than two groups, none of which accounts for more than half of the total (meaning that none of the groups constitutes a majority), the largest group is called a **plurality**. A plurality can also refer to the amount by which the largest group exceeds the next largest group in size.

- In the 1992 presidential election Bill Clinton received 42.95% of the popular vote, followed by 37.40% for George Bush, 18.86% for Ross Perot, and less than 1% for other candidates. Presidents are not elected by popular vote (in fact, two presidents—Hayes and Harrison—were elected despite losing the popular vote), but in this case the plurality voted for Clinton. Only 55.9% of eligible voters actually cast votes in the election. Thus President Clinton received the votes of about 24% of the voting-age population (because 42.95% of 55.9% equals 0.4295 × 0.559, which is 0.24, or 24%—a plurality, but not a majority).

**3. Tipping** Tips for service are calculated either as a flat fee (for valet parking or coat checking) or as a percentage of a bill. A standard tip is 15% of the pretax total for good service, and 20% of the bill for exceptional service. In most situations, tips must be computed mentally and quickly, and therefore certain rules of thumb can be useful.

In states where the meal tax is 5%, triple the amount of the tax listed on the check in order to compute a 15% tip. (Note: Unfortunately, this method will result in a disappointingly low tip in states where the alcohol tax is already included in the menu price—that is, where the meal tax is based on the price of the food but not on the drinks.) An alternative is to compute 10% of the pretax total (a simple matter of moving the decimal point one place to the left) and add half of that amount again.

- You want to add a 15% tip to the following restaurant check:

  | | |
  |---|---|
  | food and drink total | $31.55 |
  | tax (on food only) | 1.53 |
  | total | $33.08 |

First, round the pretax total upward to $32. Ten percent of $32 is $3.20, to which half is added:

3.20 + 1.60 = \$4.80. The tip should be about
\$5.00. Since the check totals just over \$33, it would
be reasonable to leave \$38. In each of these cal-
culations, the totals are rounded *up*, which errs on
the side of generosity. By rounding the pretax food
and drink total up, the tip is certain to be at least
15%.

**4. Sales Tax/Meal Tax** The taxability of various
types of purchases differs from state to state. While
food purchased in grocery stores is usually not
taxed, food served in restaurants generally is
(though listed prices occasionally include the tax).
Nonfood items sold in food stores are usually subject to state sales tax. Consider the following grocery-store receipt:

| | |
|---|---|
| cookies | \$2.49 |
| milk | 1.12 |
| eggs | 0.99 |
| apples | 2.53 |
| wax paper | 1.98 |
| liquid detergent | 3.49 |
| subtotal | 12.60 |
| tax | 0.27 |
| total | 12.87 |

The tax amounts to 5% of the cost of the nonfood
items: $0.05 \times (1.98 + 3.49) = 0.2735$, which
rounds to 27 cents.

  A 5% sales tax or meal tax is typical, but the
percentage varies from state to state and from

country to country. As a benchmark, 5% can easily be calculated as half of 10%. Thus 5% of $25.89, for example, is half of 2.589, or about $1.30.

**5. Discounts** A sale sign will often make a claim such as: "UP TO 60% OFF." In theory, this means that as much as 60% (or three fifths) of a tagged price will be deducted from that price at the register (before sales tax is computed) for selected items. This deduction is called a *discount*.

- A pair of shoes that lists for $145 is advertised at 60% off. The discount is 60% of $145, or $0.60 \times 145 = \$87.00$. Thus the cost of the shoes will be $145 - 87 = \$58$, plus tax if applicable.

Another way to compute the sale price (as opposed to the amount of the discount) is to subtract the percent discount from 100 and multiply the result by the list price.

- A $65 shirt is advertised at 30% off. It will cost 70% of $65, which is $45.50.

**6. Markups** A *markup* is a fraction (or percentage) of a base price that is added on to the base price. Markups are generally not advertised as enthusiastically as discounts. They arise in the case of difficult-to-obtain items (such as popular car models) or products that require a considerable amount of extra service to deliver to the market. A markup usually occurs in the transition from wholesaler to retailer, and again in the transition from retailer to consumer. But some retailers will mark up a suggested retail price yet again if the demand is sufficient.

- A popular sports car is priced for the national market at \$15,500 with no options. Because of demand, a local dealer marks this price up 6%. The amount of the markup is 6% of 15,500, or $0.06 \times 15,500 = \$930$. Thus the local market price is $\$15,500 + 930 = \$16,430$. This represents $(100 + 6)\%$, or 106%, of the original base price.

*Note:* A 25% markup followed by a 25% reduction does not restore the original price. This is because the base amount changes. A simple example shows that this is true in general for all percent changes.

- A \$1000 snowblower is marked up 25% so that its price increases by $0.25 \times 100 = \$250$, to become \$1250. The price is then marked down 25%. But 25% of \$1250 is $0.25 \times 1250 = \$312.50$. The adjusted price is $\$1250 - 312.50 = \$937.50$. By the same token, a 25% decrease in price followed by a 25% increase in price would result in a net loss in price.

**7. Inflation**  The *rate of inflation* reflects the buying power of one dollar, which tends to diminish with the passage of time. The process is not irreversible, but the prevailing trend in most countries is for prices to steadily rise over time. (The word *inflation* is meant to describe a long-term trend. A seasonal trend such as the rising price of gasoline in the summer months is not considered inflationary because the price declines to normal levels in the fall.)

The amount of the average inflationary increase in prices is marked each year by a number referred to as an *index*. In its mathematical sense, an index is a percent, ratio, or reference number that is used to measure the growth or decline of a quantity over a given time period. In the case of inflation, the U.S. Department of Labor regularly calculates a *cost of living index* known as the *Consumer Price Index* (or *CPI*). This index reflects changes in the market prices of a wide range of commodities (food, clothing, and household supplies mostly), and thus measures the cost of living for an average consumer. The *Producer Price Index* (or *PPI*) measures the cost of goods to producers. Because these costs ultimately filter down to the consumer, the PPI is a *leading indicator*, and tracks changes that show up later in the CPI.

The CPI and PPI, like all indexes, are numbers that have no intrinsic meaning, but are used to indicate *percent change over time*. This increase or decrease is called *relative change*.

• If the price of a gallon of orange juice increases from $1.79 to $1.89 in one year, the increase is 10 cents. The *relative change* is the increase divided by the original price. Here the original price is 179 cents, so the relative increase is 10/179, which is about 0.056, or 5.6%.

An index can be used to find the percent change between any two years. In Table 1.2 below, the CPI values for the years 1970 and 1990 are 38.8

**9. After-Tax Earnings** Earnings on stock-market investments, as well as interest earned on bank accounts, constitute taxable income (unless the money is tax-sheltered, as explained in Chapter 5). Consequently, the earnings after taxes—the net earnings—will be reduced somewhat. To calculate the after-tax earnings as a percent of the amount invested, use this formula:

$$rate\ of\ return\ (after\ taxes) = i \times (1 - t)$$

where $i$ is the annual percent interest earned (or annual yield), and $t$ is the tax rate.

- An investor in a 28% tax bracket earns 15% in one year in a mutual fund. The after-tax rate of return is

$$5\% \times (1 - 28\%) = 0.15 \times (1 - 0.28) = 0.108$$
$$= 10.8\%$$

## ounding Off

re are several schemes for deriving an approx-
ed or rounded value. These are employed
ever a number is more precise than is nec-
y for the purpose it is intended to serve, or
the accuracy of a number is in doubt. To
rstand how these schemes work, it is useful
ine the idea of a **significant digit**.

he decimal representation of a number, all
o digits are significant. Zeros at the begin-

and 130.5, respectively. The change is $130.5 - 38.9 = 91.6$. The *percent change* is $91.6/38.9$, which is 2.35, or about 235%. This means that prices have more than tripled over this period.

**Table 1.2. Consumer Price Indexes and Producer Price Indexes**

| Year | PPI | CPI | Year | PPI | CPI |
|------|------|------|------|-------|-------|
| 1950 | 28.2 | 24.1 | 1972 | 41.8 | 41.8 |
| 1951 | 30.8 | 26.0 | 1973 | 45.6 | 44.4 |
| 1952 | 30.6 | 26.6 | 1974 | 52.6 | 49.3 |
| 1953 | 30.3 | 26.8 | 1975 | 58.5 | 53.8 |
| 1954 | 30.4 | 26.9 | 1976 | 60.8 | 56.9 |
| 1955 | 30.5 | 26.8 | 1977 | 64.7 | 60.6 |
| 1956 | 31.3 | 27.2 | 1978 | 69.8 | 65.3 |
| 1957 | 32.5 | 28.2 | 1979 | 77.6 | 72.5 |
| 1958 | 33.2 | 28.9 | 1980 | 88.0 | 82.3 |
| 1959 | 33.1 | 29.1 | 1981 | 96.1 | 91.1 |
| 1960 | 33.4 | 29.6 | 1982 | 100.0 | 96.6 |
| 1961 | 33.4 | 29.9 | 1983 | 101.6 | 99.7 |
| 1962 | 33.5 | 30.3 | 1984 | 103.7 | 104.1 |
| 1963 | 33.4 | 30.6 | 1985 | 104.7 | 107.8 |
| 1964 | 33.5 | 31.0 | 1986 | 103.2 | 109.5 |
| 1965 | 34.1 | 31.6 | 1987 | 105.4 | 113.6 |
| 1966 | 35.2 | 32.5 | 1988 | 108.0 | 118.2 |
| 1967 | 35.6 | 33.4 | 1989 | 113.6 | 123.9 |
| 1968 | 36.6 | 34.8 | 1990 | 119.2 | 130.5 |
| 1969 | 38.0 | 36.7 | 1991 | 121.7 | 136.2 |
| 1970 | 39.3 | 38.9 | 1992 | 123.2 | 140.2 |
| 1971 | 40.5 | 40.6 | 1993 | 124.7 | 144.5 |

An inflation rate of 4% per year means that an item priced at $100 at the beginning of the year would cost $104 at year's end. This would correspond to an index value of 100 at the beginning of the year and 104 at year's end.

**8. Constant Dollars** Increments to salaries and hourly wages are usually measured against the rate of inflation. If a salary does not increase by at least the same percentage as the inflation rate, then the employee's buying power goes down—he or she cannot buy as much as in the previous year. The use of the terms *real dollars, real wages,* or *constant dollars* reflects the fact that the buying power of a dollar changes over time, and therefore comparing today's dollars to last year's dollars requires an unchanging unit of measure. Thus "dollars" are fixed to a particular time, and are identified as "today's dollars," "1920 dollars," and so on. The term *current dollars* refers to the face value of the amount that changes hands in a transaction.

- "Since 1979, the real wages of high school dropouts have declined by 20%." This statement is about buying power, and not about actual numbers. It could be that the average wage of high school dropouts remained constant in those years, while inflation rose 20% since 1979.

Table 1.3 shows the buying power of a dollar from 1950 to 1995. The 1950 column shows that

**Table 1.3. The Value of a Current Dollar (Real Dollars in Decade Years)**

| Year | 1950 $ | 1960 $ | 1970 $ | 1980 $ | 1990 $ |
|------|--------|--------|--------|--------|--------|
| 1950 | 1 | 1.23(.81) | 1.61(.62) | 3.42(.29) | 5.42(.18) |
| 1955 | .90(1.11) | 1.11(.90) | 1.45(.69) | 3.07(.33) | 4.87(.21) |
| 1960 | .81(1.23) | 1 | 1.31(.76) | 2.78(.36) | 4.40(.23) |
| 1965 | .76(1.31) | .94(1.06) | 1.23(.81) | 2.61(.38) | 4.13(.24) |
| 1970 | .62(1.61) | .76(1.31) | 1 | 2.12(.47) | 3.36(.3 |
| 1975 | .45(2.23) | .55(1.81) | .72(1.38) | 1.53(.65) | 2.43(. |
| 1980 | .29(3.42) | .36(2.78) | .47(2.12) | 1 | 1.59( |
| 1985 | .22(4.47) | .28(3.63) | .36(2.77) | .76(1.31) | 1.21 |
| 1990 | .18(5.42) | .23(2.54) | .30(3.36) | .63(1.59) | 1 |
| 1995 | .16(6.38) | .19(5.18) | .25(3.95) | .54(1.87) | .8 |

the buying power of a 1950 dollar declin cents by 1995. That is, a dollar stashed mattress in 1950 would purchase in 1995 of what it could have purchased in 1950 bers in parentheses are multipliers. T row shows that a 1950 dollar had 6.9 buying power of a 1995 dollar, a 196 5.18 times the buying power, and so

Another way to use the table is t aries. The 1995 equivalent of a $20 ary in 1970 is found by reading column to the year 1995. The n Multiplying $20,000 by 3.95 giv 1995 annual salary of $79,000.

The values in the table are sumer Price Index. The figur mates.

*R*

The ima whe essar whe unde to def

*1.* In non-ze

ning of a number are not significant, but any zeros between other digits or at the end of a decimal number are significant.

- 17.4 has three significant digits. Therefore, as a measurement it is closer to 17.4 than to either 17.3 or 17.5.

- 17.40 has four significant digits. Thus it is closer to 17.40 than to either 17.39 or 17.41.

- 0.0174 has three significant digits.

- 0.01074 has four significant digits.

In a whole number, zeros at the end may or may not be significant, depending on the context.

- A crowd at a demonstration was estimated to be 15,000 people. This figure has two significant digits.

- The paid attendance at a baseball game was *exactly* 23,700. Because this figure is understood to be exact, the zeros are significant. The figure has five significant digits.

Each significant digit establishes the degree of accuracy in the preceding decimal place. Thus the first 0 in 1,503,000 is a significant digit because its own degree of accuracy is established by the 3 that follows it. However, the first 0 in 1,500,000 may or may not be a significant digit.

**2. Truncating and Rounding Down** The simplest method of rounding off is by **truncation**. This method generally applies to the part of a decimal number that lies to the right of the decimal point. **Truncating** a number means eliminating all of the significant digits beyond a certain place value. In the case of a mixed number, truncation involves eliminating the fractional part of the number.

- If a scientific calculator truncates numbers that have more than 10 significant digits, a repeating decimal such as 0.$\overline{12}$ would appear as 0.1212121212.

- The number 5⅔ can be truncated to 5 by eliminating the fraction.

The process of truncating at or to the left of the decimal point is referred to as rounding down. In **rounding down**, the last significant digits are replaced by zeros.

- 75,648 can be rounded down to 75,000.

**3. Rounding to the Nearest** In any measurement, the last significant digit is the least certain digit because the digit that would follow it (if a more precise measurement were possible) is unknown. But any significant digit can be used to round a number to the decimal place that precedes it. There are several ways this can be done. The most common method is called **rounding to the nearest**, which means rounding to the nearest designated significant digit.

- An interest payment is calculated by a bank to be 15.63758 dollars, which must be rounded to the nearest cent. In this instance, the "3" in the cents' position is followed by a "7", which indicates that the "3" should be rounded up to a "4", making the interest payment $15.64.

**4. Rounding to the Nearest Even Digit** When the last significant digit is 5, it is arbitrary whether to round the previous digit up or down. The standard practice is to *round to the nearest even digit*. This assures that, in a list of numbers, about half of such decisions result in rounding up and the other half in rounding down.

• 645 rounded to the nearest ten would be 640, whereas 375 rounded to the nearest ten would be 380. In this instance 645 rounds down while 375 rounds up.

# Sequences of Numbers

Certain sequences of numbers, because of their usefulness or familiarity, have acquired specific names. The **odd numbers** (1, 3, 5, 7, 9, . . . ) and the **even numbers** (0, 2, 4, 6, 8, 10, . . . ) are the most commonly encountered sequences. Both of these are examples of *arithmetic sequences*.

**1.** An **arithmetic sequence** is a list of numbers in which each number (or **term**) is derived from the preceding number by adding a constant value to it. That is, there is a common difference between any two successive terms of an arithmetic sequence.

- The common difference between even numbers is 2.

- The sequence 5, 10, 15, 20, 25, . . . is an arithmetic sequence with a common difference of 5.

- The sequence 3.5, 7, 10.5, 14, 17.5, . . . is an arithmetic sequence with a common difference of 3.5.

**2.** A **geometric sequence** is a list of numbers in which each term is derived from the previous term by *multiplying* by a fixed constant value (called a **ratio**). A common geometric sequence is: 1, 2, 4, 8, 16, 32, 64, . . . , in which the ratio is 2.

- The sequence 1, ⅔, 4/9, 8/27, 16/81, . . . is a geometric sequence. Its ratio is ⅔.

# Infinity and Infinitesimal

One of the most important and subtle concepts in all of mathematics is the idea of **infinity**. The symbol for infinity, ∞, while often thought of as the largest number, is not a number at all. It is best thought of as the numerical process of *increasing without bound*. Thus any quantity said to be infinitely large is one that cannot be contained within any boundary, and is not exceeded by any given number. A quantity which is said to be "infinitely small," or **infinitesimal**, is smaller than any number or dimension that can be named.

These concepts are necessary in order to describe the attributes of the real number line and of the real number system. Because the number line has no end in either direction, it is infinite. The idea of infinity is used to indicate the process of moving along the number line indefinitely to the right. Thus there are an infinite number of real numbers, an infinite number of counting numbers, an infinite number of odd numbers, and so on. In fact, there are an infinite number of real numbers between 0 and 1. This can be demonstrated by choosing any two numbers, no matter how close. Between the two, another number can always be found (their average, for example). This process can be repeated indefinitely.

# Arithmetic Operations

## ADDITION AND SUBTRACTION

The four basic operations of arithmetic—**addition**, **subtraction**, **multiplication**, and **division**—are associated with the four symbols: $+$, $-$, $\times$, $\div$. Although these are the standard symbols seen on simple four-function calculators, they are not the only symbols used to represent these operations. Moreover, the symbols for addition and subtraction—the plus and minus signs—are used for other purposes that can sometimes cause confusion.

**1. The Addition Sign: +** This symbol is used to indicate that two numbers are to be added together. Order is unimportant. Thus $a + b$ is the same as $b + a$. Also, if three or more numbers are to be added together, the way in which they are combined is arbitrary. Thus $a + b + c$ can be calculated as the sum $(a + b)$ added to $c$, or as the number $a$ added to the sum $(b + c)$. (Parentheses indicate that the enclosed figures are to be treated as a unit.)

The word used to describe the interchangeability in the order of an operation is **commutativity**. Addition is said to be *commutative* because $a + b$ produces the same sum as $b + a$.

The property describing the arbitrariness of grouping is called **associativity**. Addition is said to be *associative* because $(a + b) + c$ produces the same sum as $a + (b + c)$.

- $4 + 7 + 3$ can be written as $(4 + 7) + 3$ or as $4 + (7 + 3)$. The first sum is $11 + 3$, whereas the second is $4 + 10$. In both cases the final sum is the same.

**2. The Subtraction Sign: −** The minus sign indicates that one quantity is to be subtracted from another. In using this symbol, order is important. In other words, the operation of subtraction is *not* commutative. Thus $a - b$ does not equal $b - a$. Subtraction is also *not* associative, which means that the grouping of subtracted quantities is not arbitrary.

• The compound difference $35 - 14 - 6$ is meant to be read from left to right. First subtract the 14 from 35 to get 21, then subtract 6. Thus $35 - 14 - 6 = (35 - 14) - 6 = 21 - 6 = 15$. Notice that if 6 is subtracted from 14 first, the result would be $35 - (14 - 6)$, or $35 - 8$, or 27, which is incorrect.

Subtraction can be thought of as a shift along the number line. The minus sign, like the plus sign, indicates direction.

• $22 - 11$ indicates a position that is 11 units to the *left* of 22 on a number line. The result is 11.

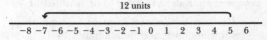

11 units

10  11  12  13  14  15  16  17  18  19  20  21  22  23

• $5 - 12$ indicates a position that is 12 units to the left of 5 on a number line. The result is $-7$.

12 units

$-8$  $-7$  $-6$  $-5$  $-4$  $-3$  $-2$  $-1$  0  1  2  3  4  5  6

**3.** The last example indicates another use of the minus sign. A minus sign before an isolated number or symbol indicates an **additive inverse**. The additive inverse of a number is another number which, when added to the first number, gives the value 0. Thus the additive inverse of a positive number is a negative number, and vice versa.

- The additive inverse of 9 is −9 (read "minus 9").

- The additive inverse of −14 is 14.

## 4. Adding and Subtracting Negative Numbers

Adding a negative number is equivalent to subtracting its additive inverse.

- 5 + (−9) is equivalent to 5 − 9, which equals −4.

Subtracting a negative number is equivalent to adding its additive inverse.

- 24 − (−14) is equivalent to 24 + 14, which equals 38.

## 5. Converting Fractions

In order for two fractions to be added or subtracted, they must first have the same denominator. Changing a fraction into an equivalent fraction with a particular denominator involves multiplying the original numerator and denominator by the same number. Thus the fraction ½ is equivalent to ²⁄₄ or ³⁄₆ or ⁴⁄₈ or ⁵⁄₁₀ or ⁶⁄₁₂.

- ²¹⁄₃₅ can be derived from ³⁄₅ by multiplying both numerator and denominator by 7.

- The fraction ⅔ can be converted to twelfths by multiplying numerator and denominator by 4.

$$\frac{2}{3} \times \frac{4}{4} = \frac{8}{12}$$

## 6. Common Denominators

The addition or subtraction of fractions with different denominators requires converting both fractions to equivalent fractions having the same (common) denominators. The product of the two denominators will serve as a **common denominator**, but may not be the *lowest* common denominator. The lowest common denominator is a multiple of each denominator, and is the smallest such number. This is also called the **least common multiple** of the denominators.

- The least common multiple of 5 and 7 is 35.
- The least common multiple of 12 and 18 is 36.

**7. Adding and Subtracting Fractions** To add two fractions with common denominators, add the numerators and place this sum over the common denominator.

- $\frac{5}{6} + \frac{11}{6} = \frac{5 + 11}{6} = \frac{16}{6}$, which reduces to $\frac{8}{3}$, or $2\frac{2}{3}$.

To subtract two fractions with common denominators, subtract one numerator from the other, and retain the common denominator.

- $\frac{11}{12} - \frac{7}{12} = \frac{11 - 7}{12} = \frac{4}{12}$, or $\frac{1}{3}$

To add or subtract fractions with unequal denominators, convert to equivalent fractions with common denominators, and add or subtract the numerators.

- $\frac{2}{3} + \frac{4}{5}$ converts to $\frac{2}{3} \times \frac{5}{5} + \frac{4}{5} \times \frac{3}{3}$, or $\frac{10}{15} + \frac{12}{15}$, which equals $\frac{22}{15}$.

- $\frac{3}{4} - \frac{11}{7}$ converts to $\frac{3}{4} \times \frac{7}{7} - \frac{11}{7} \times \frac{4}{4}$, or $\frac{21}{28} - \frac{44}{28}$, which equals $\frac{-23}{28}$.

## MULTIPLICATION AND DIVISION

**1. The Multiplication Sign: ×, \*, ·** There are many ways to indicate the multiplication of two numbers or quantities. The best-known of these, the cross, is perhaps the least used in practice. Far more common is the centered dot ·, and even the asterisk \*, which is used in computer programming and is seen on some electronic calculator screens. Perhaps the most common indicator of multiplication is no symbol at all.

- The circumference of a circle whose radius is r units is given by the expression $2\pi r$, which means $2 \times \pi \times r$.

**2.** Multiplication is nothing more than repeated addition. The sum $a + a + a + a$ can be expressed as $4 \times a$, $4 * a$, $4 \cdot a$, or simply as $4a$, and an ungainly expression such as $4 + 4 + 4 + 4 + 4$ is more succinctly expressed as $5 \times 4$, $5 * 4$, or $5 \cdot 4$.

**3.** Like addition, the operation of multiplication is both *commutative* and *associative*. This means that

$a \times b$ is equal to $b \times a$ for any values of $a$ and $b$. It also means that when multiplying three or more numbers, the way in which the numbers are grouped does not affect the final outcome. $5 \times 4 \times 3$ can be thought of as $(5 \times 4) \times 3$ or as $5 \times (4 \times 3)$; the result is the same.

Although $5 \times a$ equals $a \times 5$, the convention is to write the product as $5a$ rather than $a5$. In general: *Numbers that multiply letters are written first.*

**4. The Division Sign:** ÷ Like the multiplication symbol described above, the standard symbol for division is rarely encountered in everyday settings. The fractional form is generally preferred as a means of indicating the division of one value by another. Thus $12 \div 4$ would appear as $\frac{12}{4}$.

**5.** Division is the opposite (or **inverse**) of multiplication. Because of this, every multiplication can be written in the form of a division, and vice versa.

- $12 \div 4$ is equivalent to $12 \times \frac{1}{4}$.

- $25 \times 3$ is equivalent to $25 \div \frac{1}{3}$.

**6.** The **multiplicative inverse** of any number other than 0 is found by dividing that number into 1. Consequently, any number multiplied by its multiplicative inverse gives the result 1.

- The multiplicative inverse of 5 is $\frac{1}{5}$; thus $5 \times (\frac{1}{5}) = 1$.

Another word for the multiplicative inverse is **reciprocal**. The **reciprocal** of any counting number is 1 over that number.

- The reciprocal of 12 is $\frac{1}{12}$.

- The reciprocal of $-10$ is $\frac{1}{-10}$, which is the same as $-\frac{1}{10}$.

**7.** The reciprocal of a simple fraction can be found by flipping it.

- The reciprocal of $\frac{2}{3}$ is $\frac{3}{2}$.

- The reciprocal of $-\frac{4}{5}$ is $\frac{5}{-4}$, or $-\frac{5}{4}$.

**8.** The reciprocal of a mixed number can be found by first converting it to an improper fraction and then flipping it.

- The mixed number $5\frac{2}{3}$ is equivalent to $\frac{17}{3}$. Thus its reciprocal is $\frac{3}{17}$.

**9. Multiplying Fractions** To multiply two simple fractions, multiply their numerators and denominators separately. To multiply two mixed numbers, first convert to improper fractions, then multiply numerators and denominators.

- The product of $\frac{2}{5}$ and $\frac{7}{6}$ is $\frac{2 \times 7}{5 \times 6}$ or $\frac{14}{30}$, which reduces to $\frac{7}{15}$.

- The product of $3\frac{1}{4}$ and $5\frac{2}{3}$ is the same as the product of $\frac{13}{4}$ and $\frac{17}{3}$. The result is

$$\frac{13 \times 17}{4 \times 3} \text{ or } \frac{221}{12}, \text{ which can be expressed as } 18^5/_{12}.$$

**10. Dividing by a Fraction** To divide by a fraction is the same as to multiply by the reciprocal of that fraction.

- $2 \div \frac{1}{4} = 2 \times 4 = 8$

The idea of dividing by a fraction is conceptually more challenging than the idea of dividing by a whole number. Dividing by 2 means dividing into two equal parts. Dividing by 5 means dividing into 5 equal parts. Yet the interpretation of dividing by ¼ is not so clear. Consequently, it helps to think of division as an operation which determines how many times one number is *contained in* a second number.

For instance, the example above asks how many fourths are contained in two units. It might help to picture this procedure by visualizing the problem of finding how many quarts there are in 2 gallons. This is equivalent to dividing 2 gallons into ¼ gallons (or quarts), which in turn is the same as dividing 2 by ¼. There are 4 quarts in a gallon, and thus 2 × 4 or 8 quarts in 2 gallons. The same idea can be conveyed by asking how many quarters there are in two dollars.

**11.** To facilitate multiplying or dividing an integer by a fraction or a fraction by an integer, the integer can be expressed in fractional form by using

1 as its denominator. Thus 5 can be written as $\frac{5}{1}$.

- $\frac{7}{8} \div 5$ is equivalent to $\frac{7}{8} \div \frac{5}{1}$, or $\frac{7}{8} \times \frac{1}{5}$, which equals $\frac{7 \times 1}{8 \times 5}$, or $\frac{7}{40}$.

**12. Multiplication Shortcuts; The Distributive Law** With the advent of affordable pocket-sized calculators, the need to mentally compute or estimate sums, differences, products, and quotients has diminished, although it has not disappeared. The ability to calculate mentally is largely a matter of practice; knowing certain basic rules, one of which is the **distributive law**, can make the process much easier.

In symbols, the **distributive law of multiplication over addition** says the following:

$$a \cdot (b + c) = a \cdot b + a \cdot c$$

and

$$(a + b) \cdot (c + d) = a \cdot (c + d) + b \cdot (c + d)$$
$$= a \cdot c + a \cdot d + b \cdot c + b \cdot d$$

The usefulness of this rule relies on the ease of multiplying by powers of 10, by multiples of 10, or multiples of 5.

- The product $7 \times 15$ can be thought of as $7 \times (10 + 5)$, or 7 *tens* plus 7 *fives*. In symbols, this can be written as

$$7 \times 15 = (7 \times 10) + (7 \times 5) = 70 + 35 = 105$$

- The product $27 \times 41$ is close to $27 \times 40$, which is equivalent to 20 *forties* plus 7 *forties*.

$$27 \times 40 = (20 + 7) \times 40 = (20 \times 40) + (7 \times 40)$$
$$= 800 + 280 = 1080$$

- To find how close this is to $27 \times 41$, notice that

$$27 \times 41 = 27 \times (40 + 1) = (27 \times 40) + 27 \times 1$$
$$= 1080 + 27 = 1107$$

Thus the original estimate was low by 27.

## DIVISIBILITY

Searching for factors of a given whole number (that is, numbers that can be multiplied together to produce the number) is a matter of investigating its **divisibility**. One number is **divisible** by another when the second number is contained in the first a whole-valued number of times—that is, when dividing the first number by the second leaves no remainder. The simplest divisibility test is for divisibility by 2. Any even number (a whole number whose last digit is 0, 2, 4, 6, or 8) is divisible by 2. If the sum of the digits of a whole number is divisible by three, then so is the number itself. If the last two digits of a whole number, taken together, are divisible by 4, so is the entire number. A number whose last digit is 0 or 5 is divisible by 5.

These and other divisibility tests are summarized below in Table 1.4.

### Table 1.4. Divisibility Tests

*A whole number is divisible by* — *if*

| A whole number is divisible by | if |
|---|---|
| 2 | its last digit is 0, 2, 4, 6, 8. |
| 3 | its digits sum to a number divisible by three. (If the sum is too large to determine divisibility by 3, sum *its* digits and check again. Repeat the process as necessary.) |
| 4 | its last two digits, taken together as a single number, are divisible by 4. |
| 5 | its last digit is 0 or 5. |
| 6 | it passes the tests for divisibility by both 2 and 3. |
| 8 | its last three digits, taken as a single number, are divisible by 8. |
| 9 | the sum of the digits is divisible by 9. |
| 10 | the last digit is 0. |
| 12 | it passes the tests for divisibility by both 3 and 4. |

**1.** When the only factors of a number are 1 and the number itself, the number is called a **prime number**. Some examples of prime numbers are 2, 3, 5, 7, 11, 13, 17, 19, and 23.

**2.** Every counting number can be expressed as a product of prime numbers in exactly one way. This is called a **prime factorization**. The prime factorization of any number is found by splitting it into factors, then splitting its factors into factors until all factors are prime numbers. Below are a few examples of this process.

- $42 = 6 \cdot 7 = 2 \cdot 3 \cdot 7$
- $315 = 3 \cdot 105 = 3 \cdot 5 \cdot 21 = 3 \cdot 3 \cdot 5 \cdot 7$
- $780 = 2 \cdot 390 = 2 \cdot 2 \cdot 195 = 2 \cdot 2 \cdot 5 \cdot 39$
  $= 2 \cdot 2 \cdot 3 \cdot 5 \cdot 13$

**3. Divisibility Tests** Much mental calculation can be aided by a knowledge of powers and multiples of 10, and by a good grasp of the multiplication table. Furthermore, understanding multiplication is the key to understanding division. For example, *unit pricing* (cost per gallon, per pound, per 100 count, etc.) depends on the ability to mentally carry out short division. Although supermarkets post these unit prices, they do not always do so in the same units with comparable items. Some liquids may be priced in dollars per ounce, while other are priced in dollars per quart. Some suggestions for mentally calculating sums are given on pages 36–37 under "Multiplication Shortcuts". In addition, Table 1.4 provides some divisibility tests that may be useful in calculating ratios and other quotients.

■ **A RULE OF THUMB FOR BALANCING THE BOOKS** In any sum of numbers, a transposition error—one that involves reversing the order of digits—creates a discrepancy that

is divisible by 9. For example, the numbers 37
and 73 differ by 36, which is divisible by 9. The
numbers 327 and 732 differ by 405, which is
divisible by 9. (Recall that a number is divisible
by 9 if its digits sum to a number that is divisible
by 9.)

# The Vocabulary of Arithmetic

There exist many technical terms that describe
each part of an addition, subtraction, multiplication, or division of two numbers. Although they
have not passed out of the language entirely, many
of these terms are considered archaic. Once the
staple of arithmetic primers, they are rarely encountered today, although they describe commonly used entities for which there are no other
proper names. Here is a rundown of their meanings:

**1.** When two numbers or quantities are added together, the first number is referred to as the **addend** and the second as the **augend**. The result of
the addition is called a **sum**.

$$15 + 7 = 22$$

addend     augend     sum

**2.** In a subtraction, the number being subtracted
from is called the **minuend**, and the number being

subtracted is called the **subtrahend**. The result of any subtraction is called a **difference**.

$$8 - 5 = 3$$
minuend subtrahend difference

**3.** The result of a multiplication is called a **product**. The numbers that are multiplied to get the product are referred to as the **multiplicand** and the **multiplier**.

$$9 \times 15 = 135$$
multiplicand multiplier product

When two positive integers are multiplied together, each is called a **factor** of the product. Because $3 \times 7 = 21$, we say that 3 and 7 are **factors** of 21.

**4.** The words that describe the parts of a division are all still current. The **dividend** is the number being divided, the **divisor** is the number doing the dividing, and the **quotient** is the result. In long- or short-division procedures, the quotient might include a **remainder**, the fractional part of a mixed number.

$$32 \div 4 = 8$$
dividend divisor quotient

$$45 \div 6 = \frac{45}{6} = 7\frac{3}{6} = 7\frac{1}{2}$$
dividend divisor quotient remainder

# Exponents and Roots

**1.** Just as repeated addition can be succinctly represented by using multiplication, so can repeated multiplication be represented by another compact notation, called **exponentiation**.

- The product $3 \times 3 \times 3 \times 3 \times 3$ can be written as $3^5$.

In this example the superscripted 5 is called an **exponent**. The number 3 is referred to as the **base**. The number 5 is also referred to as the **power** of 3. The expression $3^5$ can be read as "three to the fifth," which is short for "three raised to the fifth power."

**2.** Exponents are the basis of scientific notation (see page 54), in which a given number is expressed as a number between 1 and 10 multiplied by a power of 10. A positive power of 10 in decimal form is a "1" followed by the number of zeros indicated by the exponent. $10^5$ is written in decimal form as a 1 followed by 5 zeros, or 100,000.

- Because 756,000 is 7.56 times 100,000, it can be represented in scientific notation as $7.56 \times 10^5$

**3.** Any non-zero number raised to the zero power equals 1. Also, the first power of any number is the number itself.

**4.** The second power is often referred to as the **square** of a number. The third power may be referred to as the **cube**. Thus $10^2$ can be read as "ten squared" or "the square of ten," and $10^3$ as "ten cubed" or "the cube of ten."

**5.** A **negative exponent** expresses a **reciprocal** of a power of the base. This means that a base raised to a negative power can be rewritten as 1 over the same base raised to the positive power.

- The expression $10^{-3}$ means $\frac{1}{10^3}$ or $\frac{1}{10 \cdot 10 \cdot 10}$ or $\frac{1}{1000}$.

- The expression $2^{-4}$ means $\frac{1}{2^4}$ or $\frac{1}{2 \cdot 2 \cdot 2 \cdot 2}$ or $\frac{1}{16}$.

**6.** Negative powers of 10 are converted to decimal form by starting with 1 and moving the decimal point to the left the number of places given by the negative exponent.

- $10^{-1}$ equals 0.1.
- $10^{-2}$ equals 0.01.
- $10^{-5}$ equals 0.00001.

Multiplying a decimal number by a power of 10 is carried out by moving the decimal point the number of places indicated by the exponent.

- $4.75 \times 10^{-3}$ is equivalent to 0.00475.

**7.** Another form of exponentiation is the process of taking **roots**. The **square root** of a number is a number which, when multiplied by itself (or *squared*), equals the original number. A **cube root** of a number, when *cubed*, equals the number.

- The square roots of 16 are 4 and $-4$, because $4^2 = 16$ and $(-4)^2 = 16$.

- The cube root of 125 is 5, because $5^3 = 125$.

**8.** The notation used to indicate a root is the **radical sign** $\sqrt{\phantom{x}}$ (from the Latin *radic-*, "root"). An expression containing a radical sign is called a **radical**. Whatever appears underneath a radical sign is referred to as a **radicand**.

By itself, the radical sign indicates a positive square root. Thus $\sqrt{16}$ equals 4. It is also true that $-4$ is a square root of 16, as paragraph 5 above showed. This fact is conveyed by the expression $-\sqrt{16} = -4$. To indicate both the positive and negative square roots of 16, the symbol $\pm\sqrt{16}$ is used.

- The symbol for a cube root is $\sqrt[3]{\phantom{x}}$. Thus $\sqrt[3]{125} = 5$. The symbol for a fourth root is $\sqrt[4]{\phantom{x}}$, for a fifth root $\sqrt[5]{\phantom{x}}$, and so on. $\sqrt[4]{81} = 3$ because $3^4 = 81$.

**9.** Roots can also be represented by **fractional exponents**. This avoids the use of radical signs altogether. The root is indicated by the denominator of the fractional exponent.

- The expression $4^{1/2}$ means $\sqrt[2]{4}$ or $\sqrt{4}$.
- The expression $125^{1/3}$ means $\sqrt[3]{125}$.

**10.** When a fractional exponent has a numerator other than 1, it connotes both a power and a root. In the expression $8^{2/3}$, the 2 indicates a second power (or square) and the 3 indicates a third (or cube) root. These can be taken in either order— root first and then power, or power first and then root. Thus $8^{2/3}$ can be rewritten in two ways: $\sqrt[3]{8^2}$ or $\left(\sqrt[3]{8}\right)^2$. In the first instance, 8 is first squared to get 64, then the cube root is taken, and the result is 4. In the second case, the cube root of 8 is taken first; this gives 2, which is then squared to arrive at 4.

**Table 1.5. Rules for Exponents**

|  | *example* |
|---|---|
| $a^0 = 1$ | $10^0 = 1$ |
| $a^1 = a$ | $10^1 = 1$ |
| $a^n = a \times a \times a \ldots \times a$ (n times) | $2^5 = 2 \times 2 \times 2 \times 2 \times 2 = 32$ |
| $a^{-1} = \frac{1}{a}$ | $2^{-1} = \frac{1}{2}$ |
| $a^{-n} = \frac{1}{a^n}$ | $2^{-5} = \frac{1}{2^5} = \frac{1}{32}$ |
| $a^{1/n} = \sqrt[n]{a}$ | $8^{1/3} = \sqrt[3]{8} = 2$ |
| $a^m \times a^n = a^{m+n}$ | $3^2 \times 3^4 = 3^{2+4} = 3^6 = 729$ |
| $a^m \div a^n = a^{m-n}$ | $5^4 \div 5^3 = 5^{4-3} = 5^1 = 5$ |

# Logarithms

An exponential expression, as described above, consists of a base and an exponent (or power). Such an expression has a numerical value. For example, the exponential $5^3$ has the value 125. In this scheme, the word **logarithm** refers to the exponent. The logarithm of 125 is the number 3 because this is the power of 5 which equals 125. Thus a logarithm is an exponent. But to make sense a logarithm must refer implicitly or explicitly to a base. In the above example, because $5^3 = 125$, the number 3 would be the *base-5 logarithm* of 125. This is designated $\log_5 125$. A logarithm can be defined using any positive number except 1 for the base. Thus there are base-5 logarithms, base-2 logarithms, base-7 logarithms, and so on, but in practice only two bases are used.

**1.** Base-10 logarithms, called **common logarithms**, are implied by the symbol **log**, in which no base is specified. (Any scientific calculator will compute base-10 logarithms via a key marked *log* or *logx*.)

In words, the common logarithm of a given number is the power to which 10 must be raised in order to equal that number.

- The common logarithm of 100 is 2 because $10^2 = 100$.

- The common logarithm of 100,000 is 5 because $10^5 = 100,000$.

• The common logarithm of 0.01 is $-2$ because $10^{-2} = 0.01$.

**2.** A **natural logarithm** uses the number $e$ as its base. The number $e$ is approximately equal to 2.718. Like $\pi$, it is an irrational number (a nonterminating, nonrepeating decimal) which occurs in many physical applications. The natural logarithm is designated **ln** in texts and on the calculator key pad. *ln* is essentially an abbreviated form of **log$_e$**.

The natural logarithm of a number gives the power to which $e$ must be raised in order to equal that number.

• Using a calculator, the natural logarithm of 5 comes up as 1.609437912. This means that $e$ raised to the power of 1.609437912 equals 5. These numbers are rounded off by the calculator, but are precise enough for most practical purposes.

## LOGARITHMIC SCALES

Because logarithms are a convenient way of expressing large or rapidly increasing orders of magnitude, they are commonly used in measuring schemes that would otherwise have to deal with unwieldy numbers. Here are a few examples of logarithmic scales of measurement:

**1. The Richter Scale** The Richter scale was developed by Charles Richter and Beno Gutenberg of the California Institute of Technology in 1935 to measure the magnitude of earthquakes. It is a logarithmic scale that begins at a magnitude of 0, which in Richter's time was undetectable. With each unit increase, the Richter scale of magnitude represents a *tenfold increase* in the size of the earthquake. Thus a quake measuring 2 on the scale is ten times greater than one measuring 1. A quake of 8.0 on the scale is not twice as powerful as one measuring 4.0; rather, it is $10^4$ or 10,000 times greater in magnitude. The scale, then, is logarithmic because it shows the relative sizes of quakes in terms of powers of 10.

**Table 1.6. Earthquake Magnitudes**

| Place | Year | Richter Scale Magnitude |
|---|---|---|
| Los Angeles | 1994 | 6.6 |
| Japan | 1993 | 7.8 |
| Iran | 1990 | 7.7 |
| San Francisco | 1989 | 7.1 |
| Armenia | 1988 | 6.9 |
| Mexico City | 1985 | 8.1 |
| Great Britain | 1984 | 5.5 |
| Alaska | 1964 | 8.4 |
| Chile | 1960 | 8.3 |
| Soviet Union | 1952 | 8.5 |
| San Francisco | 1906 | 8.3 |
| Colombia | 1906 | 8.6 |
| Krakatoa | 1883 | 9.9 |

The Richter scale is based on measurements collected by a device called a *seismograph,* which is located (ideally) 100 kilometers, or 62 miles, from the epicenter of the quake. Although the scale has no upper limit, the largest earthquakes measured have not exceeded 9.0 on the scale. A quake measuring 2.0 or below is barely perceptible to an observer at the epicenter. Any quake over 7.0 is considered major, although the amount of physical damage and loss of life depend largely upon the stability of buildings and the geological composition of the region. Table 1.6 shows the magnitudes of some of the most damaging earthquakes. Those that predate the Richter scale are estimates.

**2. The pH Scale**  The pH scale is used to measure the acidity or alkalinity of any solution. It is a logarithmic scale that reflects the concentration of hydrogen ions in the solution. It runs from 0 to 14. Numbers less than 7 are in the *acidic* range; numbers greater than 7 are in the *alkaline* range. The scale is logarithmic in that it represents concentration in ions per liter as expressed by reciprocals of powers of 10.

A high pH value corresponds to a large negative power of 10, meaning a weaker concentration of hydrogen ions. A low pH value indicates a small negative power of 10, which represents a high concentration.

- Pure water has a concentration of $10^{-7}$ hydrogen ions per liter. This translates into a pH factor of 7, which is neither acidic or alkaline.

• Vinegar has a concentration of $10^{-4}$ hydrogen ions per liter. Therefore its pH value is 4, which is acidic.

• Hydrochloric acid has a pH value of 0. Sodium hydroxide has a pH value of 14. These are at the outermost extremes of the scale.

Because it is logarithmic, the pH scale indicates tenfold changes in concentration with each unit increment or decrement.

• Lemon juice has a pH of about 2.1, whereas a fruit jelly might have a pH of 3.1. The juice, therefore, is 10 times more acidic than the jelly.

The burning of certain fossil fuels introduces sulfur dioxide into the atmosphere, and is thought by many scientists to affect the pH level of rainwater, and consequently the pH level in ponds and rivers. Thus the problem of *acid rain* is one in which the pH level of aquatic ecosystems is gradually being lowered and acidity is therefore increasing. Because the data supporting this phenomenon is given in pH units, the magnitude of the changes can be underestimated if the logarithmic nature of the scale is not taken into consideration.

# Factorials

**1.** A **factorial** is a procedure that applies to the set of counting numbers. It is represented by an exclamation point, which indicates the product of any counting number with all of the counting numbers below it.

- "Five factorial," written 5!, means $5 \times 4 \times 3 \times 2 \times 1$, which equals 120.

- "Seven factorial" is written 7! and equals $7 \times 6 \times 5 \times 4 \times 3 \times 2 \times 1$, or 5,040.

- By definition, "zero factorial," or 0!, is equal to 1.

**2.** Factorials are used to count the number of ways that a set of distinct objects can be arranged. Such rearrangements are called *permutations* (see page 176). For example, the number of ways of arranging 10 people in a line is 10 factorial. There are 10 possible candidates for the first position, 9 for the second, 8 for the third, and so on. The total number of possible permutations is the product of the number of possible candidates for each position: $10 \times 9 \times 8 \times 7 \times 6 \times 5 \times 4 \times 3 \times 2 \times 1$. Thus there are 3,628,800 possible permutations of 10 people.

Most scientific calculators have a special key for this operation (as they do for the four algebraic (arithmetic) operations, exponentiation, and roots or logarithms). It is marked with an exclamation point, or by *x!*

# Order of Operations

It is by no means arbitrary how one goes about performing arithmetic operations. Thus it is not always possible simply to work from left to right.

**1.** In the most basic ordering of operations, multiplication and division come before addition and subtraction.

- In the expression $8 + 7 \times 5$, the multiplication must be performed first. In words, the expression is translated as "8 plus the product of 7 and 5." This simplifies to 8 plus 35, or 43.

**2.** In the absence of any **grouping symbols** such as parentheses, brackets, radical signs, or fraction bars, multiplication and division clearly come before addition and subtraction. But if in the absence of parentheses an expression contains only multiplication and division, or is restricted to addition and subtraction alone, then the operations are carried out from left to right. Thus a string of additions and subtractions is carried out from left to right.

- $10 - 7 + 14$ is calculated as $10 - 7$ added to 14. The result is 17.

**3.** When multiplication and division appear in the same expression without parentheses, the operations are carried out from left to right.

- In the expression $20 \div 5 \times 3$, the division is carried out first: $20 \div 5$ is 4, which is then multiplied by 3 to arrive at 12.

**4.** Any operations contained within parentheses must be carried out before those operations that are outside of the parentheses.

- $(7 - 10) \times (6 + 5) = (-3) \times (11) = -33$

**5.** Expressions such as powers, roots, factorials, or logarithms must be calculated before any other algebraic operations.

- $2 \times 10^2$ equals $2 \times 100$ (and not $200^2$).

- $5 + 3!$ equals $5 + (3 \times 2 \times 1) = 5 + 6 = 11$ (not $8!$).

- $4 \cdot \log100$ equals $4 \cdot 2$, or 8 (since $\log100 = 2$).

**6.** The initials PPMDAS, which stand for "Powers and Parentheses, Multiplication and Division, Addition and Subtraction," can help you remember the order of operations. In general, beyond remembering this basic order, the best way to proceed with arithmetic computations is to calculate first the value of any expressions that are contained within grouping symbols (parentheses, brackets, or radical signs). If an expression contains **nested parentheses** (or other grouping symbols), calculation should begin with the innermost set of parentheses.

- $4 \cdot \left[ 100 \, (2 \times 3)^2 \right] = 4 \cdot \left[ 100(6)^2 \right] = 4 \cdot \left[ 100 \times 36 \right] = 4 \cdot \left[ 3600 \right] = 14{,}400.$

**7.** The fraction bar is also a grouping symbol. Thus, in the expression $\dfrac{5}{25 - 10}$ the subtraction in the denominator is carried out first, followed by the division.

$$\bullet \quad \frac{5}{25 - 10} = \frac{5}{15} = \frac{1}{3}$$

# Scientific Notation

Because the display screen of a standard calculator shows no more than 10 significant digits for any number, it would be impossible to display a number greater than 9,999,999,999 or less than 0.000000001 in decimal form. For this reason, calculators employ a notation that has long been used in scientific writing: **scientific notation**.

**1.** The representation of a number in scientific notation consists of a number between 1 and 10 multiplied by a power of 10. The most commonly encountered powers of 10 are written out in Table 1.7.

**2.** Any terminating decimal number can be expressed in scientific notation as a terminating decimal between 1 and 10 multiplied by a power of 10. The power of 10 indicates how many places the decimal point should be moved to convert the number back to decimal form. Positive powers move the decimal point to the right, negative powers to the left.

- $246 = 2.46 \times 10^2$
- $3,048,000 = 3.048 \times 10^6$
- $0.0176 = 1.76 \times 10^{-2}$
- $0.000032 = 3.2 \times 10^{-5}$

**Table 1.7. Powers of Ten**

$10^9 = 10\times10\times10\times10\times10\times10\times10\times10\times10 = 1,000,000,000$   (billions)

$10^6 = 10\times10\times10\times10\times10\times10 = 1,000,000$   (millions)

$10^5 = 10\times10\times10\times10\times10 = 100,000$   (hundred thousands)

$10^4 = 10\times10\times10\times10 = 10,000$   (ten thousands)

$10^3 = 10\times10\times10 = 1,000$   (thousands)

$10^2 = 10\times10 = 100$   (hundreds)

$10^1 = 10$   (tens)

$10^0 = 1$   (ones)

$10^{-1} = \dfrac{1}{10} = 0.1$   (tenths)

$10^{-2} = \dfrac{1}{10^2} = 0.01$   (hundredths)

$10^{-3} = \dfrac{1}{10^3} = 0.001$   (thousandths)

$10^{-4} = \dfrac{1}{10^4} = 0.0001$   (ten thousandths)

$10^{-5} = \dfrac{1}{10^5} = 0.00001$   (hundred thousandths)

$10^{-6} = \dfrac{1}{10^6} = 0.000001$   (millionths)

**3.** Because most electronic calculator displays cannot reproduce standard exponential notation, a few digital variants of the handwritten notation have arisen. One of them employs the letter E (for exponent) as follows:

- $2.46 \times 10^2$ appears as 2.46E2.
- $1.76 \times 10^{-2}$ appears as 1.76E−2.

Another notation displays the power of ten in raised (exponent) position.

- $3.048 \times 10^6$ appears as $3.048^{06}$
- $3.2 \times 10^{-5}$ appears as $3.2^{-05}$

# Calculator Calculation

Electronic calculators come in a dazzling array of sizes, shapes, and formats, and a comprehensive guide to their operation would be beyond the scope of this book. However, because of some similarities in design, and the generic nature of those calculators called *scientific calculators*, several useful generalizations concerning machine calculations can be made. More specific instructions for using a particular calculator can be found in the user's manual.

**1. Types of Calculators** Electronic calculators fall into four general types: the basic four-function calculator, the scientific calculator, the graphing calculator, and the specialized calculator, such as a business, engineering, or statistical calculator. This section covers only the use of inexpensive calculators that have become somewhat generic.

On a basic *four-function calculator* the operations are limited to the four algebraic operations ($+$, $-$, $\times$, and $\div$) and perhaps a percent key or a square-root key. Such a calculator is inadequate for all but the most rudimentary calculations, and can be replaced at low cost by a good scientific calculator.

A *scientific calculator* can be distinguished from a four-function calculator by the presence of several important keys. Among these are the keys marked $\sqrt{\phantom{x}}$ , *log*, $10^x$, *ln*, $e^x$, *sinx*, *cosx*, and $x^y$ (or $y^x$). There are many other keys on a standard scientific calculator key pad, but these ones (or variations of them) will always be present.

At five to ten times the cost of a scientific calculator, a *graphing calculator* represents the high end of the spectrum. While such a calculator can be useful for students and some specialists, it requires a good deal of practice to use. Its one advantage to the average consumer is that it allows mathematical formulas or calculations to be entered and displayed on a single screen in much the same way they would be written out on paper. Thus it can display an entire calculation, as opposed to one part of a sequence of operations, which is a limitation of most smaller calculators. (Some scientific calculators do allow a short string of symbols to be displayed at one time on their screens.)

A *business calculator* is a standard tool of investment analysts and mortgage underwriters. There are many name brands, each with a different protocol, but all of them include simple routines for calculating mortgage payments, future value of investments, and maturity dates. These procedures are described in Chapter 5.

**2. Modes** Scientific and graphing calculators allow the user to specify several modes of operation. The standard (or *default*) mode is the **decimal mode**. This mode is used for ordinary base-10 calculations. Less commonly used are the *binary mode, octal mode, hexadecimal mode*, and *statistical mode*. The decimal mode is limited to a display of nine or ten characters consisting of the ten digits, decimal points, negative signs, and a limited range of notation including some means by which to indicate scientific notation.

**3. Order of Operations in Calculator Computations** While some calculators follow a left-to-right order of operations (in the absence of parentheses), most retain the priority of multiplication and division over addition and subtraction.

• The key sequence $\boxed{5}\ \boxed{-}\ \boxed{3}\ \boxed{\times}\ \boxed{15}\ \boxed{\div}\ \boxed{6}\ \boxed{=}$ gives a result of 5 if the calculator works from left to right. This will occur if the calculator carries out each operation as it is typed in. If, however, the calculator follows the standard order of operations, it would give a result of $-2.5$.

In general, it is safest to carry out operations one at a time by pressing = after each operation. This will assure the operator's control over how the calculation is carried out. A calculator such as a graphing calculator, which allows an entire expression to be typed into the display, will follow a standard order of operations. For clarity, it is a good idea to use parentheses to insure that the desired order is followed.

**4. Operator Keys** Several keys carry out operations on numbers displayed on the screen. The simplest examples are the squaring key $\boxed{x^2}$, the square-root key $\boxed{\sqrt{x}}$, and the logarithm key $\boxed{\log}$. Depending on the calculator one uses, these keys should be pressed before or after a given number is entered; in most instances the number must be entered first.

- The sequence $\boxed{16}$ $\boxed{\sqrt{x}}$ will give the *positive* square root of 16, which is 4.

- The sequence $\boxed{100}$ $\boxed{\log}$ will give the log of 100, which is 2.

**5. The Additive-Inverse Key $+/-$** This key is used to change any number into its additive inverse by changing its sign from positive to negative or negative to positive.

**6. The Multiplicative-Inverse or Reciprocal Key** This key displays the symbol $1/x$. It changes any number except 0 into its multiplicative inverse. Because the result is given in decimal form, it may not be easily recognizable as a reciprocal. For example, the key sequence $\boxed{.}$ $\boxed{4}$ $\boxed{1/x}$ returns the value 2.5. This is because 0.4 equals $4/10$ or $2/5$, and the reciprocal of $2/5$ is $5/2$, which in decimal form is 2.5.

**7.** To calculate compound interest, population-growth estimates, or the **geometric mean** (see page 204), it is essential to know how to raise a number to an integer or fractional power. This can be done in many ways with a scientific calculator. There are four keys that can be used to find powers and roots of numbers. Because the most frequently used roots are square roots and cube roots, and the most frequently used powers are squares and cubes, there are special keys for each of these operations. But there is a more versatile pair of keys that can be used to find any powers or roots. The first is labeled either $x^y$ or $y^x$, and its counterpart is labeled $x^{1/y}$ or $y^{1/x}$.

**8.** To raise one number to the power of another, enter the first number and press $x^y$, then enter the exponent. Some calculators require that the equal sign be pressed; others do the calculation without it.

- To compute $5^4$, press the sequence $\boxed{5}\boxed{x^y}\boxed{4}$. The answer is 625.

- To compute $2^{10}$, press the sequence $\boxed{2}\boxed{x^y}$ $\boxed{10}$. The answer is 1024.

**9.** To find a square root or cube root, use the keys labeled $\sqrt{\phantom{x}}$ and $\sqrt[3]{\phantom{x}}$ respectively. For a 4th, 5th, or higher root, use the key labeled $x^{1/y}$.

- To compute the fifth root of 24, enter $\boxed{24}\boxed{x^{1/y}}$ $\boxed{5}$. This key sequence represents $24^{1/5}$ or $\sqrt[5]{24}$.

The calculation of $\sqrt[5]{24}$ would give the answer 1.888175023, which is not exact but is sufficiently close that, if it is then raised to the 5th power by pressing the sequence $\boxed{x^y}\boxed{5}$, the answer displayed on most calculators will be exactly 24. This will not always happen. Depending on the method of computation and rounding that is programmed into the calculator, some roundoff errors will be propagated through subsequent computations, and some will not. In general, the degree of accuracy on most calculators is more than sufficient for any practical purposes.

**10.** To raise a number to a fractional exponent, both the $\boxed{x^y}$ and the $\boxed{x^{1/y}}$ keys may be needed.

- The expression $8^{2/3}$ indicates either the *square* of the *cube root* of 8 or the *cube root* of the *square* of 8. The order is not important. In this case, either process results in a value of 4. To carry out such a calculation on the calculator, press the sequence $\boxed{8}\ \boxed{x^{1/y}}\ \boxed{3}\ \boxed{=}$ followed by $\boxed{x^y}\ \boxed{2}\ \boxed{=}$. (The equal signs may not be necessary, depending on the calculator.)

**11. Degree vs. Radian Measure of Angles** Scientific calculators have the capability of working with angle measures in **degrees** (in which 360 degrees is a full revolution) or **radians** (in which $2\pi$ radians represents a full revolution). The default setting is degree measure. The distinction between these two modes only matters when angles are being used with trigonometric functions (see page 98).

**12. Digital Representation of Numbers** In decimal mode, numbers that can be entered are limited to 6 to 10 digits (depending on the calculator).

When a calculator completes a computation, it will resort to scientific notation for numbers that go beyond 10 digits. It is also possible to enter a number in scientific notation with most calculators. Such numbers, however, cannot have more than 10 significant digits.

- $\boxed{1}\,\boxed{\div}\,500\,\boxed{=}$ will result in a display of $2^{-03}$ or 2E-3 on a calculator screen. A simple trick that will convert this number to decimal form is to add 1. The result is 1.002. Thus $1 \div 500$ is 0.002.

**13. Error** Every time a rounded figure is used in a computation, an error is **propagated**, which means it gets passed on to the result of a computation. A general rule for rounding such a result to the proper number of significant figures is to make sure it does not contain more significant digits than any of the measurements that produced it.

- On a calculator, $2.718 \times 3.1416$ equals 8.5388688. If the numbers being multiplied are exact, then the answer is also exact. But if the computation is meant to represent $e \times \pi$, it should be rounded. Because the first figure (the multiplier) is rounded to three decimal places, the answer should be rounded to 8.539 at best, or 8.54 to be safe.

Electronic calculators do not take significant digits into account. In general, decimal numbers that are entered or displayed on calculator screens are assumed to be exact.

# Chapter 2

# Algebra and Geometry

## Basic Algebra

Algebra is the language of quantity. It allows quantitative expressions, ideas, information, or questions that can be expressed in plain English to be expressed in mathematical symbols. The most basic tool of algebra is the **equation**, which is nothing more than a sentence that states that two quantities are equal, where at least one quantity contains a variable or unknown. The goal of many algebraic procedures is to solve equations.

### EQUATION SOLVING

**1.** Algebra allows physical situations to be translated into abstract symbols and solved. To **solve** means to find the solution set of an equation. A **solution set** consists of all values or numbers which, when substituted for unknown quantities in any equation, make the equation a true statement.

• In 1863 Abraham Lincoln began his most famous speech with the words "Four score and seven years ago." Many people who realize that he was referring to the year 1776 and the signing of the Declaration of Independence might not remember what a *score* is. The sentence can be converted to an equation that will lead to the answer.

If a score is designated by the letter $x$—the unknown quantity—then "four score and seven" means $4x + 7$. This should equal the number of years between 1776 and 1863. The fact that "four score and seven years ago" is equivalent to "87 years ago" is expressed by the equation $4x + 7 = 1863 - 1776$ or $4x + 7 = 87$. This equation has the solution $x = 20$. This means that when 20 is substituted for $x$, the equation becomes a true statement. Four times twenty plus seven does indeed equal 87, and thus "four score and seven years ago" is equivalent to "87 years ago."

**2. The equal sign** The use of the equal sign is somewhat ambiguous in mathematics. In the simple arithmetic expression $2 + 3 = 5$, the equal sign is a statement of fact. In the expression $x + 3 = 5$, however, it is a conditional expression of possibility, since $x + 3 = 5$ depends for its truthfulness on the value chosen for $x$. Similarly, the statement $x = 5 - 3$ is a conditional statement which is true only if $x$ equals 2.

**3. Terms** are groups of numerical and alphabetical characters that are separated by the symbols $+$, $-$, and $=$. In simple equations the variable or unknown is contained in one term. In more complex equations there can be several terms that contain the variable.

- In the equation $3x + 5 = 26$, the terms are $3x$, $5$, and $26$.

- In the equation $-2y^2 + 7y + 5 = 13$, the terms are $-2y^2$, $7y$, $5$, and $13$.

**4.** The numerical multiplier preceding the variable part of a term is called a **coefficient**.

- In the term $5x^3$ the coefficient is $5$.

- In the term $\frac{1}{3}\pi r^2$ the coefficient is $\frac{1}{3}\pi$.

**5. Like terms** Many equations feature several terms that contain the unknown or variable. Any terms that contain the same power of the variable are called **like terms**.

- $5x$ and $8x$ are like terms.

- $10x^2$ and $-4x^2$ are like terms.

- $4\pi r^3$ and $-2r^3$ are like terms.

**6.** Like terms can be combined into a single term by combining their coefficients.

- $5x + 8x$ becomes $(5 + 8)x$ or $13x$.

- $10x^2 - 4x^2$ becomes $(10 - 4)x^2$ or $6x^2$.

**7. Solving** an equation is the process of isolating the term or terms containing the variable on one side of the equal sign. Thus the goal of simple equation solving is to *isolate the unknown*. This involves identifying which term or terms of the equation contain the unknown, and then using algebraic operations to bring these terms together on the same side of the equation. There are four basic rules that can be used to carry this out.

   i. The same number or quantity may be added to both sides of an equation.

   ii. The same number or quantity may be subtracted from both sides of an equation.

   iii. The equation may be multiplied by the same non-zero number or quantity on both sides.

   iv. The equation may be divided on both sides by the same non-zero number or quantity.

Any one of these four procedures will produce a new equation that is equivalent to the original equation. By definition, **equivalent equations** have the same solution set. Thus the process of equation solving is one in which a succession of equivalent equations is derived from the original equation. In the final step of this process the unknown is completely isolated, and the equation is thereby solved.

- To solve the equation $2x + 7 = 15$,
    First subtract 7 from both sides:
    $2x + 7 - 7 = 15 - 7$.
    Then simplify: $2x = 8$.

    Then divide both sides by 2: $\frac{2x}{2} = \frac{8}{2}$

The solution is contained in the last equation, which simplifies to $x = 4$.

**8.** Solving an equation in which the variable appears in several terms requires combining like terms, then isolating the term that contains the variable.

- To solve the equation $5x - 4(x - 4) = 6 + 3x$:

    First simplify the left side:
    $5x - 4x + 16 = 6 + 3x$.
    Then combine like terms:
    $x + 16 = 6 + 3x$.
    Subtract $x$ from both sides:
    $x - x + 16 = 6 + 3x - x$.
    Then combine like terms again:
    $16 = 6 + 2x$.
    Subtract 6 from both sides: $10 = 2x$.
    Divide both sides by 2: $\dfrac{10}{2} = \dfrac{2x}{x}$.
    And simplify to find the solution $x = 5$.

**9. Rate-Time-Distance Problems** A car leaves Toledo heading west at 55 mph. Two hours later another car starts out in pursuit at 65 mph. How long will it take the second car to catch up to the first?

This type of question is fairly typical of rate-time-distance problems. Its solution begins with the recognition that the distances traveled by each car will be the same at the time the second car overtakes the first, yet the second car will have traveled for two hours less time overall.

|        | rate | × | time | = | distance |
|--------|------|---|------|---|----------|
| 1st car | 55 |   | $t$ |   | $55t$ |
| 2nd car | 65 |   | $(t-2)$ |   | $65(t-2)$ |

• Set the distances equal to each other and solve for $t$.

$$65(t - 2) = 55t$$
$$65t - 130 = 55t$$
$$65t - 55t - 130 = 0$$
$$65t - 55t = 0 + 130$$
$$10t = 130$$
$$t = 13 \text{ hours}$$

# Coordinate Geometry

**1.** The geometry of two- and three-dimensional figures can be investigated by means of **graphs**. The most common method of two-dimensional graphing uses a grid on which two perpendicular lines—a **horizontal** and a **vertical axis**—establish a frame of reference that can be used to specify the exact location of any point. The two axes intersect at a point called the **origin**. From this reference point, all points in two-dimensional space can be uniquely identified by means of two coordinates—a horizontal displacement and a vertical displacement. In the standard orientation, the positive directions are *up* and *right*, while the negative directions are *left* and *down*. This is called a **rectangular coordinate system**.

• The point (2, 5) can be found by starting at the origin—which is identified by the coordinate pair (0, 0)—and moving 2 units to the right and 5 units up. The point (−3, −7) is located by moving from the origin 3 units left and 7 units down.

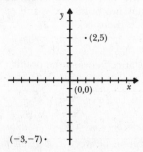

**2.** Many geographical systems use **rectangular coordinates** to identify locations. For example, in a city laid out in a grid pattern, any address can be located by specifying the nearest intersection of named, numbered, or lettered streets or avenues. The corner of 40th and Spruce streets in Philadelphia is a place identified using two coordinates; so is Fifth Avenue and 52nd Street in New York. Similarly, games that employ grids use two coordinates to identify squares on those grids by specifying a row and a column. In chess, Q7 is the 7th square in the queen's column. In reading maps, as in the game of Battleship, a grid location is specified by giving a letter and a number. Letters usually run horizontally across the grid, while numbers typically run from top to bottom.

**3.** The **distance** between any two points on a rectangular grid can be found by using a formula derived from the Pythagorean Theorem (see page 84). Given any two points $(a, b)$ and $(c, d)$, the distance between them is

$$\sqrt{(a - c)^2 + (b - d)^2}.$$

• The distance between the points $(7, -2)$ and $(3, 5)$ is

$$\sqrt{(7 - 3)^2 + (-2 - 5)^2} = \sqrt{4^2 + (-7)^2}$$
$$= \sqrt{16 + 49} = \sqrt{65}.$$

**4.** The **midpoint** between two given points $(a, b)$ and $(c, d)$ has the coordinates

$$\left( \frac{a + c}{2}, \frac{b + d}{2} \right).$$

• The midpoint between $(2, -7)$ and $(8, 13)$ has coordinates

$$\left( \frac{2 + 8}{2}, \frac{-7 + 13}{2} \right), \text{ or } (5, 3).$$

• New York is located at 40°45′N latitude, 74°1′W longitude, and Los Angeles is located at 34°3′N latitude and 118°15′W longitude. Their midpoint can be located by treating latitude and longitude readings as rectangular coordinates.

*latitude of midpoint:*

$$\frac{1}{2}(40°45' + 34°3') = \frac{1}{2}(74°48') = 37°24'N$$

*longitude of midpoint:*

$$\frac{1}{2}(74°1' + 118°15') = \frac{1}{2}(192°16') = 96°8'W$$

These are approximately the coordinates of Kansas City.

*Note:* Lines of latitude and longitude are not technically a rectangular coordinate system because they are drawn on a sphere instead of a plane. Projections of the sphere onto a plane, such as a Mercator projection map (see page 166), do convert lines of latitude and longitude into a grid, but there is some distortion. Thus, on a flat map of the United States, Kansas City does not appear to be the midpoint of the line that connects New York and Los Angeles, whereas on a globe it does.

**5.** Given the coordinates of two points—*(a, b)* and *(c, d)*—the **slope** of the line passing through them is given by the formula

$$m = \frac{d - b}{c - a}$$

(The letter *m* is typically used to designate slope.)

- A line passing through the points $(2, -5)$ and $(6, 3)$ has the slope

$$m = \frac{3 - (-5)}{6 - 2} = \frac{8}{4} = 2$$

The choice of which coordinates to subtract does not matter as long as the coordinates of one point subtract the corresponding coordinates of the other. The slope found above could also be calculated as

$$m = \frac{-5 - 3}{2 - 6} = \frac{-8}{-4} = 2$$

**6. Slope** is a numerical measure of the inclination of a line with respect to the horizontal. A horizontal line has a slope of 0. A vertical line does not have a slope, since it is infinitely steep. A line that is not vertical or horizontal—an **oblique line**—will have a non-zero slope. A line that is 45° above horizontal and climbing to the right has a slope of 1. A line that climbs to the left at an angle of 45° has a slope of −1. Slopes of lines that climb to the right are positive, and slopes of lines that climb to the left are negative.

**7.** The numerical value of slope is calculated as a ratio or quotient. Taking any two points on a line, the slope of the line is defined as the ratio of the vertical displacement, called the **rise**, to the horizontal displacement, called the **run**. This ratio is the same for any two points on the line.

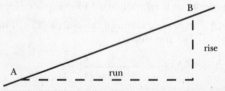

When designing a set of stairs, an architect must keep within certain limits on tread width and riser height in order to meet building codes. In other words, the slope or steepness of a flight of stairs, which is determined by the ratio of rise (riser height) to run (tread width), is confined within certain limits.

$$slope = \frac{riser\ height}{tread\ width}$$

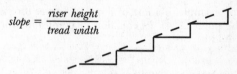

**8.** Outside of coordinate geometry, slopes are referred to more informally, usually by using degree measure. The words that are used instead of *slope* are **grade**, which applies to roads, and **pitch**, which applies to roof lines. A 45° pitch is equivalent to a slope of 1. A 6° grade is equivalent to a slope of about 0.105. The conversion of angle measure to slope is taken up in the section on trigonometry (see page 98).

## EQUATIONS OF LINES

The equation of a line can be found when either:

  i. the coordinates of two points are given, or
  ii. the slope of the line and the coordinates of a single point are given.

In the first instance, the two given points can be plugged into the slope formula (see paragraph 5 above), which will reduce the problem to the second case. When a point and a slope are given, the equation of the line can be found using **point-slope form** as follows:

**1.** Given that a line has slope $m$ and passes through the point $(a, b)$, the equation of the line in point-slope form would be:

$$y - b = m(x - a).$$

For example, if a line of slope $-2$ passes through the point $(1, 4)$, its equation in point-slope form would be

$$y - 4 = -2(x - 1).$$

This equation simplifies to

$$y - 4 = -2x + 2,$$

and finally, adding 4 to both sides,

$$y = -2x + 6.$$

**2.** An equation in the form $y = mx + b$ is said to be in **slope-intercept form.** In this form the slope is still designated with the letter $m$, and the value $b$—called the $y$-intercept—indicates where the line crosses the vertical axis.

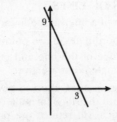

The equation $y = -3x + 9$ describes a line of slope $-3$ that crosses the $y$-axis at 9.

**3.** An equation of a line states a **linear relationship** between two quantities. In the above examples, where the quantities are designated $x$ and $y$, the value of $y$ is said to be **linearly related** to $x$, and vice versa. This type of relationship between two quantities is very common.

- The conversion formula from degrees Fahrenheit to degrees Celsius is a linear relationship. It is expressed by the conversion formula:

$$F = \frac{9}{5}C + 32.$$

Solved for C, the formula looks like this:

$$C = \frac{5}{9}F - \frac{160}{9}.$$

Both formulas are of the form $y = mx + b$.

Knowing that 0°C is equivalent to 32°F, and that 100°C is equivalent to 212°F, it is possible to draw

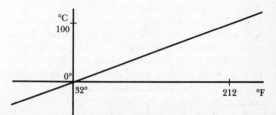

a linear graph that visually represents the conversion from Fahrenheit to Celsius, and vice versa. (For more on temperature conversions, see page 149.)

# Classical Geometry

Classical geometry, which originated with the ancient Greeks, is the study of the properties of points, lines, and lengths, from which are derived theorems concerning angles, shapes, surfaces, and solids. The subject was formalized by Euclid, the Greek author whose *Elements* brought together all the known geometrical knowledge of the era (c. 300 B.C.). Euclid's text established geometry as a coherent subject, and it remains the basis of the course called *Euclidean geometry* (or *plane geometry*) as it is taught today.

Euclidean geometry is not entirely concerned with drawn figures. It also deals with the way in which a hypothesis leads to a conclusion through a process known as **proof.** That is, although it deals with points and lines, Euclid's geometry is essentially the study of logic—of deductive reasoning. Its theorems rest mostly on basic assumptions called **postulates** and **axioms.** These, along with the definitions of *point, line, plane,* and *length,* combine to form a vast array of conclusions of increasing complexity about circles, triangles, squares, rectangles, trapezoids, three-dimensional solids, and so on, which in turn support the theory of architectural and engineering design. This section is a brief outline of some of the more important geometric definitions and theorems.

## DEDUCTIVE REASONING

**1. Deductive reasoning**, which is the heart of classical geometry, is based on the idea of a conditional statement. A **conditional statement** is a sentence that puts forth a **hypothesis**, in the form of an "if" clause, followed by a **conclusion** or "then" clause. A typical conditional statement is of the form

if $a$, then $b$,

which can also be written symbolically as

$$a \rightarrow b$$

(that is, statement $a$ implies statement $b$).

**2.** Any conditional statement may be true or false, but those upon which other conclusions are based are assumed to be true. Most conditional statements used in the course of proving other conditional statements either are obviously true or become evident after a proof has established their validity. The following are examples of nongeometrical conditional statements whose truth is debatable.

- If the car is green, then it is a Ford.

- If the car was made in Japan, then it is an import.

- If it is raining, then it is not sunny.

**3.** Given any conditional statement, three related conditional statements can be constructed from it by reversing the order of hypothesis and conclusion and/or negating both hypothesis and conclusion.

Given the conditional statement "If a, then b," there exists

the **converse**: "If b, then a."

the **contrapositive**: "If not b, then not a."

the **inverse**: "If not a, then not b."

**4.** A conditional statement and its contrapositive are **logically equivalent**, which means that, if one is true, then the other must also be true.

*conditional statement:* If today is Thanksgiving, then today is a Thursday.

*contrapositive:* If today is not a Thursday, then today is not Thanksgiving.

**5.** While the contrapositive of a conditional statement must be true, the converse and inverse are not necessarily true.

*conditional statement:* If today is Thanksgiving, then today is a Thursday.

*converse:* If today is Thursday, then today is Thanksgiving.

*inverse:* If today is not Thanksgiving, then today is not a Thursday.

Because the inverse is the contrapositive of the converse, the inverse and the converse are logically equivalent statements. Thus, if one is true the other must be true, or (as in the above example) if one is false the other is also false.

**6.** The truth of a conditional statement is often established by the definitions of objects and concepts. In geometry, however, the most basic building blocks—*point, line,* and *plane*—are **undefined terms** because they cannot be described using terms whose own definitions do not rely on these very terms. Therefore general descriptions of these terms must suffice.

> A **point** is represented as a dot. It is a location in space and it has no dimension.

> A **line** can be thought of as a straight thin wire that goes indefinitely in both directions. It has no thickness.

> A **plane** is a flat surface that extends infinitely in all directions. It has no thickness.

> A **ray** is a line that begins at a point and continues indefinitely in one direction.

> An **angle** consists of two rays that share the same endpoint.

**7.** A **definition** is a true conditional statement whose converse is also true. The definition "A right angle is an angle measuring 90°" can be put in the form of a conditional statement as "If an angle measures 90°, then it is a right angle." The converse of this would be "If it is a right angle, then it measures 90°." Because the conditional statement and its converse are both true, this constitutes a definition.

## DEFINITIONS

The definitions given below are stated in abbreviated form, not as conditional statements.

### Angles

**acute angle**   an angle whose measure is less than 90°.

**right angle**   an angle whose measure is exactly 90°.

**obtuse angle**   an angle whose measure is greater than 90°.

**complementary angles**   a pair of angles whose measures add up to 90°.

**supplementary angles**   a pair of angles whose measures add up to 180°.

### Triangles

**acute triangle**   a triangle with three acute angles.

**obtuse triangle**   a triangle with one obtuse angle.

**right triangle**   a triangle with one right angle.

**scalene triangle**   a triangle with no equal sides.

**isosceles triangle**   a triangle with at least two equal sides.

**equilateral triangle**   a triangle with three equal sides.

**equiangular triangle**   a triangle with three equal angles.

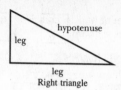

Isosceles triangle

Right triangle

**vertex** the point of intersection of two sides (informally, a "corner" of the triangle, although *corner* properly refers only to a right angle).

**altitude** (**height**) the perpendicular distance from a side to the opposite vertex.

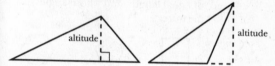

## Four-Sided Figures

**quadrilateral** any four-sided figure (the sum of its four angles is 360°).

**parallelogram** a quadrilateral in which both pairs of opposite sides are equal in length.

**rhombus** a quadrilateral with equal sides (the angles do not have to be equal).

**rectangle** a quadrilateral with four right angles.

**square** a quadrilateral with four equal sides and four equal angles.

**trapezoid** a quadrilateral with exactly one pair of parallel sides.

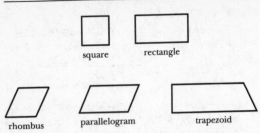

square   rectangle

rhombus   parallelogram   trapezoid

## Regular Polygons

**regular polygon** a multisided figure whose sides are of equal length, and whose angles are of equal measure.

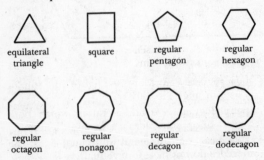

equilateral
triangle

square

regular
pentagon

regular
hexagon

regular
octagon

regular
nonagon

regular
decagon

regular
dodecagon

## Circles

**circle** the set of points in a plane all of which are the same distance from a given point.

# BASIC POSTULATES

Euclid's *Elements* builds upon five basic postulates (or assumptions), which appear below in paraphrased form.

   i. A unique straight line can be drawn between any two points.

  ii. Such a line can be extended indefinitely in either direction.

 iii. A circle can be drawn using a given point (center) and a given distance (radius).

 iv. All right angles are equal.

  v. Given a line and a point not on the line, there exists exactly one line parallel to the original line passing through the given point.

The fifth postulate, the famous **parallel postulate**, is controversial because, unlike the first four postulates, it is not self-evident, nor can it be proven from the axioms. The acceptance of this postulate leads to what is called **Euclidean geometry**; rejection of it opens doors to many other kinds of geometries, which are referred to as **non-Euclidean geometries**.

The postulates and axioms lead to many conclusions that are familiar to most students of geometry. Below are a few of the more important observations.

   Two points uniquely determine a line.

   Three points not lying on the same line uniquely determine a plane.

To every pair of points there corresponds a unique positive number referred to as the **distance** between the points.

To every angle there corresponds a unique number called the **measure** of the angle. (Angle measurements may be in *degrees* or *radians;* see page 105.)

To every region in a plane there corresponds a unique positive number which is called the **area** of the region.

## BASIC THEOREMS

Here are a few examples of statements whose truth is established by the definitions and postulates.

If a triangle is equilateral, then it is isosceles.

If a triangle is not isosceles, then it is not equilateral.

The sum of the measures of the three angles of any triangle is 180°.

The shortest distance from a point to a line is along a perpendicular.

## THE PYTHAGOREAN THEOREM

The famous **Pythagorean Theorem** is the basis of the study of right triangles. In words, it says:

The sum of the squares of the lengths of the legs of a right triangle is equal to the square of the length of the hypotenuse.

In symbols: $a^2 + b^2 = c^2$

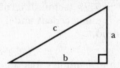

A **Pythagorean triple** consists of three numbers that satisfy the conclusion of the Pythagorean Theorem: $a^2 + b^2 = c^2$. There are an infinite number of Pythagorean triples; Table 2.1 lists those that involve numbers up to 50.

**Table 2.1. Pythagorean Triples**

| | |
|---|---|
| 3, 4, 5 | 14, 48, 50 |
| 5, 12, 13 | 15, 20, 25 |
| 6, 8, 10 | 15, 36, 39 |
| 7, 24, 25 | 16, 30, 34 |
| 8, 15, 17 | 18, 24, 30 |
| 9, 12, 15 | 20, 21, 29 |
| 9, 40, 41 | 21, 28, 35 |
| 10, 24, 26 | 24, 32, 40 |
| 12, 16, 20 | 27, 36, 45 |
| 12, 35, 37 | 30, 40, 50 |

# Ratios and Proportions

**1.** A **ratio** of two numbers is a way of expressing their quotient. The ratio of $a$ to $b$ can be written $a : b$ or $\frac{a}{b}$. The ratio of 20 to 35 is $\frac{20}{35}$, which is equivalent to $\frac{4}{7}$. Thus a ratio of 20 to 35 is the same as a ratio of 4 to 7. In technical terms, 4 would be referred to as the **antecedent** and 7 as the **consequent** of the ratio.

**2.** A ratio of $a$ to $b$ implies that a given group of objects can be broken into $a + b$ parts, where $a$ objects fall into one subgroup, and $b$ objects fall into another. The first subgroup is $\frac{a}{a + b}$ of the whole, and the second is $\frac{b}{a + b}$ of the whole.

- A ratio of 4 to 7 implies a group that can be divided into 11 parts. 4 of them fall into one category, 7 fall into the other. For example, if a social club has 55 members and the ratio of smokers to nonsmokers is 4 to 7, then 4/11 of the group are smokers, and 7/11 are nonsmokers. 4/11 of 55 equals 20, and 7/11 of 55 equals 35. Thus the ratio of smokers to nonsmokers is 20 to 35, which is equivalent to 4 to 7, because 20/35 equals 4/7.

**3.** A **proportion** is a statement of equality between two ratios. "$a$ is to $b$ as $c$ is to $d$" is a proportion. It can be written symbolically as $a : b :: c : d$, or as $\frac{a}{b} = \frac{c}{d}$. A proportion can also refer to the numerical value of a ratio. Thus a ratio of 6 to 10 implies a quotient of 6/10, or a proportion of 0.6. Such a proportion may also be given in percent form as 60%.

**4.** When two quantities are said to be **proportional** or **directly proportional**, their ratio is a constant value. This ratio, in its reduced form, is sometimes referred to as a **constant of proportionality**. Thus another way to express the fact that quantity A and quantity B are proportional is to say that their ratio is a constant ($A/B = k$, where k stands for constant) or that the first quantity is a multiple of the second ($A = kB$).

• The number of gallons of paint needed to paint the rooms in a house is directly proportional to the square footage of the rooms. If one gallon of paint will cover 400 square feet, then the amount of paint required to cover 5 rooms that have a total of 2300 square feet of wall surface can be found by setting up a proportion.

$$\frac{1 \text{ gallon}}{400 \text{ square feet}} = \frac{x \text{ gallons}}{2300 \text{ square feet}}$$

This proportion translates to the equation: $x = \frac{1}{400} \cdot 2300$. Thus, to find the amount of paint required, multiply the total square footage to be painted by $\frac{1}{400}$. In this case the amount would be 5.75 gallons.

**5.** Two triangles are **similar** if they are identical in shape (but not necessarily in size). Consequently, the measures of corresponding angles of similar triangles are the same. In addition, the ratios of corresponding sides of similar triangles are the same. Thus similar triangles are **proportional** in size.

$$\frac{a}{d} = \frac{b}{e} = \frac{c}{f}$$

$$\frac{b}{a} = \frac{e}{d}, \frac{c}{a} = \frac{f}{d}, \text{ and } \frac{c}{b} = \frac{f}{e}$$

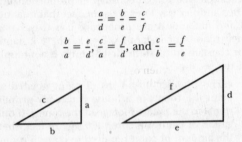

**6.** The proportions of similar triangles can be used to make measurements. A simple sighting device in the form of a 3-4-5 right triangle can be used to set up proportions from which the heights of distant objects can be calculated.

• The height of a tree can be calculated by pacing off the distance from the base of the tree to the observer. If this distance is 60 feet when the top of the tree is lined up in the sighting device, then the ratio of the tree height to 60 feet must be 3 to 4. The height can be found by solving this equation:

$$\frac{h}{60} = \frac{3}{4} \text{ or } h = \frac{3}{4} \times 60 = 45$$

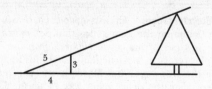

# EXAMPLES OF RATIOS AND PROPORTIONS

**1. Gear Ratios** When one gear turns another gear, the number of teeth on the driving gear and the number of teeth on the driven gear form a ratio called the *gear ratio*. This ratio determines how the rotary force is transmitted from one gear to the next.

A high gear ratio is one in which the driving gear is larger than the driven gear. For example, in the gear ratio 2 to 1, the drive gear has twice as many teeth as the driven gear and has twice the circumference. One revolution of the drive gear will produce two revolutions of the driven gear.

A low gear ratio involves a smaller drive gear. In a 1 to 2 ratio, the drive gear has half as many teeth as the driven gear and must make two revolutions in order to produce one revolution in the driven gear.

In an automobile transmission, the gear ratios of different gears determine how the rotation of the engine's crankshaft is transmitted to the wheels.

■ **Bicycle Gears** Cyclists have their own way of calculating the gear ratios that determine a bicycle's performance. A *100-inch gear*, for example, refers to a particular gear ratio. In this case the front gear has 52 teeth and the rear-wheel gear (or drive gear) has 14 teeth. The ratio of 52 to 14 is multiplied by the wheel diameter, which is 27 inches on racing bikes, to come up with the value 100.

$$\frac{52 \ (front)}{14 \ (rear)} \times 27 \text{ inches } (wheel \ diameter) = 100.3''$$

A 100.3-inch gear is typically referred to as a 100-inch gear.

**2. Housing Ratios** Anyone who has applied for a mortgage has heard of the ratio numbers 28% and 36%. The first is the *housing ratio*, which is the ratio of monthly ownership costs to gross monthly income. This is a maximum threshold which limits the total value of monthly mortgage, property tax, and insurance payments to 28% of gross monthly income.

The second ratio is called the *total obligation ratio*. It takes into account *all* monthly debt, which cannot exceed 36% of gross monthly income.

These ratios were established by the Federal National Mortgage Association (Fanny Mae), which regulates how mortgages are resold on the secondary market. Some lenders have relaxed these requirements in recent years. (For more details, see pages 256-59.)

## 3. SPF Factors

Suntanning lotions are graded according to an *SPF* (or Sun Protection Factor) scale. The numbers range from 2 to 30. The scale represents a proportion which is a multiplicative factor of extra protection from the sun. An SPF of 2 is supposed to mean that a person can remain in the sun twice as long as usual without burning. An SPF of 30 allows the same person to remain in the sun 30 times as long without burning, which means almost indefinitely.

• A person who can remain in the early afternoon sun for 15 minutes without burning can theoretically remain in the sun safely for one hour by using a number 4 SPF lotion.

Scientific evidence of the effectiveness of sun creams is highly suspect. Even though the SPF scale was promulgated by the U.S. Food and Drug Administration, its meaning should be interpreted with caution. It does not provide as much protection as common sense.

## 4. Vision Testing

Tests to measure vision consider two abilities—distance focusing and close-up focusing. The ratio $20/20$ refers to objects viewed at a distance of 20 feet. "Normal" distance vision is defined as $20/20$. Thus a person with $20/20$ vision can read a line of text of a certain size from 20 feet away. A person with $20/30$ vision can only focus on objects at 20 feet that a person with normal vision could focus on at 30 feet. Thus a person with $20/30$ vision can read a line of text at 20 feet that a person with normal vision could read from 30 feet away. If the viewer has $20/15$ vision, he or she can focus on objects at 20 feet that a normal viewer could only focus on at 15 feet.

A similar test and ratio is used for close-up vision, but with a distance of 14 inches. $14/14$ is defined as normal, whereas $14/36$ means that the viewer can focus on a line of print at 14 inches that a normal viewer could focus on at 36 inches.

**5. Ohm's Law**   In the study of electric circuits, one of the most important theorems is *Ohm's Law*, which says that *the voltage is proportional to the current and the resistance.* If V is the voltage, I the current, and R the resistance, then Ohm's Law can be written as

$$V = I \times R, \text{ or } I = \frac{V}{R}$$

The voltage in most household circuits is 120V. The resistance is a feature of the appliance or device, and is measured in units called *ohms.* The current is measured in *amperes,* or *amps,* and gives an idea how much electricity is used.

• A toaster has a resistance of 10 ohms and is plugged into a 120-volt circuit. The current that the toaster draws can be computed using Ohm's Law as follows:

$$current = \frac{120 \text{ volts}}{10 \text{ ohms}} = 12 \text{ amps.}$$

The circuit breaker in a house limits the amount of amperage that can be drawn on any given circuit. Most of these are set to break the circuit at 15 amps, 20 amps, or 30 amps. A standard current for an entire house is 100 amps (although in older homes it was usually set at 60 amps).

Electrical power usage is measured in *watts*, or in thousand-watt units called *kilowatts*. Power usage is proportional to the current, and is defined by the equation

*power* (watts) = *current* (amps) × *voltage* (volts).

The toaster in the above example draws a current of 12 amps on a 120-volt circuit. Thus

$$
\begin{aligned}
power &= current \times voltage \\
&= (12 \text{ amps}) \times (120 \text{ volts}) \\
&= 1440 \text{ watts} \\
&= 1.44 \text{ kilowatts}
\end{aligned}
$$

Power usage in kilowatts over time leads to the unit of electrical energy use called a *kilowatt-hour*.

- A 75-watt lightbulb burns for 24 hours. Thus the power usage is 75 watts, or 0.075 kilowatts, and the total energy usage is

$$(0.075 \text{ kW}) \times (24 \text{ hrs}) = 1.8 \text{ kWh}$$

The electric utility companies set rates per kilowatt-hour that vary with the amount of usage. The national average is around 9 cents per kilowatt-hour.

**6. f-numbers** The *f-stop* setting on a camera reduces or enlarges the *aperture*, or lens-opening size, effectively enlarging or reducing the diameter of the lens. Thus it controls the amount of light that is admitted when the shutter is opened. The shutter speed, by controlling the amount of time the shutter remains open, also controls the amount of light to which the film is exposed. Thus the *f*-stop and the shutter speed must be used together to define the quality and quantity of light that will create the photographic image.

The *f-stop*, or *f-number*, refers to the ratio of the *focal length* of the lens (the distance from the lens to the film plane when the camera is focused at infinity) to the diameter of the aperture. The *f*-numbers on a typical camera are $f/1.4$, $f/2$, $f/2.8$, $f/4$, $f/5.6$, $f/8$, $f/11$, $f/16$, $f/22$, $f/32$, and $f/45$. Each setting in this series admits half as much light as the setting that precedes it.

- A camera with a focal length of 50 mm is set so that its aperture size is 25 mm. The focal-length-to-aperture ratio is 50 to 25, which is equivalent to 2 to 1. The number 2 here is referred to as the *f*-number (designated $f/2$).

  Reducing the aperture to 12.5 mm creates a ratio of 50 to 12.5, or 4 to 1. The *f*-number corresponding to this is $f/4$.

In most cameras the focal length is fixed. Consequently, as the *f*-number increases, the aperture size decreases. A higher *f*-number setting implies a higher focal-length-to-aperture ratio, which can only happen if the aperture size is reduced. To maintain the amount of light admitted, the shutter speed can be adjusted to keep the shutter open longer.

The $f$-numbers are square roots of a series of numbers that represent the area of the aperture (and thus the amount of light admitted by the lens). Each time the aperture area is reduced by half, it generates the next setting.

**7. Binocular Numbers** Binoculars are given two identifying numbers—one that indicates the amount of magnification and another that gives the diameter of the front lens or lenses. A front lens is known as an *objective lens*, or simply as the *objective*. A pair of 6 × 30 binoculars magnify six times (6×) using an objective lens of 30-mm diameter.

The light-gathering capability—or *relative brightness*—of a pair of binoculars can be found by squaring the ratio of lens size to magnifying power.

$$relative\ brightness = \left(\frac{diameter\ of\ objective\ lens}{magnification}\right)^2$$

A 6 × 30 pair of binoculars has a lens-to-magnification ratio of 30 to 6. This can be expressed as the fraction $^{30}\!/_6$, which reduces to 5. The square of this ratio is 25. A pair of 7 × 25 binoculars has a relative brightness of $(^{25}\!/_7)^2$, which is about 13. On a relative scale, the second pair of binoculars has about half the brightness of the first.

**8. Aspect Ratio Aspect ratio** refers to the dimensions of a rectangle—usually a motion-picture screen, a photograph, a film negative, or some projected image. It is the ratio of the width divided by the height. The aspect ratio of television screens is 4 to 3, or about 1.33 to 1. This was also the original standard in the motion-picture industry, and is known as the *Academy ratio*. Wide-screen moviemaking introduced higher aspect ratios. In the 1950s, systems such as CinemaScope, Cinerama, and Todd AO produced motion pictures that were shot in ratios varying from 1.65 to 1 up to 2.35 to 1. In 1963, Cinerama adopted a new technique that resulted in an aspect ratio of 2.75 to 1. Currently, the image ratio in the U.S. film industry is about 1.85 to 1. In Europe, the standard varies from 1.66 to 1 up to 1.75 to 1.

**9. The Golden Ratio and Golden Section** A ratio of particular importance in classical architecture is the **golden ratio**. If a line segment is divided into two pieces such that the ratio of the whole to the longer piece is the same as the ratio of the longer piece to the shorter piece, the division is called a **golden section** and the ratio thus created is called the *golden ratio*.

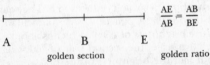

$$\frac{AE}{AB} = \frac{AB}{BE}$$

A       B      E

golden section       golden ratio

The numerical value of the golden ratio is exactly

$\frac{1}{2}\left(1 + \sqrt{5}\right)$, which is about 1.618 to 1, but it is easier to picture as a ratio of about 1.6 to 1, or 8 to 5.

**10. The Golden Rectangle** The **golden rectangle** represents the ideal of proportion in classical design. Its dimensions are considered the most aesthetically pleasing of all rectangles, and it was widely used by the ancient Greeks in designing temples such as the Parthenon.

The aspect ratio of a golden rectangle is a golden ratio: that is, the exact ratio of width to height is $\frac{1}{2}\left(1 + \sqrt{5}\right)$ to 1. The approximate ratio is 8 to 5. To construct a golden rectangle, begin with a square, such as square ABCD below. Find the midpoint of AB and call it M. Draw the diagonal from M to C. Use this diagonal as the radius of an arc centered at M and drawn down to intersect the extension of line AB. Label the intersection E. Extend a perpendicular from AE to where it intersects the extension of DC at point F.

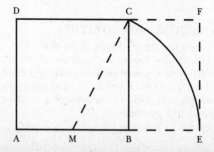

In the diagram, $\frac{BE}{AB}$ is a golden ratio, as is $\frac{AE}{EF}$.

# Trigonometry

The word **trigonometry** means "triangle measurement." Thus trigonometry is primarily the study of the relations between the lengths of the sides of a triangle and the measures of its angles. It is used for the calculation of heights, distances, and angles in architecture, engineering, surveying, and navigation. It is a direct extension of the geometry of familiar triangles such as the 30°-60°-90° and the right isosceles triangles.

This section is not a survey of trigonometry. Instead it focuses on the smaller subject of the analysis of right triangles and their use in measurement and estimation. It defines the trigonometric functions of sine, cosine, and tangent, and explores how electronic calculators can be used in solving trigonometric problems.

## DEFINITIONS AND NOTATION

A **triangle** has three angles, three sides, and three vertices. Capital letters are traditionally used to label each vertex, lowercase letters to label the sides, and lowercase Greek letters to label the angles, as in triangle ABC below. (The symbol $\alpha$ is *alpha*, $\beta$ is *beta*, and $\gamma$ is *gamma*.)

*angles:* $\angle\alpha$, $\angle\beta$, $\angle\gamma$

*sides:* AB has length *c;* AC has length *b;*
BC has length *a.*

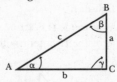

Each angle of the triangle has an **opposite side**
and two **adjacent sides**. For ∠α, the opposite side
is side *a,* and sides *b* and *c* are the adjacent sides.

**1. Right Triangles** By definition, a **right triangle**
contains one right angle. Because the three angles
of a triangle must sum to 180 degrees, the two
other angles must sum to 90 degrees. Thus they
are both **acute angles,** and also **complementary angles**.

**2.** In a right triangle, the two sides adjacent to the
right angle are called the **legs**. The side opposite
the right angle is called the **hypotenuse**. By the
Pythagorean Theorem, the sum of the squares of
the legs of a right triangle equals the square of the
hypotenuse.

$$a^2 + b^2 = c^2$$

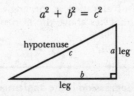

**3.** A **right isosceles triangle** has angles measuring 45°, 45°, and 90°. The ratios of its sides are illustrated in this figure.

The ratio of the legs is 1 to 1.

The ratio of the hypotenuse to a leg is $\sqrt{2}$ to 1.

**4.** A **30°-60°-90°** right triangle has sides whose ratios are illustrated in this figure. The short leg is half the length of the hypotenuse. The longer leg is $\sqrt{3}$ times the length of the shorter leg.

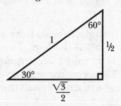

**5.** An **angle of elevation** is the angle made by a line of sight that lies above the horizontal.

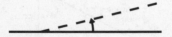

An **angle of depression** is the angle made by a line of sight that lies below the horizontal.

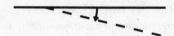

Any object whose angle of elevation or depression is being measured can be considered a vertex of a right triangle.

If the angle of elevation of the sun is 30°, a tall object such as a tree, flagpole, or building will cast a shadow that forms a 30°-60°-90° triangle.

- A flagpole casts a 90-foot shadow when the sun is at a 30° angle of elevation. The height of the flagpole can be found by using the property of similar triangles and writing a ratio.

$$\frac{\sqrt{3}/2}{1/2} = \frac{\text{length of shadow}}{\text{height of pole}} = \frac{90}{x}$$

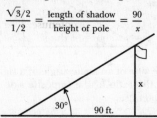

The ratio of the long leg to the short leg of a 30°-60°-90° triangle is $\sqrt{3}$. Therefore the ratio of shadow length to pole height is $\sqrt{3}$.

$$\frac{90}{x} = \sqrt{3}$$

Thus the height of the pole is given by

$$x = \frac{90}{\sqrt{3}} \approx 51.96, \text{ or about 52 feet.}$$

(The sign $\approx$ means "approximately equals.")

# TRIGONOMETRIC FUNCTIONS

The **trigonometric functions**—sine, cosine, and tangent—are based on the ratios of the sides of right triangles. The values of these functions can be used to solve problems that arise with triangles other than the 30°-60°-90° triangle and the 45°-45°-90° (right isosceles) triangle. Thus the sine (sin), cosine (cos), and tangent (tan) of an angle are numerical values that "measure" certain properties of the angle. The acute angle is symbolized by the Greek letter θ, or *theta*.

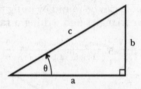

The **sine** of an acute angle of a right triangle is the ratio of the opposite side to the hypotenuse.

$$\sin\theta = \frac{b}{c}$$

The **cosine** of an acute angle of a right triangle is the ratio of the adjacent side to the hypotenuse.

$$\cos\theta = \frac{a}{c}$$

The **tangent** of an acute angle of a right triangle is the ratio of the opposite side to the adjacent side.

$$\tan\theta = \frac{b}{a}$$

Notice that the tangent of an angle is the quotient of its sine to its cosine.

$$\tan\theta = \frac{\sin\theta}{\cos\theta}$$

**1. Solving Right Triangles** The value of the sine, cosine, and tangent of an angle can be used to solve for the dimensions of a triangle. Table 2.2 shows several common values.

**Table 2.2. Trigonometric Function Values**

| angle θ | sinθ | cosθ | tanθ |
|---------|------|------|------|
| 0° | 0 | 1 | 0 |
| 15° | .2588 | .9659 | .2679 |
| 30° | 0.5 | .8660 | .5774 |
| 45° | .7071 | .7071 | 1.000 |
| 60° | .8660 | 0.5 | 1.7321 |
| 75° | .9659 | .2588 | 3.7321 |
| 90° | 1 | 0 | — |

Although the table does not go beyond four decimal places, it is accurate enough to show that the sine of an angle is equal to the cosine of its complement (sin15° = cos75°, sin30° = cos60°, etc.). As noted above, the tangent is the quotient of the sine and the cosine of any angle.

Below are two examples of how the trigonometric functions are used to solve for the dimensions of right triangles.

• An airplane is flying at a height of 5000 feet. An observer on the ground measures its angle of elevation to be 32°12′. How far is the plane from the observer?

In the diagram below,

$$\sin\theta = \frac{opposite}{hypotenuse} = \frac{5000}{x}$$

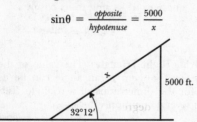

But sin 32°12′ can be found using a scientific calculator. Look for a key marked ° ′ ″. This key allows angle measurements to be entered in degree-minute-second mode. The sine of 32°12′ is 0.532876. Thus

$$0.532876 = \frac{5000}{x} \text{ or } x = \frac{5000}{0.532876} \approx 9383 \text{ feet.}$$

• A car descends a 15° grade for 3.5 miles. How much altitude has it lost, and how many miles has it covered on the map?

The diagram indicates two unknown values that can be found using trigonometric relations.

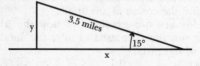

$\sin 15° = \frac{y}{3.5}$ or $\frac{y}{3.5} = 0.2580$, so $y = 0.9059$.

$\cos 15° = \frac{x}{3.5}$ or $\frac{x}{3.5} = 0.9659$, so $x = 3.38$.

Thus the car has descended just over 0.9 miles and has traveled 3.38 horizontal miles.

**2. Degrees and Radians** A **degree** is an angle measurement equivalent to $\frac{1}{360}$th of a full revolution. A **radian** is another angle measure. Radian measure equates a full revolution with the measure $2\pi$. Thus $2\pi$ radians is equivalent to $360°$. The conversion formulas for degrees and radians are

$$1 \text{ degree} = \frac{\pi}{180} \text{ radians}$$

$$1 \text{ radian} = \frac{180}{\pi} \text{ degrees}$$

A $30°$ angle is equivalent to an angle of $30 \times \frac{\pi}{180}$ radians, or $\frac{\pi}{6}$ radians.

Most electronic calculators allow angle measurements to be entered in degree-minute-second format or in radian measure. When an angle is entered using the degree-minute-second (° ′ ″) key, it is usually converted to a decimal form. A *minute* is $\frac{1}{60}$th, or 0.0167, of a degree; a *second* is $\frac{1}{60}$th of a minute, or $\frac{1}{3600}$th of a degree.

• $30°\,12'$ is equivalent to 30 and $\frac{12}{60}$ degrees. But $\frac{12}{60}$ equals $\frac{1}{5}$, or 0.2. Thus the angle measure of $30°12'$ will be displayed by a calculator as 30.2 degrees.

• $56°6'36''$ would be displayed as the equivalent of $56 + \frac{6}{60} + \frac{36}{3600}$, or $56 + 0.1 + 0.01$, or 56.11 degrees.

Most electronic calculators can easily switch back and forth between degree and radian modes.

The screen will usually indicate the mode by showing the symbols *DEG* or *RAD*. It is important to enter angle measures in the proper mode when calculating values of trigonometric functions.

**Table 2.3. Degree and Radian Measure Equivalents**

| | |
|---|---|
| 0° | 0 radians (rad) |
| 15° | $\pi/12$ rad |
| 30° | $\pi/6$ rad |
| 45° | $\pi/4$ rad |
| 60° | $\pi/3$ rad |
| 75° | $5\pi/12$ rad |
| 90° | $\pi/2$ rad |

**3. Tangent and Slope** The tangent function can be used to determine the slope of a line based on its angle of elevation. The tangent of angle $\theta$ is $a/b$, which is the rise over the run of segment AB. Thus the slope of a line with a pitch of $\theta$ degrees is the tangent of $\theta$.

$$\text{slope AB} = \frac{a}{b}$$

$$\tan\theta = \frac{a}{b}$$

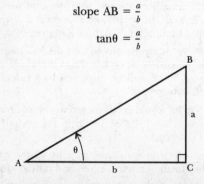

Thus tanθ = slope AB.

• A 45° pitch is the same as a slope of 1, which equals tan45°.

• A line with a 60° angle of elevation has a slope of 1.732, which equals tan60°.

**Table 2.4. Conversion of Pitch to Slope**

| Angle of Elevation | Slope |
|---|---|
| 0° | 0.0000 |
| 5° | 0.0875 |
| 10° | 0.1763 |
| 15° | 0.2679 |
| 20° | 0.3640 |
| 25° | 0.4663 |
| 30° | 0.5774 |
| 35° | 0.7002 |
| 40° | 0.8391 |
| 45° | 1.0000 |
| 50° | 1.1918 |
| 55° | 1.4281 |
| 60° | 1.7321 |
| 65° | 2.1445 |
| 70° | 2.7475 |
| 75° | 3.7321 |
| 80° | 5.6713 |
| 85° | 11,4301 |
| 90° | infinite |

Table 2.5 provides basic formulas for all the common geometrical figures.

**Table 2.5. Length, Area, and Volume Formulas**

## circle

circumference = $2\pi r$

area = $\pi r^2$

area of a sector:

$(\theta/360) \times \pi r^2$ (degree measure)

or $\theta r^2/2$ (radian measure)

length of an arc:

$\pi r\theta/180$ (degree measure)

or $r\theta$ (radian measure)

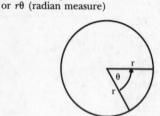

## triangle

area = $\frac{1}{2}bh$

angle/side relationships:

$\dfrac{\sin\alpha}{a} = \dfrac{\sin\beta}{b} = \dfrac{\sin\gamma}{c}$ (Law of Sines)

$c^2 = a^2 + b^2 - 2a \times b \times \cos\gamma$ (Law of Cosines)

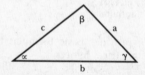

**Table 2.5** *(continued)*

**square**
  area = $x^2$
  perimeter = $4x$

**rectangle**
  area = *(length)* × *(width)* = $xy$
  perimeter = $2x + 2y$

**parallelogram**
  area = $b \times h$

**trapezoid**
  area = $\frac{1}{2}(a+b) \times h$

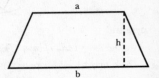

**rectangular box**
  volume = *(length)* × *(width)* × *(height)* = $xyz$
  surface area = $2xy + 2xz + 2yz$

**Table 2.5** *(continued)*

**cylinder**
  volume = *(area of base)* × *height* = $\pi r^2 h$
  surface area = $2\pi rh + 2\pi r^2$

**cone**
  volume = $\frac{1}{3}\pi r^2 h$

  surface area = $\pi rs$
  (not including base)

**pyramid**
  volume = $\frac{1}{3}$ *(area of base)* × *height*

  (Base may be any shape.)

**sphere**
  volume = $\frac{4}{3}\pi r^3$
  surface area = $4\pi r^2$

# Chapter 3

# Everyday Mathematics

## Household Mathematics

### PRODUCT LABELING—NUTRITIONAL REQUIREMENTS

New Food and Drug Administration guidelines issued in 1994 put forth two sets of dietary recommendations—one a set of *maximum daily values* of food groups, the other of *minimum daily values* of vitamins and minerals. The guidelines also mandated the labeling of food. These *nutrition facts*, which are listed on every packaged grocery-store product, relate the contents of a single serving to the maximum and minimum daily values as they are listed in the tables below.

When viewed with the tables of maximum and minimum values, the statement of nutrition facts is supposed to be self-explanatory. Still, a few observations are worth emphasizing.

**Table 3.1. FDA Recommendations, based on a daily diet of 2000 calories**

| Food group | Maximum daily value |
|---|---|
| fat | 65 g |
| saturated fatty acids | 20 g |
| cholesterol | 300 mg |
| sodium | 2400 mg |
| total carbohydrate | 300 g |
| fiber | 25 g |
| potassium | 3500 mg |
| protein | |
|     infants | 14 g |
|     children 1 to 4 yrs. | 16 g |
|     pregnant women | 60 g |
|     nursing mothers | 65 g |
|     others | 50 g |

The percentages of fat, cholesterol, sodium, carbohydrate, and protein need to be understood as percents of *maximum* recommended amounts. Seven grams of fat, for example, constitutes 11% of the maximum recommended intake of 65 grams (7 grams divided by 65 grams is about .1077, which is rounded to 11%).

The percentages of vitamins and minerals are calculated from *minimum* allowances. Thus one serving of this food delivers 6% of one's iron requirements for one day. At the bottom of the nutrition facts, the table in small print makes allowances for different body types, and also indicates how many calories are accounted for by fat, carbohydrate, and protein.

### Table 3.2 FDA Minimum Daily Values of Vitamins and Minerals

| | |
|---|---|
| vitamin A | 5,000 IU (international units) |
| vitamin B6 | 2 mg |
| vitamin B12 | 6 micrograms |
| vitamin C | 60 mg |
| vitamin D | 400 IU |
| vitamin E | 30 IU |
| folic acid | 0.4 mg |
| thiamin | 1.5 mg |
| niacin | 20 mg |
| riboflavin | 1.7 mg |
| calcium | 1.0 g |
| iron | 18 mg |
| phosphorus | 1 g |
| iodine | 150 micrograms |
| magnesium | 400 mg |
| zinc | 15 mg |
| copper | 2 mg |
| biotin | .3 mg |
| pantothenic acid | 10 mg |

A typical statement of nutrition facts looks like the one shown on page 114.

## PRODUCT LABELING—ALCOHOL CONTENT

**1. Proof (alcohol)** The *proof,* or alcohol content, of distilled liquor is a number between 0 and 200 representing twice the percent alcohol content by volume. Pure ethyl alcohol is 200 proof. A 90 proof whiskey is 45% alcohol.

# Nutrition Facts

Serving Size 3 biscuits (34 g)
Servings per Container About 6

Amount Per Serving

## Calories 170  Calories from Fat 60

|  | % Daily Value* |
|---|---|
| **Total Fat** 7g | 11% |
| Saturated Fat 3g | 15% |
| **Cholesterol** 10mg | 3% |
| **Sodium** 170mg | 7% |
| **Total Carbohydrate** 24g | 8% |
| Dietary Fiber 1g | 4% |
| Sugars 5g | |
| **Protein** 2g | |

Vitamin A 0%  ·  Vitamin C 0%

Calcium 0%   ·  Iron 6%

*Percent Daily Values are based on a 2,000 calorie diet. Your daily values may be higher or lower depending on your calorie needs:

| | Calories: | 2,000 | 2,500 |
|---|---|---|---|
| Total Fat | Less than | 65g | 80g |
| Sat Fat | Less than | 20g | 25g |
| Cholesterol | Less than | 300mg | 300mg |
| Sodium | Less than | 2400mg | 2400mg |
| Total Carbohydrate | | 300mg | 375mg |
| Dietary Fiber | | 25g | 30g |

Calories per gram:
Fat 9  ·  Carbohydrate 4  ·  Protein 4

A *proof spirit* is an alcoholic liquor or a mixture of alcohol and water which contains 50% alcohol by volume. In the United States, this would be 100 proof. In Great Britain the definition is somewhat different. Proof spirits there are defined to be 48.24% alcohol by weight, or 57.06% alcohol by volume. The two are equivalent.

The amount of alcohol in beer and wine is usually measured by the percent of liquid content, and not by proof. This measure, called *percent by volume*, is not the same as *percent by weight* for all liquids. Because alcohol is lighter than water, the percent alcohol by volume will always exceed the equivalent percent alcohol by weight.

By law, all European Union countries require the alcohol content of beers, wines, and spirits to be displayed in terms of percent alcohol by volume. In the United States, beer is sometimes labeled in terms of percent volume by *weight*, which is lower than percent by volume. For example, 3.5% by weight is equivalent to about 4.4% by volume. But because some states have laws banning the display of alcohol content, most nationally distributed U.S. beers are not labeled at all.

Table 3.3 shows the percentages of alcohol by volume for types of beer, wine, and spirits.

**2. Liquor Measures**  Beer, wine, and liquors come in a dazzling array of serving and container sizes. There are few, if any, universal standards. The base unit for a serving of liquor is the *shot*, but smaller servings—a *dram*, a *nip*, a *finger*—are possible. Below, roughly ordered by size, is a short glossary of the ways alcoholic beverages may be purchased.

**dram**  a small quantity, a sip.

**nip**  a sip (as in "a nip of spirits"); in the case of ale, up to a half-pint serving (as in "a nip of ale"); also a small (about 50 ml) bottle of liquor.

**finger**  a serving of liquor filling a small whiskey glass to the depth of a finger's width—about ¾

**Table 3.3. Alcohol Content of Distilled and
Fermented Drinks**

| Type | Percent alcohol by volume |
| --- | --- |
| whiskey | 40 |
| gin | 40 |
| rum | 40 |
| sherry | 20 |
| port | 20 |
| Madeira | 20 |
| table wines (white, red, rosé) | 7–15 |
| sparkling wines | 7–15 |
| dessert (or fortified) wines | 16–23 |
| lager beers | 3–5 |
| top-fermented beers (ales, porters, and stouts) | 4–6.5 |
| malt liquor | up to 8 |

inch or 19 mm. A two-finger serving is filled to
the depth of two fingers—about 1½ inches.

**shot**   the amount that pours out of a bottle with
a practiced twist of the wrist; about 1½ ounces or
45 ml. The capacity of a shot glass.

**a double**   a drink consisting of two shots.

**a triple**   a drink consisting of three shots.

**pony**   a 1-ounce glass of liquor (much like a
shot); a 7-ounce bottle of ale or beer (similar to
a nip in both of its meanings).

**jigger**   a small whiskey glass or cocktail measure
containing 1½ ounces or 45 ml; similar to a shot.

**fifth** a fifth of a gallon, or ⅘ quart; approximately 750 ml.

**split** a half-size bottle, 6 to 8 fluid ounces; originally a soda drink in which the soda bottle was split in making a serving for two people.

**flagon** one quart.

**yard, yard-of-ale** a trumpet-shaped glass 3 feet long and containing just over a half gallon.

**magnum** large wine bottle equivalent to 2 standard bottles or 1.5 liters.

**jeroboam** a large wine bottle equivalent to 4 standard bottles, or about 3 liters; also used for christening ships.

**demijohn** a wicker-covered glass bottle holding anywhere from 2 to 12 gallons.

**keg** a small cask or barrel holding 5 to 10 gallons.

**firkin** a quarter of a barrel.

**barrel** a container holding 43¼ gallons of beer (31½ gallons of ordinary liquids, 42 gallons of oil)

## UNIT PRICING

Most supermarkets are required by law to display a *unit price* for each item they sell. Following the tradition of street markets, they list prices of goods by the pound, by the gallon, or by some measure or count, depending upon how the product may happen to be packaged. By a simple formula

$$unit\ price = \frac{total\ cost}{total\ amount}$$

For purposes of comparison, the units chosen for amounts are kept uniform for competing items. Brands of honey are all priced in cents per ounce, napkins in cents per 100 count, juices in dollars per gallon, and so on.

Unit pricing is not typically provided in dry-goods stores. Therefore, when choosing between stores and between brand names (or generic brands) the consumer should carefully compute the unit price in order to make an informed comparison.

## MONTHLY BILLS—ELECTRICITY

The basic units used to measure electrical potential, current, and resistance are *volts, amps,* and *ohms.* These are often described using an analogy between the flow of electricity through a wire and the flow of water through a pipe. The *voltage* is equivalent to the water pressure, the *current* (in amps) to the rate of flow, and the *resistance* (in ohms) to the size or resistance of a waterwheel or some other device that the flow is driving.

The voltage in any household outlet is either 120 volts, for standard outlets, or 240 volts for heavy-duty outlets required by dryers and air conditioners. (Although this figure should remain constant, electric companies occasionally have to decrease the voltage during periods of peak demand. During critical power shortages, this results in a brownout.)

Voltage and current can be multiplied together to find electric power usage, which is measured in kilowatts. Usage over time is measured in kilowatt-hours. This section explains each of these units and shows how they relate to a monthly electric bill.

**1.** A *kilowatt-hour* (kWh) is the basic unit of electric power consumption used by electric utility companies to calculate electric bills. It is defined as the amount of power used by a device that draws 1 kilowatt over 1 hour. Every electrical appliance or device carries a label indicating the amount of power it consumes. A 75-watt bulb, for example, requires 75 watts of power to light. Given the wattage and the duration of use, the cost of operation can be calculated by estimating kilowatt-hour usage and multiplying by the usage charge indicated on an electric bill.

Not all devices are labeled by wattage, however. Some are labeled by amperage, resistance, and even horsepower. But all of these can be converted to wattage through simple formulas.

**2. Wattage** The number of watts used by a device can be calculated in a number of ways. Once the wattage has been calculated, it can easily be converted to kilowatts, and then to kilowatt-hours by the following formula:

$$(\text{watts} \div 1000) \times \text{hours} = \text{kilowatts} \times \text{hours}$$
$$= \text{kilowatt-hours (kWh)}$$

- A 100-watt bulb uses $100/1000 = 0.1$ kilowatts. If it burns for 20 hours, it uses $(0.1 \text{ kW}) \times (20 \text{ hours}) = 2$ kWh.

• A string of twenty 15-watt Christmas light-bulbs requires $20 \times 15 = 300$ watts of power. If the lights are turned on for 5 hours each day, they use $(300 \text{ watts} \div 1000) \times 5 \text{ hours} = 1.5$ kilowatt-hours each day.

## 3. Amperage

Electric current is measured in units of *amperes* (or simply *amps*). A typical house has 100-amp electrical service, although many are now outfitted with 200-amp service. The circuit-breaker box distributes this current through various circuits that may be rated at 15, 20, or 30 amps. If the total amperage on a circuit exceeds the rating, the circuit breaker will open in order to prevent the circuit from overheating.

Current (in amps) can be converted to power usage (in watts) by using this formula:

$$power = voltage \times current$$

When expressed in units of measurement, this formula becomes:

$$watts = volts \times amps$$

The standard household outlet supplies 120 volts, so the conversion from amps to watts reduces to multiplication by 120. With a heavy-duty outlet, the conversion requires multiplying by 240 volts.

• A 10-amp toaster drawing 120 volts uses $120 \times 10 = 1200$ watts of power. If the toaster is used 15 minutes per day, then it is used $30 \times 15$ or 450 minutes per month, which is equivalent to 7½ hours. The number of kilo-watt-hours used would be

$$(1200 \text{ watts} \div 1000) \times 7.5 \text{ hours} = 9 \text{ kilowatt-hours}$$

**4. Resistance** Some appliances are rated by their electric resistance, which is measured in *ohms*. A simple formula known as *Ohm's Law* relates voltage, resistance, and current. It says:

$$amps = volts \div ohms$$

• A microwave oven with a resistance of 8 ohms operating on a standard 120-volt circuit uses (120 volts ÷ 8 ohms) = 15 amps.

As described above, once the current (in amps) is known, the power in watts can be calculated using the fact that *watts = volts × amps*. Combining this with Ohm's Law results in two formulas that can be used to convert current and resistance to wattage, or voltage and resistance to wattage.

$$watts = volts \times volts \div ohms$$

$$watts = amps \times amps \times ohms$$

• The power used by the microwave oven in the previous example can be calculated using either of the above formulas, where voltage is 120, amperage is 15, and resistance is 8 ohms:

$$amps \times amps \times ohms = 15 \times 15 \times 8$$
$$= 1800 \text{ watts, or about } 1.8 \text{ kW}$$

The voltage supplied to household outlets does vary, generally between 110 and 120 volts, but it should be thought of as constant. Therefore the power usage is directly related to the current. By Ohm's Law, the current (amperage) is inversely related to the resistance (ohms). Thus the power usage increases as the resistance falls—an appliance with a low resistance dissipates a lot of power compared to one with high resistance for a given applied voltage. Telephones, for example, have a very high resistance, and consequently draw little power. Some low-power systems use a low-voltage transformer or power adapter to convert 120 volts to about 24 volts or less. Such a transformer might be used to power a doorbell, an electric train set, or a laptop computer.

- A laptop computer has an AC (current) adapter that converts 120 input volts to 24 output volts. It is rated at 1.04 amps. Its power usage is found by multiplying voltage times current:

$$24 \text{ volts} \times 1.04 \text{ amps} \approx 25 \text{ watts}$$

**5. Horsepower** Electric power is sometimes measured in *horsepower*. This is usually the case with electric motors. One horsepower is the power required to lift a 500-pound weight 1 foot in 1 second. It is equivalent to 746 watts of power. To convert horsepower to watts, multiply by 746.

- Assume a table saw has a 2½-horsepower motor. The wattage required to run the saw would be (2½ × 746), or 1865 watts. If the saw runs for 15 minutes, its power usage would be

(1865 watts ÷ 1000) × 0.25 hours = 0.46625
kilowatt-hours

**6. Electric Meters** There are several types of electric meters. Some have digital readouts, but older meters use four or five dials that indicate kilowatt-hour usage in 1-kWh, 10-kWh, 100-kWh, 1000-kWh, and 10,000-kWh units. The dials alternate in their direction of numbering. One is numbered clockwise from 0 to 9, the next counterclockwise from 0 to 9, and so on. The indicator on each dial should be read like an hour hand—it indicates the digit most recently passed. A hand between the 5 and the 6, even if it is closer to the 6, indicates 5.

Digital or dial meters show a cumulative total of kilowatt-hour usage. The digits on the dials can be written from left to right to form a number. This number can be checked against the reading for the previous month to find the total usage for each month.

31,641 Kilowatt-hours

**7. Cost of Electrical Usage** A monthly electric bill will show the number of kilowatt-hours used during a month-long period, and perhaps the average household usage per day. A majority of that usage will come from heating and air-conditioning systems and large appliances. It is possible to estimate the monthly cost of operating any household electrical device by calculating its power usage. This task is simplified in the case of large appliances, which are required to display an energy efficiency rating and estimated annual cost of operation. For smaller appliances, in those cases where the approximate usage can be estimated, operating cost can be determined directly.

• An electric dryer uses a 220-volt outlet. If it draws a current of 20 amps, the power usage would be

$$(220 \text{ volt}) \times (20 \text{ amp}) = 4400 \text{ watts.}$$

A load requiring 45 minutes to dry would use

$$(4400 \text{ watts} \div 1000) \times (.75 \text{ hours}) =$$
$$(4.4 \text{ kWh}) \times (.75 \text{ hours}) = 3.3 \text{ kWh.}$$

At about 9.5 cents per hour, this would cost

$$(3.3) \times (\$0.095) = \$0.3135, \text{ or about 31 cents.}$$

If the dryer is used to dry four loads each week, the annual cost of operation would be

$$(4 \text{ loads per week} \times 52 \text{ weeks}) \times (\$0.31 \text{ per}$$
$$\text{load}) = \$64.48.$$

**8. Sliding Scales** Electric bills are generally calculated on a sliding scale. The first one or two hundred kilowatt-hours are the most expensive (perhaps 9 or 10 cents per kWh), but after that the rate drops considerably.

• An electric bill indicates a monthly usage of 215 kWh. The first 100 units are priced at $0.098, the next 100 at $0.072, and anything over that at $0.062. The cost of electrical usage would be

$$100 \times (0.098) = \$9.80$$
$$100 \times (0.072) = \$7.20$$
$$\underline{15 \times (0.062) = \$0.93}$$

total                $17.93

A monthly service charge would also appear on the bill.

## MONTHLY BILLS—NATURAL GAS

Most gas companies measure gas usage in units of *therms*. A therm is about 100 cubic feet of gas, although this can vary. Consequently a gas bill will often indicate a *conversion factor* from units of 1000 cubic feet of gas to therms of gas. The gas meter measures usage in cubic footage, but billing is done on the basis of therms used. The two measures are always very close. A therm or CCF of gas converts to about 100,000 BTUs (British Thermal Units). A BTU is the amount of heat required to raise the temperature of 1 pound of water 1 degree Fahrenheit.

To calculate a gas bill, the gas company reads the gas meter on the same day each month, and subtracts the previous month's reading in order to find the total therms used during the month.

The gas bill includes a monthly fee, and also incorporates a sliding scale. It might look something like this:

monthly charge     $5.70
first 30 therms       .6523
additional therms     .3871

If the customer used 47 therms during the month, the bill would look like this:

| | |
|---|---:|
| Oct 17 meter reading | 6659 |
| Sept 17 meter reading | 6612 |
| therms billed | 47 |
| monthly charge | 5.70 |
| 30 therms @ .6523 | 19.57 |
| 17 therms @ .3871 | 6.58 |
| total | 31.85 |

## PROPERTY TAXES

Most cities and towns generate revenue for public services by levying a *property tax*. The tax is stated as a dollar amount per thousand dollars of assessed value. The *assessed value* is based upon such factors as the lot size, the square footage of the house, its condition, and the value of surrounding properties. The assessed value is not necessarily the market value. In some localities, the assessed value is calculated directly as a percent of the market price—perhaps 80%.

- If a house sold for $140,000 and is assessed at 80% of market value, its assessed value would be ($140,000) × (0.8) = $112,000. If the tax rate is $15 per thousand, the annual property tax would be ($15) × (112) = $1,680 per year.

Property-tax bills are generally collected semi-annually rather than monthly. Often a bank holding a mortgage establishes an escrow account for the purpose of paying property taxes. The accumulated six months of payments are paid to the city or town by the bank at the end of the fiscal year (usually September 30) and at the midpoint (March 31).

# Construction

## CALCULATING SQUARE FOOTAGE AND CUBIC FOOTAGE

In order to estimate the amount of wallpaper, flooring, tile, paint, carpet, roofing, or driveway sealer needed for a job, it is necessary to calculate the square footage to be covered.

It is worth noting that contractors almost never estimate materials by calculating completely from scratch. There are a few whose experience allows them to "eyeball" the job and order material without making any written computations. Most contractors, however, make use of simple slide-rule–style calculators provided by building material suppliers. These give quick and accurate totals based on the dimensions of the job. Lumberyards use a modified yardstick to calculate board feet. There are also calculators for asphalt, concrete, roofing and siding shingles, and insulation. With a concrete calculator, for example, the user lines up the measured length, width, and thickness dimensions, and then reads off the number of cubic yards required for the job. All of these carry out simple calculations based on the formulas outlined below.

**1.** Household square-footage calculations for everything but circular regions are based on the areas of rectangles (area = length × width) and areas of triangles (area = base × height/2). Because of the complexity of most floor plans and wall profiles, it may be necessary to break irregularly shaped spaces (L-shaped rooms, for example) into two or more rectangles.

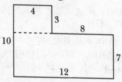

• The floor plan shown above can be broken into two rectangles: a 7' by 12' and a 3' by 4'. These have areas of 84 and 12 square feet, respectively, which add up to 96 square feet. An alternative is to subtract the area of the cutout—that is, to think of the room as a 10' by 12' rectangle minus a 3' by 8' piece. The area by this method would be 120 minus 24, or 96 square feet.

• A gallon of paint covers approximately 400 square feet (this may vary considerably—the exact figure is always given on the can).

If a room is 12 feet long and 14 feet wide with 8-foot-high ceilings, its total wall space would be:

2 walls @ 8' by 12', or 2 × 96 = 192 sq. ft.
2 walls @ 8' by 14', or 2 × 112 = <u>224 sq. ft.</u>

total   416 sq. ft.

Assuming there are door and window openings that can be subtracted from the total, the surface area could safely be covered by a gallon labeled to cover 400 square feet.

**2. Legal Square Footage** The *square footage* of a home, as used in tax assessments or in descriptions of the house used by realtors and contractors, is the total amount of interior living space. It does not include the basement, attic, or garage. If any of these are finished spaces, their square footage is usually noted separately from the figure for the house.

Total square footage is computed using the *exterior* dimensions of the house. This can be done from a blueprint or from measurements made and recorded onto a sketch of the footprint of the house. Some houses have simple rectangular footprints, but those that do not can usually be broken into rectangular sections by drawing dotted lines as shown below. Using the formula for the area of a rectangle, the total square footage for each level can be easily calculated.

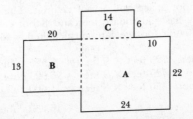

- The footprint of the house drawn here can be broken into three rectangles.

$$\text{Area of A} = 22 \times 24 = 528 \text{ square feet}$$
$$\text{Area of B} = 13 \times 20 = 260$$
$$\underline{\text{Area of C} = \phantom{0}6 \times 14 = \phantom{0}84}$$

1st-floor total         872 square feet

If the second level has the same footprint, and there are no other levels, the total square footage would be double the first-floor total, which comes out to 1,744 square feet.

**3.** To calculate the *cubic footage* of a house, find the total area of the floor plan (or footprint), and multiply by the ceiling height. If each floor has the same floor plan and the same ceiling height, multiply the cubic footage of the first floor by the number of floors. Otherwise, calculate the area of the floor plan for each level, and multiply by its ceiling height.

- A three-story house has identical first and second floors, each of which has 725 square feet of floor space and 9-foot ceilings. The third story has 450 square feet and 8-foot ceilings. The cubic footage can be calculated as follows:

1st floor: 725 feet $\times$ 9 feet =   6,525 cubic feet
2nd floor: 725 feet $\times$ 9 feet =   6,525 cubic feet
3rd floor: 450 feet $\times$ 8 feet =   $\underline{3,600 \text{ cubic feet}}$

total                  16,650 cubic feet

## UNITS OF MEASURE

**1. Roofing** Roofing shingles are sold in units called *squares.* A square is equivalent to a 10' × 10' area, which totals 100 square feet. To estimate the number of squares needed for a job, find the square footage of the roof and divide by 100.

- An 80-foot-long building has a simple pitched roof that measures 25 feet from gutter to peak. Thus the roof consists of two 25' × 80' rectangles. Each has a square footage of 25 × 80 = 2000, for a total of 4000 square feet. Divide by 100 to find the number of squares:

$$\frac{4000}{100} = 40 \text{ squares}$$

Roofs generally have rectangular surfaces, although there are many types of roof designs that have irregularities such as window dormers. Dormers are not difficult to estimate because they can be broken into triangles. In fact, the two sides of a dormer can be combined to form a rectangle.

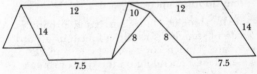

- The roof pictured above has a single dormer. The two roof surfaces of the dormer can be pieced together to make an 8' × 10' rectangle, which has 80 square feet of area. The dormer divides the roof into two principal surfaces that can also be arranged to form a rectangle—in this case with length 19.5′ and width 14′. The total area of this rectangle is 14 × 19.5, or 273 square feet.

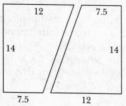 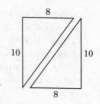

The total surface area of the dormer and the roof (on this side of the house) is 80 + 273, or 353 square feet. If the opposite side is identical, the job would require twice this amount, or 706 square feet of shingles. Seven squares of shingles would not be enough to do the job if some allowance for waste is included (as it should be). But it would not be necessary to buy another square.

Extra shingles can be purchased in bundles. A *bundle* of shingles is usually a fourth or a third of a square. Thus it covers anywhere from 25 to 35 square feet, depending on the type of shingle.

**2. Board Feet** Lumber, in the form of siding, flooring, studs, joists, and other boards, is sold by the *board foot*. A board foot is the equivalent of a piece of wood 12 inches long by 12 inches wide by 1 inch thick. The volume of a board foot is 144 cubic inches.

To calculate the number of board feet in a piece of wood, compute its volume. This may require converting its length from feet to inches.

- A 10-foot $1'' \times 4''$ oak board has a length of $10 \times 12 = 120$ inches. Its volume is $(120'') \times (1'') \times (4'')$ or 480 cubic inches.

Dividing by 144 gives $3\frac{1}{3}$ board feet. If the oak costs \$2.75 per board foot, the cost of the piece would be

$$(3\frac{1}{3}) \times (\$2.75) = \$9.17.$$

A simpler but equivalent formula is:

*board feet = (length in feet) × (width in feet) ×
(thickness in inches)*

- A 12-foot $2'' \times 10''$ joist contains

$$(12') \times (^{10}/_{12}) \times (2'') = 20 \text{ board feet.}$$

(Notice that the 10″ width dimension is expressed in feet as $^{10}/_{12}$.)

1-inch, ⅞-inch, and ¾-inch stock are all calculated as 1 inch thick in the board-feet formula. To calculate board feet for thinner stock—½″ thick or less—use a thickness of ½″.

**3. Lumber Dimensions** Lumber comes in a few general classifications:

A *board* is wood that is milled less than 2 inches thick.

*Dimension lumber* can be 2 to 5 inches thick. This includes framing lumber such as 2 × 4's, joists, and planks.

*Timbers* are more than 5 inches in thickness and width. This includes most beams.

There is also *millwork* (moldings, casing, tongue and groove, flooring) and *sheathing* (plywood and particleboard).

Prices of millwork and sheathing are set by the linear foot (or running foot), by the 4' × 8' sheet, or by the square foot. Other lumber prices are set by the board foot, which is calculated from the dimensions of the piece.

Although a board, a timber, or a piece of dimension lumber is finished, or *dressed,* to dimensions that are smaller than the named dimensions, it is the named dimension that is used in the calculation of board feet.

A two-by-four, for example, is dressed to 1⅝ by 3⅝ inches. Yet the board-footage of a 12-foot 2 × 4 is calculated using a full 2 inches for the thickness and 4 inches for the width.

$$board\ feet = (12\ feet) \times \left(\frac{1}{3}\ feet\right) \times (2\ in)$$
$$= 8\ board\ feet$$

Other dressed dimensions are given in the table below. The rough dimension is the named dimension. In a 2 × 4, the 2″ thickness is the rough thickness of the board before it is dressed to about 1⅝″.

### Table 3.4. Nominal Size and Dressed Dimensions of Boards, with Board Feet per Linear Foot

| Nominal Size (in inches) | Actual Size (dressed) | Board Feet per Linear Foot |
|---|---|---|
| 1 by 2 | ¾×1½ | .1667 |
| 1 by 4 | ¾×3½ | .3333 |
| 1 by 6 | ¾×5½ | .5000 |
| 1 by 8 | ¾×7½ | .6667 |
| 1 by 10 | ¾×9½ | .8333 |
| 1 by 12 | ¾×11½ | 1.000 |
| 2 by 2 | 1½×1½ | .3333 |
| 2 by 3 | 1½×2½ | .5000 |
| 2 by 4 | 1½×3½ | .6667 |
| 2 by 6 | 1½×5½ | 1.000 |
| 2 by 8 | 1½×7½ | 1.333 |
| 2 by 10 | 1½×9½ | 1.667 |
| 2 by 12 | 1½×11½ | 2.000 |

Some types of lumber are rough-cut, and their named dimensions are the same as their true dimensions. A 4 × 4 cedar fencepost, for example, is a true 4 inches by 4 inches, whereas a finished, pressure-treated 4 × 4 post is dressed to 3⅝ inches by 3⅝ inches.

**4. Heating with Wood** Wood for home heating is measured in units of cords. A *cord* is the equivalent of a stack of wood 4 feet wide by 4 feet high by 8 feet long. Its total volume is 4 × 4 × 8, or 128 cubic feet. A *cord foot* is a stack 4 feet wide by 4 feet high by 1 foot thick. Thus there are 8 cord feet in a cord.

**5. Yards of Concrete** Concrete is measured and sold by the cubic yard, which is referred to simply as a *yard*. A yard is a volume that is 3 feet long, 3 feet wide, and 3 feet high. Thus it contains $3 \times 3 \times 3 = 27$ cubic feet.

In order to estimate the amount of concrete needed for a job, it is necessary to find the cubic footage of the area to be filled.

• A 50-foot driveway, 10 feet wide, is to be poured to a depth of 6 inches. The volume is (50 feet) $\times$ (10 feet) $\times$ (½ foot) = 250 cubic feet. Divide this by 27 to obtain the number of cubic yards.

$$\frac{250}{27} \approx 9.3 \text{ yards of concrete}$$

If concrete is selling for \$62 per yard, the job would cost $9.3 \times 62 = \$576.60$. To add a 5% sales tax, multiply the total by 1.05. Total billed amount: $\$576.60 \times 1.05 = \$605.43$

In practice, concrete jobs are estimated using a *concrete calculator*, a slide-rule–like device that transforms the measured dimensions (length, width, thickness) into the number of yards required. Any concrete supply company can provide one.

**6. Nails** Below is a table of standard wire nail lengths with counts per pound. The abbreviation for *penny* is the letter *d*. With nail sizes, there is far more unanimity as to lengths than to counts per pound. Still, even the length measurements given here should not be relied on as universal standards.

**Table 3.5. Nail Sizes**

| designation | length (inches) | count per pound |
| --- | --- | --- |
| 2d | 1 | 900 |
| 3d | 1¼ | 615 |
| 4d | 1½ | 325 |
| 6d | 2 | 200 |
| 8d | 2½ | 105 |
| 10d | 3 | 75 |
| 12d | 3¼ | 60 |
| 16d (spike) | 3½ | 45 |
| 20d | 4 | 30 |
| 30d | 4½ | 20 |
| 40d | 5 | 14 |
| 50d | 5½ | 10 |
| 60d | 6 | 8 |

A *keg* of nails is a 100-pound container.

# Automobiles

A car's engine generates a rotational speed of several thousand revolutions per minute. This must be transmitted to the wheels by some mechanism that reduces the speed of rotation. The *transmission* (or *gearbox*) not only does this, but at the same time it transfers the rotational force, or *torque*, from the engine to the wheels in such a way that the driver can regulate the acceleration and speed of the car. This process is accomplished with *gear ratios*.

The numbers involved in this process—the actual gear ratios—are not of much interest or use to the average driver. Nor are many of the technical specifications of automobile engines. But in the course of shopping for, buying, maintaining, and driving a car, a car owner is confronted with many confusing numbers that are either taken for granted or taken at face value. The purpose of this section is to explain a few basic principles of automotive engineering which generate meaningful numbers that come into play in acquiring and operating a car.

**1.** The *speed* or *velocity* of a car is a measure of its change in position with respect to time. For any trip a car makes, its *average velocity* is calculated as the ratio of total distance traveled to time the trip required.

$$average\ velocity = \frac{\text{distance traveled}}{\text{elapsed time}}$$

(Notice that this is a form of the familiar algebraic formula: *rate* × *time* = *distance*.)

• A car makes a trip in 6.4 hours. The odometer reading was 65,488 at the start of the trip, and 65,744 at the end. The average velocity of the car on the trip was

$$\frac{\text{distance traveled}}{\text{elapsed time}} = \frac{65744 - 65488}{6.4} = \frac{256}{6.4}$$
$$= 40\ \text{miles per hour.}$$

The *instantaneous velocity* is simply the speed of the car as indicated by the speedometer at any instant of time. The instantaneous velocity can be thought of as the average velocity over a very short time interval.

- If a car travels a distance of 88 feet in 1 second, its average velocity (88 feet per second) is very close to its instantaneous velocity because the time interval is so short. Because there are 5280 feet in a mile, and 3600 seconds in an hour, the conversion to miles per hour would look like this:

$$1 \text{ foot} = \frac{1}{5280} \text{ miles, so } 88 \text{ feet} = 88 \times \frac{1}{5280} \text{ miles}$$

$$= \frac{1}{60} \text{ mile.}$$

$\frac{1}{60}$ mile in 1 second converts to $3600 \times \frac{1}{60}$ miles per hour, because there are 3600 seconds in an hour. The simplified result is 60 miles per hour.

**2.** *Acceleration* is the rate of change of velocity. A car whose velocity is increasing (which means that the car is speeding up) is said to be *accelerating*. A car whose velocity is decreasing (slowing down) is *decelerating*.

A falling object has an acceleration of 32 feet per second per second. This means that the velocity increases every second by 32 feet per second. At 1 second, the velocity would be 32 feet per second, at 2 seconds it would be 64 feet per second, at 3 seconds it would be 96 feet per second, and so on.

The same principle applies to an automobile. The acceleration can be estimated by taking speed readings at regular time intervals. The standard measure of acceleration is the time it takes a car to go from 0 to 60 miles per hour. If a car accelerates at 6 miles per hour *per second,* it will go from 0 to 6 mph in 1 second, 0 to 12 mph in 2 seconds, and, ultimately, 0 to 60 mph in 10 seconds.

**3.** In their annual rating of new automobiles, *Consumer Reports* uses two key indicators of engine performance. These are the *final-drive ratio* and the *engine revolutions per mile.* Both these numbers are based on the performance of the car in high gear.

The *final-drive ratio* is the number of engine revolutions for each revolution of the wheels.

*Engine revolutions per mile* is the same as revolutions per minute at 60 miles per hour. (This is because 60 miles per hour is equivalent to 1 mile per minute.)

A low value for either measure relative to other models in the same class generally means better gas mileage and lower engine noise, but less accelerating power.

**4.** An engine's size is measured by the volume of *displacement* of its cylinders. This is directly related to the amount of power it generates. The power derives from the combustion of fuel in the cylinder, which causes a piston to move down (and then back up). The pistons are attached to a crankshaft in a way that transforms their up-and-down motion into the rotational motion of the shaft. This is ultimately transferred to the wheels through the transmission and the drive train.

The displacement of a cylinder is the volume through which the piston moves between its highest and lowest positions in the cylinder. This volume is determined by the length of travel of the piston (the *stroke*) and the diameter of the cylinder (the *bore*). If a cylinder is likened to a simple tin can, its volume can be found by multiplying its height (or stroke) by the area of its circular cross-section. The formula is

$$volume = \pi \times r^2 \times h$$

where the radius *r* is half of the bore, and the height *h* is the stroke.

• A 1988 Toyota Camry four-cylinder engine has identical bore and stroke measurements of 3.39 inches. The radius is half of the bore—about 1.69 inches. The cylinder displacement can be calculated from the formula given above.

$$volume = \pi \times (1.69 \text{ in})^2 \times (3.39 \text{ in})$$
$$\approx 30.4 \text{ cubic inches}$$

An engine's total displacement is the displacement of all of its cylinders. This is expressed in cubic inches, cubic centimeters, or liters.

• The Camry's total engine displacement is found by multiplying one cylinder's displacement by 4.

*total displacement* = 4 × (30.6 cubic inches)
≈ 122 cubic inches

The conversion factor from cubic inches to liters (given in the conversion table on page 336) is 0.06387. Thus

122 cubic inches = (0.06387 × 30.6) liters
≈ 1.95 liters

The Camry's engine would therefore be referred to as a 2-liter engine.

The displacement of an American automobile may be given in cubic inches or liters. A luxury-class 8-cylinder car will often exceed 300 cubic inches. A compact will usually not exceed 120 cubic inches.

One way manufacturers use engine displacement numbers is to differentiate among types of motorcycles. The number of cubic centimeters, or cc's, is usually part of the name. A 250-cc motorcycle is a small bike, possibly a dirt bike, while a 1000-cc motorcycle would be a large road bike.

**5. Compression Ratio** The *compression ratio* of a cylinder measures the amount by which the fuel mixture is compressed before combustion. The fuel begins to enter the cylinder when the piston is at the bottom of the stroke. The fuel is compressed as the piston moves toward the top of the stroke. The space into which the fuel is compressed when the piston is at the top of the cylinder is referred to as the *combustion chamber.* If D is the cylinder displacement and V is the volume of the combustion chamber, then

$$compression\ ratio = \frac{D + V}{V} = \frac{maximum\ chamber\ volume}{minimum\ chamber\ volume}$$

A typical compression ratio for passenger cars is about 8 to 1 or 9½ to 1. The ratios for special-performance cars fall into the range from 11 to 1 up to 13 to 1.

**6. Horsepower** Engine output is most often measured in units of horsepower. One *horsepower* is defined to be the power required to lift a 500-pound weight 1 foot in 1 second. This standard was established by James Watt, the pioneer in steam-engine design for whom the electrical unit of power is named. To rate his steam engines, Watt decided upon a measure equivalent to 33,000 foot-pounds per minute, which is the power capacity of about 1½ real horses. An engine's horsepower is related to its displacement, but the way engine power is tested leads to several categories of horsepower.

When a braking device is placed on an engine's output shaft, the measure of resistance is called *brake horsepower (bhp)*. While there is no exact conversion formula for automobile engines, as a rule of thumb, 1 liter of engine capacity converts to between 50 and 70 bhp. (One liter is equivalent to 1000 cc.) Higher ratios are attained by turbocharged engines, which can generate as much as 150 bhp per liter of displacement. Motorcycle engines can also achieve high performance. A

Honda 1100-cc motorcycle, for example, has an output of 175 bhp for its 1.1 liters.

Another measure of engine power—*indicated horsepower*—is based on the pressure developed in the cylinders. Indicated horsepower exceeds brake horsepower by about 10 percent, reflecting the internal friction in the engine.

Finally, the *manufacturer's horsepower* is the advertised horsepower. This, like all power ratings, varies with the speed at which the car is tested. Thus the figure used by manufacturers is the *advertised net horsepower at rpm*, which specifies the horsepower generated at the engine's maximum rpm (and is thus the engine's maximum horsepower). A race car, for example, generates its highest horsepower in the highest 1500 rpm of its range (which may go as high as 7000). A sedan, such as a four-cylinder Toyota Camry, with its two-liter engine, is listed at about 120 horsepower, which it generates at top speed.

**7. Gas mileage**  A car's *gas mileage* is the average ratio of miles traveled to fuel consumed. Because driving conditions affect gas mileage, it is best to make this calculation using a full tank of gas, and to repeat the calculation many times in different weather and traffic conditions.

To find the gas mileage, fill the gas tank and zero out the trip odometer. After running the car somewhere near empty, refill the tank and record the number of gallons it takes to refill. Divide the odometer mileage by the number of gallons, and record the result. Repeat this for several tanks of gas.

- A car travels 364 miles on 13.45 gallons of gas. The gas mileage for that tank is 364 ÷ 13.45, or about 27 miles per gallon.

## 8. Tire Sizes

The numbers printed on the sides of automobile tires are mandated by the U.S. Department of Transportation. They refer not only to tire size but to certain performance tests. None of these indicators are self-explanatory. The standardized designations for tire sizes, for example, display a curious mixture of metric and U.S. systems of measurements. Three numbers are used to indicate the *tire width* in millimeters, the tire's *cross-sectional aspect ratio* (a dimensionless figure given as a percent), and the *rim diameter* in inches.

The *tire width* is the width of the tire when seen from the front.

The *aspect ratio* is a ratio of two dimensions: the distance from the bottom of the rim to the road (also known as the sidewall height), and the tire width.

The *rim diameter* is the inner diameter of the tire.

- In a tire size given as P205/70 R 14, *P* stands for *passenger* car; *205* is the tire width in millimeters; *70* is the aspect ratio, indicating that the sidewall height *y* is 70 percent of the tire width *w*; *R* stands for *radial* tire; and the last

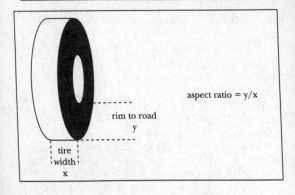

aspect ratio = y/x

rim to road
y

tire
width
x

number indicates that the tire fits a *14*-inch-diameter rim.

Other numbers that appear on the tire are:

1. The *load index* and *speed rating*. In a load/speed rating such as 87S, the 87 is a coded number that indicates a maximum weight the tire can carry at a speed designated S. The S stands for *standard load,* which is the recommended rating for a passenger car. A tire salesman may try to push a sports-car owner toward a higher rating (which will increase the price), but a rating in the vicinity of 85S is adequate for most cars and drivers. The range of speed ratings are:

> S - 112 mph
> T - 118 mph
> H - 130 mph

        V - 149 mph

        Z - 149 mph or more

2. *Date of manufacture.* This is given in a string of symbols following the DOT code. A number such as 0495 indicates the fourth week of 1995.

3. The *tread-wear index.* This is intended to indicate how long the tread will last. It is an index number which rates every tire against a reference tire with a rating of 100. A rating of 400 means that a tire will last 4 times as long as the reference tire. An index in the 100s is considered low, near 500 is considered high. *Consumer Reports* notes that manufacturers are allowed to conduct this test themselves, so there is no independent verification.

4. *Traction and temperature rating.* The traction rating is a test of straight-line stopping distance on wet pavement. The possible ratings are A, B, and C. According to *Consumer Reports,* the test is not very demanding, and about half of all passenger-car tires achieve a rating of A. The temperature rating, also an A–B–C scale, gauges a tire's ability to withstand the heat generated under driving conditions; most tires rate at least B.

**9. Braking Distance** The time required for a car to come to a stop depends first on the reaction time of the driver, which averages ¾ of a second.

The distance covered during this time depends on the speed of the car. At 60 miles per hour, which is equivalent to 88 feet per second, a car will travel 66 feet in ¾ of a second. After that, the braking distance depends on the reliability and type of brakes. Table 3.6 gives average values for braking distances at different speeds.

**Table 3.6. Braking Distances**

| Speed (mph) | Reaction time | Braking distance | Stopping distance |
|---|---|---|---|
| 10 | 11 feet | 9 feet | 20 feet |
| 20 | 22 | 23 | 45 |
| 30 | 33 | 45 | 78 |
| 40 | 44 | 81 | 125 |
| 50 | 55 | 133 | 188 |
| 60 | 66 | 206 | 272 |
| 70 | 77 | 304 | 381 |

[Source: *Automotive Encyclopedia*, rev. ed. (South Holland, Ill.: Goodheart-Wilcox, 1989)]

As a rule of thumb, the proper distance for following behind another car at any speed should be at least a full two-second count. That is, a driver should be able to count off "one thousand one, one thousand two" before passing some landmark that the leading car has just passed.

# Weather and the Environment

**1. Temperature Scales** There are three basic temperature scales. The one upon which the other two are based is the *Kelvin scale*, a scientific scale that is rarely encountered in anything but scientific settings. It is sometimes referred to as *absolute temperature*. Its base temperature—0° Kelvin—is called *absolute zero;* it is the temperature at which all molecular motion stops.

The *Celsius scale* (also known as the *centigrade scale*) uses the freezing and boiling points of water as the basis of a scale divided into 100°. It is also the temperature scale used in the metric system. The relationship between Celsius and Kelvin is:

$$C = K - 273.15°$$

Thus the freezing point of water is 0°C or 273.15°K, and the boiling point is 100°C or 373.15°K.

In the United States, the *Fahrenheit scale* is used. On this scale, the freezing point of water is 32° and the boiling point is 212°. Converting temperatures from Fahrenheit to Celsius or vice versa involves either of two conversion formulas.

$$C = \frac{5}{9} \times (F - 32)$$

$$F = \frac{9}{5} \times C + 32$$

• A temperature of 68° Fahrenheit converts to 20° Celsius as follows:

$$C = \frac{5}{9} \cdot (68 - 32) = \frac{5}{9} \cdot 36 = 20$$

• A temperature of 15° Celsius is equivalent to 59° Fahrenheit:

$$F = \frac{9}{5} \times 15 + 32 = 59$$

**Table 3.7. Fahrenheit/Celsius/Kelvin Equivalents**

| Fahrenheit | Celsius | Kelvin |
|---|---|---|
| 0 | −18 | 255.15 |
| 14 | −10 | 263.15 |
| 32 | 0 | 273.15 |
| 41 | 5 | 278.15 |
| 50 | 10 | 283.15 |
| 59 | 15 | 288.15 |
| 68 | 20 | 293.15 |
| 77 | 25 | 298.15 |
| 86 | 30 | 303.15 |
| 95 | 35 | 308.15 |
| 212 | 100 | 373.15 |

A fair and mild day thus falls into the range of 20°C to 25°C.

**2. Windchill Factors** Because the human body gives off heat, exposed skin enjoys a thin insulating layer of warm air that serves as protection from hot or cold air. But wind has the effect of removing this protection. This is why any rapid movement in a sauna seems to intensify the sensation of heat, and also why it feels colder on a windy 30° day than on a calm 30° day. The latter effect is called *windchill*. It is a perception rather than something measurable by instruments, but it is a relevant consideration when deciding how to dress for a cold day.

The National Weather Service has compiled a table that gives an idea of what various combinations of wind and cold temperatures *feel* like. For example, on a 10° day, a 15-mile-per-hour wind will cause it to feel like a −18° day.

**Table 3.8. Windchill Factors**

Wind
speed
(mph)       *Outdoor temperature (degrees Fahrenheit)*

| | 30 | 25 | 20 | 15 | 10 | 5 | 0 | −5 | −10 | −15 | −20 | −25 | −30 | −35 |
|---|---|---|---|---|---|---|---|---|---|---|---|---|---|---|
| 0 | 30 | 25 | 20 | 15 | 10 | 5 | 0 | −5 | −10 | −15 | −20 | −25 | −30 | −35 |
| 5 | 27 | 22 | 16 | 11 | 6 | 0 | −5 | −10 | −15 | −21 | −26 | −31 | −36 | −42 |
| 10 | 16 | 10 | 3 | −3 | −9 | −15 | −22 | −27 | −34 | −40 | −46 | −52 | −58 | −64 |
| 15 | 9 | 2 | −5 | −11 | −18 | −25 | −31 | −38 | −45 | −51 | −58 | −65 | −72 | −78 |
| 20 | 4 | −3 | −10 | −17 | −24 | −31 | −39 | −46 | −53 | −60 | −67 | −74 | −81 | −88 |
| 25 | 1 | −7 | −15 | −22 | −29 | −36 | −44 | −51 | −59 | −66 | −74 | −81 | −88 | −96 |
| 30 | −2 | −10 | −18 | −25 | −33 | −41 | −49 | −56 | −64 | −71 | −79 | −86 | −93 | −101 |
| 35 | −4 | −12 | −20 | −27 | −35 | −43 | −52 | −58 | −67 | −74 | −82 | −89 | −97 | −105 |
| 40 | −5 | −13 | −21 | −29 | −37 | −45 | −53 | −60 | −69 | −76 | −84 | −92 | −100 | −107 |

**3. Heat and Humidity Index** Just as wind can make cold temperatures feel even colder, high levels of humidity can make high temperatures seem especially unbearable. This is because the body regulates heat through the evaporation of sweat, which causes cooling. In low humidity, perspiration readily evaporates, whereas high humidity conditions retard the evaporation process. Consequently a body retains more heat in humid conditions, and feels hotter. Wind can provide some relief by aiding sweat evaporation, although muggy days tend to be windless days, with only an occasional cool breeze.

The effect of humidity on the perception of temperature has been summarized in a table prepared by the National Oceanic and Atmospheric Administration. Matching the temperature given in the top row to a relative humidity reading (see below) gives the *apparent* temperature. Whenever this temperature exceeds 100°, people are advised to remain indoors, or at least to minimize outdoor activities in the middle of the day.

**Table 3.9. Heat and Humidity Factors**

*Relative humidity*          *Perceived temperature (degrees Fahrenheit)*

|      | 70 | 75 | 80 | 85 | 90 | 95 | 100 | 105 | 110 | 115 | 120 |
|------|----|----|----|----|----|----|-----|-----|-----|-----|-----|
| 0%   | 64 | 69 | 73 | 78 | 83 | 87 | 91  | 95  | 99  | 103 | 107 |
| 10%  | 65 | 70 | 75 | 80 | 85 | 90 | 95  | 100 | 105 | 111 | 116 |
| 20%  | 66 | 72 | 77 | 82 | 87 | 93 | 99  | 105 | 112 | 120 | 130 |
| 30%  | 67 | 73 | 78 | 84 | 90 | 96 | 104 | 113 | 123 | 135 | 148 |
| 40%  | 68 | 74 | 79 | 86 | 93 | 101| 110 | 123 | 137 | 151 |     |
| 50%  | 69 | 75 | 81 | 88 | 96 | 107| 120 | 135 | 150 |     |     |
| 60%  | 70 | 76 | 82 | 90 | 100| 114| 132 | 149 |     |     |     |
| 70%  | 70 | 77 | 85 | 93 | 106| 124| 144 |     |     |     |     |
| 80%  | 71 | 78 | 86 | 97 | 113| 136|     |     |     |     |     |
| 90%  | 71 | 79 | 88 | 102| 122|    |     |     |     |     |     |
| 100% | 72 | 80 | 91 | 108|    |    |     |     |     |     |     |

**4. Relative Humidity** *Relative humidity* is a measure of how well air can absorb moisture. It is calculated as a ratio of the amount of moisture actually in the air compared to the amount of moisture the air can potentially hold under its present temperature and pressure conditions. In other words, relative humidity is the water-vapor content of the air as a percent of what it *could* be. A relative humidity of 60% means that the outdoor air is 60% saturated with moisture.

Cold air cannot hold as much moisture as hot air. On cold days the moisture in a drafty house tends to be sucked out, leaving the indoor air very dry. In the same way, when cold outdoor air is heated to room temperature without adding any moisture, its relative humidity drops to a very low level, which is why in winter the indoor air can become uncomfortably dry.

When the water content of air reaches a certain level of saturation, it will condense. Thus the relative humidity helps determine when water vapor will condense into clouds, fog, or moisture on objects. Generally, when a cold object such as a bottle of milk is placed in warm surroundings, moisture from the air condenses on the bottle. If the bottle is warm enough, no moisture will collect on it. The exact temperature of the bottle at which moisture would begin to collect is called the *dew point*.

**5. Dew Point and Frost Point** The *dew point* is the temperature at which an object will collect condensation (or dew). When outside temperatures are below freezing, the temperature of an object on which ice or frost will begin to form is called the *frost point*.

In essence, the dew or frost point is a temperature at which leaves or blades of grass will become wet with dew or covered with frost. Because it represents the temperature at which moisture in the air will condense, the dew point is also the temperature of fog or a cloud formation. Thus it is also known as the *cloud point*. Both the frost point and the dew point are directly related to the relative humidity of the air.

**6. The Greenhouse Effect**  A greenhouse permits radiation from the sun to enter and be converted to heat, while its glass panes prevent much of this heat from escaping. In the earth's atmosphere, the same effect is created by carbon dioxide, water vapor, and other gases, which allow the sun's rays to pass through, but reflect back the heat that tries to escape. This trapping of heat is what maintains the earth's temperature within a range that supports life. In contrast, the dense atmosphere of Venus exaggerates the greenhouse effect and causes surface temperatures to reach almost a thousand degrees Fahrenheit.

The burning of fossil fuels has produced a 25% increase in the amount of carbon dioxide in the atmosphere over the last century and a half. This, along with increasing levels of "greenhouse gases" such as methane and chlorofluorocarbons, has contributed to a rising average global temperature of about a half degree Celsius since temperature records began in 1860. Scientists are warning that the rate of change is increasing. They predict that a change of even a few degrees in this average would lead to catastrophic environmental changes.

**7. Barometric pressure** Atmospheric pressure can be seen at work whenever a suction cup is depressed. Because the air pressure is not equalized on both sides, it is the outside air pressure that keeps the suction cup on the wall. A more reliable indicator of atmospheric pressure, which operates on the same principle, is the measuring device known as the *barometer.*

Originally, barometers were constructed as tubular glass columns filled with mercury and then inverted. The weight of the mercury creates a vacuum at the top of the tube. The size of this vacuum, and thus the height of the mercury, is determined by the outside air pressure. Because barometers were originally marked off in inches, barometric pressure was also given in units of inches, and often still is. But for official purposes, other units of measure are used.

One *atmosphere* is defined to be the air pressure at sea level. This corresponds to about 30 inches, or 760 millimeters, of mercury. In the metric system, the base unit of pressure is the *pascal.* Atmospheric pressure can be expressed in pascals or *kilopascals,* which are units of 1000 pascals; in *bars,* which are equivalent to units of 100 kilopascals; or in *millibars,* which are units of 100 pascals. Although the accepted standard unit of measurement for barometric pressure is the kilopascal, weather reporters still like to refer to inches of mercury.

Zones of pressure on weather maps are indicated by *isobars.* Each isobar represents a region of uniform pressure. In general, low-pressure weather systems are associated with stormy weather, and high-pressure systems with clear, calm weather.

**Table 3.10 Conversion of Air-Pressure Units**

1 kilopascal = 10 millibars = .295 inches of mercury

1 atmosphere = 760 mm of mercury
= 29.92 inches of mercury

1 atmosphere = 101,325 pascals = 1013.25 millibars
= 1.01325 bar

1 millibar = 0.75 mm of mercury $\approx \frac{1}{32}$ inch of mercury

1 inch of mercury = 0.03342 atmospheres

# Measuring Time

## UNITS OF TIME

60 seconds = 1 minute
60 minutes = 1 hour
24 hours = 1 day
7 days = 1 week
4 weeks $\approx$ 1 month
12 months (52 weeks) = 1 year
10 years = 1 decade
100 years = 1 century
1000 years = 1 millennium

The units of time given above, as they are commonly understood, are based on conventions of timekeeping that are not entirely scientific. There are not exactly four weeks in a month, for example. And while the year is divided into 12 months, a month is not a fixed or unchanging unit of time.

If one year is defined as the basic time unit, then months, weeks, days, hours, minutes, and seconds can all be defined in relation to it. But there are many kinds of years, all of slightly different lengths. There is the calendar year, the lunar year, the sidereal year, the solar year, and the fiscal year. Consequently there are calendar days, sidereal days, lunar months, sidereal months, and so on. Below, the methods of determining lengths of time are briefly described.

*Solar* time refers to the motion and elevation of the sun, or, more properly, the earth's motion with respect to the sun. A *solar year* or *tropical year*, for example, is the average duration of the earth's orbit around the sun. It lasts 365 days, 5 hours, 48 minutes, and 45.51 seconds.

*Sidereal* refers to timekeeping based on the movement of the stars. Because the stars are the most consistent long-term timekeepers, astronomers and other scientists use them to measure time. Sidereal time is used as the basis for scientific clocks. A sidereal year is about 20 minutes longer than a solar year.

*Lunar* time is based on the phases of the moon. A complete lunar cycle lasts about 29½ days. Technically, a *lunar month* is the time it takes the moon to complete an orbit around the earth—about 27⅓ days. This is the same as a lunar day because it coincides with a single rotation of the moon about its axis. (The same side of the moon always faces the earth. Thus a lunar orbit coincides with one lunar rotation.)

*Synodic* time refers to another way of calculating a lunar cycle. A *synodic month* is the period from one new moon to the next, which takes about 29½ days.

## CALENDARS

The word *calendar* comes from the Latin *kalends,* meaning the day on which accounts were due. In its modern sense, a calendar is a convenient division of a year into months, weeks, and days. But the urgency of its Latin origin remains. The calendar is largely a means of scheduling meetings, assigning deadlines, and setting due dates, and its consistency has always been an important issue.

**1.** The calendar currently in use is called the *Gregorian calendar,* after Pope Gregory XIII, who instituted it in the year 1582. This calendar features a *leap year* every fourth year (it occurs in years divisible by 4, although it skips those century years that are not divisible by 400). The need for such a seemingly complicated arrangement arises because neither the sun's nor the moon's cycle comprises a whole number of days.

**2.** A *lunar cycle* is the time required for the moon to complete one set of *phases*. It begins with a *new moon,* which occurs when the moon is between the earth and the sun and thus reflects no sunlight. As the cycle progresses, the moon *waxes* (or increases in size and visibility) each night until it reaches its full stage two weeks later. It then *wanes,* or gradually decreases back to crescent stage, and to the next new moon. A full moon rises at sunset, and each night thereafter rises later and later as it wanes. The new moon rises at dawn.

**3.** The lunar cycle lasts about 29½ days, so 12 lunar cycles last about 354 days, which is 11¼ days short of a full year as measured by one earth revolution about the sun. Consequently the moon is not a suitable long-term timekeeper.

**4.** Calendars acknowledge the lunar cycle by dividing the year into 12 units. But each month does not begin with a new moon. This is because a full year is determined by the movement of the sun, or, more accurately, by the movement of the earth around the sun.

A *solar year* is the duration of one earth orbit around the sun. It is exactly 365 days, 5 hours, 48 minutes, and 45.51 seconds long. Within the solar year are 4 important days—the two *equinoxes* and the two *solstices.* The summer and winter solstices are the longest and shortest days of the year in terms of amount of daylight. Each equinox (literally, "equal night") falls midway between the solstices and marks the days when the day and night are of equal length. These four days divide the year into the four seasons.

> Spring equinox: March 21
>
> Summer solstice: June 21
>
> Autumnal equinox: September 21
>
> Winter solstice: December 21

(In some years, these divisions fall on the 20th or 22nd of the month.)

**5.** The *Julian calendar,* which was instituted by Julius Caesar in the year 45 B.C., established the calendar still in use today (except for a few significant changes). It originated the idea of a *leap year*—a year with an extra day occurring once every four years. In Caesar's era the new year began on March 1. The extra day in leap years was added at the end of the year, which is how it came to fall on February 29.

This innovation was inspired by the assumption that there are exactly 365¼ days in a solar year. In reality, the solar year is about 11 minutes shorter than this. What Caesar and his advisers overlooked was that the Julian calendar would gain a full day every 120 years, and this would cause calendar dates to fall behind corresponding solar events. The spring equinox, for example, was occurring 8 days short of March 21 by the year 1000. Because this time lag made it nearly impossible for the Church to schedule its movable feasts, a revision of the Julian calendar became necessary.

In 1582, Pope Gregory ordered that 10 days be dropped from the calendar so that the spring equinox would fall on March 21. And to correct the error in the Julian calendar, the Pope's decree eliminated three leap years in every 400 years (specifically, on those century years not divisible by 400). Because it works, the *Gregorian calendar* has become the worldwide standard, although it took several centuries to take hold globally (it was not adopted in Britain and the American colonies, for example, until 1752).

# Geography and Navigation

## MAPS

A *map* is a way of representing space. The most familiar maps represent the whole or part of the earth's surface. But there are also maps that represent the moon, the surfaces of other planets, the heavens, as well as interior spaces (such as building directories), or prevailing conditions (such as weather maps, population-density maps, or other statistical maps).

This section focuses on the mathematical problem of representing the spherical surface of the earth on the flat surface of a map.

**1.** For mapmaking purposes, the earth is modeled as a perfect sphere that rotates on a *polar axis*, and is encircled by an *equator.*

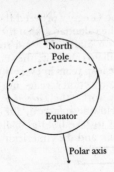

**2.** Any place or point on the globe can be specified using two numbers. The first denotes the point's angular elevation above or below the equator. This is called *latitude*. Zones of latitude are designated on a globe by circles that run parallel to the equator.

Any circle of latitude can be identified by its angle of elevation above the horizontal from the earth's center. The North Pole is at ninety degrees north latitude, or 90°N. The South Pole is at 90°S.

In geographical measures, 1 degree is divided into 60 minutes, and each minute into 60 seconds. The minutes symbol is ', and the seconds symbol is ". At the equator, a degree of latitude is equivalent to about 110 km, a minute to 1.8 km, and a second to about 31 meters. (U.S. equivalents are 69 miles, 1.15 miles, and 34 yards.) These distances vary slightly at latitudes further to the north

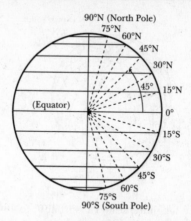

LATITUDES

or south because the earth is not a perfect sphere.
New York City is at about 40°45′N.

**3.** The second number used to locate a point on
the earth's surface denotes how far east or west
the point lies from Greenwich, England. This
measure is called *longitude*. The line that runs directly north and south through the Greenwich Ob-
servatory ultimately encircles the globe, passing
through both poles. This is called the *prime meridian*. In general, a *meridian* is a line that circles the
globe north to south and passes through the poles.
Every point on the globe lies on a meridian, which
places it at a certain angle east or west of Greenwich.

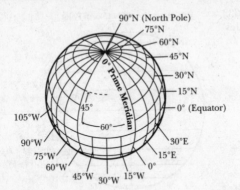

The longitude scale runs from 0° to 180° East, and 0° to 180° West, the two designations meeting at the opposite side of the globe from the prime meridian. New York has a longitude of 74°W. Moscow has a longitude of 37°30′E.

One degree of longitude at the equator is equivalent to about 110 km or 69 miles. This diminishes steadily as longitude lines converge to the north and south.

**4.** The idea of a map is inseparable from the idea of scale. A *scale* is the size of the representation of an object relative to its actual size. A map, for example, might use one centimeter to represent one kilometer. The scale in this case would be 1 cm to 100,000 cm. This is written as ¹⁄₁₀₀₀₀₀, or as 1 : 100,000. A map on which 1 inch represents 10 miles has a scale that can be written as "1 in. to 10 mi." or as

1:633,600 (because there are 633,600 inches in 10 miles).

In general, a scale is a ratio of the number 1 to some larger number (a 1 to 1 ratio would be actual size). The larger the second number, the smaller the scale of the map. A trade-off arises between scale and precision. A smaller scale allows a greater area to be represented. A larger scale allows greater detail to be shown.

U.S. Geological Survey maps are produced in several scales, from detailed local maps (1:24,000) to more inclusive regional maps (1:250,000). These maps come in two forms: planimetric and topographic.

A *planimetric map* includes outlines of those physical features, natural and manmade, that the scale permits. These may include rivers, streams, roads, houses, and buildings, airports, and so on.

A *topographic map* has the same features, but also includes elevations indicated by contour lines. A *contour line* indicates a path of constant elevation above sea level. The simplest and most visible example of a contour line is provided by the boundary of a lake or pond. On maps, contour lines are drawn at intervals of 10 feet or 100 feet, depending on the scale. The spacing of the line is an indication of the steepness of the terrain: the closer the lines, the steeper the slope.

**5.** *Density maps,* like topographical maps, associate a numerical quantity (such as population, mean income, incidence of disease) with a geographical region. This can be done by color coding, by using dots to represent some numerical count, or by sizing the region to correlate with its percent representation. On a population-density map done this way, North Dakota would appear much smaller than it really is, and New Jersey much larger.

**6. World Maps and Projections** The problem of representing the surface of the entire globe on a flat map cannot be successfully solved by any single method. In any scheme, there will either be distortion of area or distortion of the distance between points. One map that distorts both area and distance is the most commonly used by navigators. It is called a *Mercator projection.*

The Mercator projection is named for Gerardus Mercator (1512–94), the Flemish mathematician and astronomer who invented it. His idea can be visualized by imagining a transparent globe with a light source at its center. If a rectangle of paper is rolled into a tube and placed around the

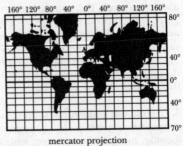

mercator projection

globe so that it touches the equator all the way around, the outlines of the continents would be projected onto the inner surface of the tube. Points near the equator would suffer little distortion, but further to the north and south, land masses would become exaggerated in size. Latitude lines would become horizontal lines, longitude lines would project onto vertical lines, and together they would form a rectangular grid.

**7. Time Zones** Time zones originated in the United States in 1883 at the request of railroad executives who needed a standard time by which to coordinate their train schedules. From this were born the four U.S. time zones—Eastern, Central, Mountain, and Pacific. Passing westward into a new time zone entails moving the clock back one hour. Therefore clocks in the Pacific time zone are set 3 hours earlier than those in the Eastern time zone. Time zones extend both east and west around the globe, so Paris is 6 hours ahead of New York, and Hawaii is 6 hours behind New York.

Because this procession of time zones has to end somewhere, an *international date line* was arbitrarily established at about the 180° meridian (opposite Greenwich, England). Passing over this line from east to west results in moving forward a calendar day. The line does not follow the meridian precisely. It actually zigzags in order to avoid land masses and archipelagoes.

The difference between time zones is further complicated by *daylight saving time*. This was instituted early in this century to adjust for the lengthening of daytime in the summer months. The change between standard time and daylight saving time occurs in the United States at 2:00 A.M. on the first Sunday in April, and ends at 2:00 A.M. on the last Sunday in October.

The changing of the clocks is not observed everywhere in the United States, and although other countries also have daylight saving time, there is no universal agreement as to when it should begin and end. (European countries use the last Sunday in March and the last Sunday in September.)

# Chapter 4

# Probability and Statistics

Statistics is the branch of mathematics that deals with collecting, analyzing, interpreting, and presenting numerical data. Part of its purpose is to summarize what *has* happened in order to predict what *will* happen or what *might* happen. In this way statistics is closely connected with probability, which is the science of predicting the likelihood of events.

Statistics is perhaps the area of mathematics that is most commonly used in everyday life. Probability and statistics determine how insurance companies set their rates, how brokers make investment decisions, how casinos reap their profits, and how planning strategies are designed. When a baseball manager sends in a left-handed pinch hitter, or an insurance company offers lower rates for nonsmokers, they are playing the laws of averages—using statistics to try to give themselves the best chance of coming out ahead.

Though statistics terminology tends to use words in a way that retains their everyday meaning, some technical language is necessary. While statistics, when properly used, can clearly summarize complex information, it can also be used to bolster a weak argument or to create a false impression. Thus it is all the more important for the consumer to understand its concepts.

# Probability

**1.** In the context of probability, an *experiment* is a situation whose outcome is uncertain but not entirely unknown. At the very least, an experiment must involve an observer who can anticipate, identify, or at least record every possible *outcome* in a given situation. Every time the observer records the result of an experiment, it is referred to as a *trial* of the experiment.

**2.** An *outcome* is one of the possible results of an experiment. It is the basic unit of possible occurrences. In a coin toss, the outcomes are *heads* and *tails*. In the toss of a die, the outcomes consist of the six sides representing the numbers 1 through 6. In a horse race, the outcomes are the possible orders of finish.

**3.** An *event* is some combination of possible outcomes in one trial of an experiment. If one of the outcomes constituting the event occurs, then the event is said to have occurred.

• In picking a card from an ordinary deck of cards, the *outcomes* are the 52 cards themselves. Examples of *events* are:

"Pick a 4"—that is, one of the four cards numbered 4.

"Pick a diamond"—that is, one of the 13 cards in the suit of diamonds.

"Pick a face card"—that is, one of the 12 cards showing a king, queen, or jack.

**4.** Someone who tosses a die or a coin 100 times is conducting 100 trials of the same experiment. The number of times a 1 comes up is called the *frequency* of this outcome. The *relative frequency* of an outcome is the ratio of the frequency of the outcome to the number of trials that have been conducted.

• 100 coin tosses result in 47 heads and 53 tails. The relative frequency of *heads* is $^{47}/_{100}$, or 0.47. The relative frequency of *tails* is $^{53}/_{100}$, or 0.53.

**5.** In situations in which the possible outcomes or events in an experiment can be listed, the *probability* of an outcome or event is its *long-run relative frequency*. This supposes an infinite number of trials, which is clearly impossible. But it is usually possible to establish what the long-run relative frequency *would* be by assessing the intrinsic physical properties of the experiment. If a coin is tossed many times, for example, experiments prove that heads comes up half the time and tails the other half. The long-run relative frequency of heads would thus be 0.5.

# Finding Probabilities

Probability is a numerical assessment of likelihood. It is a number between 0 and 1, where 0 means that an event is impossible, and 1 means that it is absolutely certain to happen. Between 0 and 1 is a range of possible values that can be given in decimal, fraction, or percent form. A probability of ½ (or 0.5, or 50%) means that an event will occur half the time whenever the experiment is performed. But to say that there is a 50% chance that a coin toss will result in a head is not the same as saying that there is a 50% chance of rain tomorrow. In one instance, the experiment is repeatable, and the event (flipping a head) either will or will not happen. Experience shows that it can be expected to happen about half the time. By contrast, a 50% chance of rain means that, based on past experience with similar conditions, there is a 50% chance that *some* rain will fall somewhere in the local area at *some* time during the day.

Some probabilities are more reliable than others. Predicting the weather is less precise than stating the chances of winning at a roulette table. In the same way, predicting the behavior of the stock market, the outcome of a professional sports contest, or the chances that a new movie will be a hit are highly speculative. Still, there are some mathematical principles at work in all predictions of likelihood. These can be summed up as three basic approaches to finding probabilities.

The probability of an event can be computed by:

i. *A logical assessment of the physical properties of the experiment.* This applies to experiments such as picking a card, guessing a number, flipping a coin, or spinning a dial. It assumes that the basic outcomes are all equally likely, or at least consistent from trial to trial. Predicting whether a football team will win, and by how much, does not fall into this category.

ii. *Experiment and observation.* When the characteristics of the mechanism at the heart of an experiment are unknown, a large number of trials can reveal its long-run patterns. How often a baseball player is likely to get a hit in one situation is judged by how well he has performed in similar situations. The chance that a mass-produced object is defective can be found by analyzing a large number of production runs and counting the number of defective units. This method of assessing probabilities is one rationale for keeping statistics.

iii. *Informed judgment.* Some situations have no precedent, and their most probable outcome can only be found by exercising the best possible judgment based on experience, the available information, and the properties of the experiment. Examples include forecasting the chance of rain, predicting whether a new movie will be a hit, and playing the stock market.

There are many schemes used to find probabilities, but the most elementary ones are based on ratios. Such schemes rely on the idea that what is *probable* depends on what is *possible*.

**1. The First Principle of Probability** If an experiment has a set of distinct outcomes, each of which is equally likely to occur, then the probability of an event is the ratio of the number of outcomes that constitute the event to the total number of possible outcomes.

- Picking a card from a deck of cards has 52 distinct outcomes. The event "Pick a diamond" consists of 13 of these outcomes—the 13 cards in the suit of diamonds. Thus the probability of picking a diamond is given as

$$P(\text{diamond}) = \frac{no.\ of\ diamonds}{no.\ of\ cards} = \frac{13}{52} = \frac{1}{4}, \text{ or } 0.25.$$

**2. Probability as Relative Frequency** The relative frequency of an event is the ratio of the number of occurrences of the event to the number of trials.

$$relative\ frequency = \frac{no.\ of\ occurrences}{no.\ of\ trials}$$

In many situations that are not well understood initially, a large number of trials can reveal what the probabilities of the possible outcomes should be. This is the principle used in the computation of batting averages, product reliability (and failure rates), and manufacturing defects.

• A production run of 5000 silicon wafers reveals that 143 are defective. Therefore, the probability that a wafer chosen at random is defective would be $^{143}\!/_{5000}$, or 0.0286.

# Counting Methods

The probability of an event can often be found by counting the number of outcomes that can happen. Because this usually involves very large numbers, many people play hunches instead of taking advantage of calculable odds. This happens most often in games of chance, in which the sheer number of possible outcomes makes it difficult to calculate probabilities mentally, and the game often unfolds very fast. Some familiarity with the principles of counting could help in these situations.

For example, imagine a lottery game that involves matching five numbers. To find the probability of winning, it is necessary to calculate how many five-number arrangements are possible. This involves counting. But because so many arrangements are possible, some counting method is needed. The method will involve nothing more than multiplication and division, but the way it is done will depend on how the arrangements are made. If the order of the five numbers is important, the arrangement is called a **permutation**. If order is unimportant, it is a **combination**. If any number can be used more than once, the possible orderings are here referred to as **assortments**. The methods of counting permutations, combinations, and assortments are explored below.

## THE PRINCIPLE OF MULTIPLICATION

In general, if a group of objects is to be assembled by choosing one object at a time, the number of ways of choosing the needed number of objects is found by multiplying the number of possible choices for each position.

total number of ways of choosing =
(no. of choices for 1st position)
× (no. of choices for 2nd position)
× (no. of choices for 3rd position)
× · · · × (no. of choices for last position)

This is called the **principle of multiplication**.

## PERMUTATIONS

**1.** A permutation is an ordering of objects. In any permutation, an object can only be used once.

The six possible permutations of the letters A, B, and C, for example, are

ABC, ACB, BAC, BCA, CAB, CBA.

The number of permutations of three objects can be found by noting that there are 3 choices for the first position, 2 for the second, and 1 for the third. By the principle of multiplication, the number of possible permutations is $3 \times 2 \times 1$, or 6. The expression $3 \times 2 \times 1$ is called "three factorial" and is written in compact notation as 3!. (See page 000 for more on factorials.)

In general, the number of permutations of $n$ objects is $n!$ Ten people can be lined up in 10! ways. This amounts to $10 \times 9 \times 8 \times 7 \times 6 \times 5 \times 4 \times 3 \times 2 \times 1$, or 3,628,800 ways. There are 7! possible orders of finish in a horse race involving 7 horses. This amounts to 5040 possible finishes.

**2.** Whenever some of the objects in a group of objects are chosen, the number of possible arrangements (or permutations) of these objects can be found by using factorials.

• In a 12-horse field, the number of win-place-show combinations can be found by noting that there are 12 possibilities for the winner, 11 for second place, and 10 for third. By multiplying, the number of possibilities turns out to be $12 \times 11 \times 10$, or 1320. This is the same as 12 factorial divided by 9 factorial.

In general, the number of ways of arranging $r$ objects chosen from a set of $n$ objects, designated $P_{n,r}$, is given by

$$P_{n,r} = \frac{n!}{(n-r)!}$$

• A disk jockey has to play nine songs from a playlist of 15 songs during an hour-long broadcast. The total number of possible song combinations (in which order is important) is given by

$$\frac{15!}{(15-9)!} \text{ or } \frac{15!}{6!}$$

This equals 1,816,214,400 possible playlists.

## COMBINATIONS

**1.** A **combination** is the number of ways of choosing some objects out of a group of objects, where the order is unimportant. ABC, BAC, and CBA, for example, are considered the same combination of the first three letters of the alphabet. As with a permutation, no object in a combination can be used more than once. But unlike a permutation, ordering doesn't matter. A poker hand, for example, represents a combination of five objects chosen from a set of 52 objects. Even if the order of the five cards is rearranged, it remains the same combination, and the same hand.

Because order is unimportant in a combination, there are fewer combinations than permutations of a given number of objects. If five basketball players are chosen from an eight-man roster, the number of *permutations* would be

$$\frac{8!}{(8-5)!} = \frac{8!}{3!} = 8 \times 7 \times 6 \times 5 \times 4 = 6720.$$

Because the ordering of the five players doesn't matter, some of these permutations are simply re-arrangements of the same five players. The number of these duplications is 5!, or $5 \times 4 \times 3 \times 2 \times 1$, which is the number of ways of arranging five players. So the number of *combinations* of five players on an eight-man roster is found by dividing the number of permutations of the players by the number of duplications of five objects. This would be

$$\frac{8 \times 7 \times 6 \times 5 \times 4}{5 \times 4 \times 3 \times 2 \times 1} = 56$$

**2.** In general, the number of combinations of $r$ objects taken from a set of $n$ objects, in which an object can be used just once and order is unimportant, is designated $C_{n,r}$, where

$$C_{n,r} = \frac{n!}{r! \times (n-r)!}$$

• The number of ways that a committee of three can be chosen from a group of 15 people is

$$\frac{15!}{3! \times (15-3)!} = \frac{15!}{3! \times 12!} = \frac{15 \times 14 \times 13}{3 \times 2 \times 1} = 455$$

## ASSORTMENTS

If a group of objects is selected from a larger group in such a way that an object can be used more than once, the number of possible groupings is neither a permutation nor a combination.

Writing a number, for example, involves writing a string of digits. Any digit can be used any number of times. Choosing a password involves writing a string of letters of the alphabet with repetition of letters allowed. Because the digits and letters can be used more than once, this way of combining objects is unlike a permutation or a combination, and it requires a special counting method.

The number of arrangements, or **assortments**, of numbers that can be made from the 10 digits, or of words that can be made from the 26 letters of the alphabet, is found using the principle of multiplication.

> no. of assortments =
> (no. of choices for 1st position)
> × (no. of choices for 2nd position)
> × · · · × (no. of choices for last position)

• To find how many three-digit numbers there are, begin with the 10 possible choices for the first digit, multiplied by the 10 possible choices for the second digit and the 10 possible choices for the third digit. There are $10 \times 10 \times 10$, or 1000 such combinations. These combinations include numbers that begin with 0, such as 001, 015, and 090. The entire list includes all of the counting numbers from 0 (or 000) to 999.

• The number of possible license plates containing three letters followed by three digits is: $26 \times 26 \times 26 \times 10 \times 10 \times 10 = 17,576,000$. This is because there are 26 choices for each letter and 10 choices for each digit.

To summarize: To count the number of ways that *r* objects can be chosen from a set of *n* objects, proceed as follows:

If an object can be used more than once, use the principle of multiplication. The number of ways equals:

(no. of choices for 1st position)
$\times$ (no. of choices for 2nd position)
$\times \cdots \times$ (no. of choices for last position)

If an object cannot be used more than once, but order *is* important:

$$no.\ of\ permutations = P_{n,r} = \frac{n!}{(n-r)!}$$

If an object cannot be used more than once, but order *is not* important:

$$no.\ of\ combinations = C_{n,r} = \frac{n!}{r! \times (n-r)!}$$

*Note:* Most scientific calculators have not only a key for factorials (usually marked *x*!) but a key for permutations and combinations. These are marked *n*P*r* and *n*C*r*, which are equivalent to $P_{n,r}$ and $C_{n,r}$. For example, to calculate the number of *permutations* of four objects chosen from a set of nine objects, press $\boxed{9}$ $\boxed{nPr}$ $\boxed{4}$. The result is 3024, which is 9! divided by $(9-5)!$.

• To calculate the number of *combinations* of four objects chosen from a set of nine objects, press $\boxed{9}$ $\boxed{nCr}$ $\boxed{4}$. This gives the result 126, which is 9! divided by the product of 4! and $(9 - 4)!$. The process of finding the number of combinations of four objects chosen from a set of nine is called "9 choose 4."

## COIN TOSSES

**1.** Events or outcomes are said to be *independent* if, in a series of trials, the occurrence of one event has no effect on the results of any other trial. In a series of coin tosses, each toss is independent of the others. In picking a card from a deck of cards, each outcome is independent of any other if the card is replaced each time. If the card is not replaced, then the probabilities change with each repetition.

**2.** The probability of the occurrence of a set of independent events is the product of their probabilities.

• The probability of throwing two heads in a row is $\left(\dfrac{1}{2}\right) \times \left(\dfrac{1}{2}\right) = \left(\dfrac{1}{4}\right)$.

• The probability of throwing three heads in a row is $\left(\dfrac{1}{2}\right) \times \left(\dfrac{1}{2}\right) \times \left(\dfrac{1}{2}\right) = \left(\dfrac{1}{8}\right)$.

• The probability of throwing $n$ heads in a row is $\left(\dfrac{1}{2}\right)^{n}$ or $\left(\dfrac{1}{2^{n}}\right)$.

These are probabilities calculated *before the fact*. If someone has just thrown 10 consecutive heads in a coin-toss game, the probability that the next toss will result in a head is still ½, or 50%. The previous throws have no effect on this. However, the probability that someone will throw 11 heads in a row, calculated *before* any tosses have been made, is $\frac{1}{2^{11}}$, which is $\frac{1}{2048}$.

## CARD GAMES

A standard deck of cards contains 52 cards divided into four suits—spades, hearts, diamonds, and clubs. Each suit consists of 13 cards, labeled Ace, 2, 3, 4, 5, 6, 7 8, 9, 10, Jack, Queen, and King. This composition dates from about the year 1500, and was adapted from tarot cards by the French. Not all card games use this deck; some use only a portion of it, others use more than one deck. Only games that involve drawing cards from a single, standard deck will be considered here.

**1.** The probability of drawing any particular card from a standard deck is 1 in 52. This assumes that the order of the deck is completely random. Studies have shown that at least five standard shuffles are necessary to randomize a deck. Seven shuffles is safer.

**2.** Probabilities associated with card games vary considerably in degree of complexity. The simplest probabilities are those associated with the chance of drawing specific card combinations such as poker hands. This involves selecting or dealing five cards face down. Once the cards have been viewed, the probabilities of subsequent draws will change.

Table 4.1 shows a list of poker hands, in order from best to worst, with the number of ways they can be dealt and their probabilities of being dealt. A *straight* means any five cards in sequence. A *flush* is five cards of the same suit. A *straight flush* is five cards of the same suit that are also in sequence. A *full house* means a pair and three of a kind. The other names are self-explanatory.

This table reflects the fact that there are 2,598,960 possible five-card combinations in a deck of 52 cards. (In the notation of combinations, this is $_{52}C_5$, or $C_{52,5}$.) The probability of being dealt any one hand is the number of ways the hand can be dealt divided by the number of

**Table 4.1. Poker Hand Probabilities**

| Hand | No. of ways | Probability |
|------|-------------|-------------|
| straight flush | 40 | 0.0000154 |
| four of a kind | 624 | 0.0002401 |
| full house | 3744 | 0.0014406 |
| flush | 5108 | 0.0019654 |
| straight | 10,200 | 0.0039246 |
| three of a kind | 54,912 | 0.0211285 |
| two pair | 123,552 | 0.0475390 |
| one pair | 1,098,240 | 0.4225690 |
| none of the above | 1,302,540 | 0.5011774 |
| totals | 2,598,960 | 1.0000000 |

possible combinations. Of the 40 possible straight flushes, for example, only four are *royal flushes* (10, J, Q, K, and A in the same suit). So the probability of getting a royal flush is 4 out of 2,598,960, or about 0.00000154. Any hand that can be dealt must fall into one of the above categories. Thus, although a straight flush is both a straight and a flush, it is in its own category, and does not count in either of the other two categories. Keeping in mind that high cards beat low cards, winning hands are determined by the order listed above.

## TWO-DICE PROBABILITIES

Table 4.2 below reflects the fact that the number of possible combinations that can be thrown with two distinct dice (one black and one red, for example) is 36. For example, there are four ways for two dice to total 5 (specifically: 1 and 4, 2 and 3, 3 and 2, 4 and 1), so the probability of throwing a total of 5 is $\frac{4}{36}$.

**Table 4.2. Two-Dice Probabilities**

| Two-dice total | 2 | 3 | 4 | 5 | 6 | 7 | 8 | 9 | 10 | 11 | 12 |
|---|---|---|---|---|---|---|---|---|---|---|---|
| probability | $\frac{1}{36}$ | $\frac{2}{36}$ | $\frac{3}{36}$ | $\frac{4}{36}$ | $\frac{5}{36}$ | $\frac{6}{36}$ | $\frac{5}{36}$ | $\frac{4}{36}$ | $\frac{3}{36}$ | $\frac{2}{36}$ | $\frac{1}{36}$ |

## Craps

Craps is a betting game played with two dice. The basic rules are as follows:

　　i. A total of 7 or 11 on the first roll results in a win.

ii. A total of 2, 3, or 12 on the first roll produces an immediate loss. These outcomes are referred to as *craps*.

iii. A first roll of 4, 5, 6, 8, 9, or 10 (each of which is called a *point*), allows the player to roll again.

iv. If a point from the first roll is matched before the player rolls a 7, the player wins.

v. If a 7 is rolled before a point is matched, the player loses.

The probability of a win or loss on the first roll is easy to compute. From the table above,

$$\text{probability of } 7 = \tfrac{6}{36}$$
$$\text{probability of } 11 = \tfrac{2}{36}$$

probability of winning on first roll = $\tfrac{8}{36}$, or $\tfrac{2}{9}$

$$\text{probability of } 2 = \tfrac{1}{36}$$
$$\text{probability of } 3 = \tfrac{2}{36}$$
$$\text{probability of } 12 = \tfrac{1}{36}$$

probability of losing on first roll = $\tfrac{4}{36}$, or $\tfrac{1}{9}$

The probability of rolling a point on the first roll is $\tfrac{24}{36}$, or $\tfrac{2}{3}$.

The goal of craps—winning the game—is called "making a pass." The probability of making a pass is remarkably close to ½. It is precisely $\tfrac{244}{495}$, or about 0.493. Conversely, the probability of losing is $\tfrac{251}{495}$, or about 0.507. In craps, as in most casino games, the outcome of one play is independent of the outcome of the next. There are no guaranteed winning strategies. From a purely mathematical point of view, the best risk is to bet "pass." This will be explained in the following section on odds.

# Odds

The term *odds* can refer to the probability that an event occurs, but it can also be used to indicate the payoff on a winning bet. These two meanings do not necessarily coincide; thus the term is ambiguous. Although *odds* in its everyday sense is synonymous with *chances,* it does not have to coincide with the true probability of an event, as a simple example will show.

A coin toss has a 50% chance of coming up heads or tails. This would be referred to as *1-to-1* or *even odds.* If a casino were to pay even odds on such a game, it would pay one dollar for each dollar bet. But chances are it wouldn't. It might instead pay 95 cents, which would give it an advantage on each play. In that case it would be offering odds of 95 to 100. Thus the "true odds" are not always the same as the "payoff odds."

## DEFINITIONS

**1.** The probability that an event A will occur is denoted P(A). The probability that an event A will not occur can be denoted P(*not*A). Because either event A will occur or event A will not occur (either something happens or it doesn't), it must be the case that P(A) + P(*not*A) = 1. Thus, the probability that event A will *not* occur is 1 − P(A).

**2.** The *odds* that an event will occur is the ratio of the probability that it will occur to the probability that it will not occur. This is referred to as the *odds for* the event.

$$odds\ for\ event\ A = \frac{P(A)}{1 - P(A)} = \frac{probability\ that\ A\ will\ occur}{probability\ that\ A\ will\ not\ occur}$$

- In tossing two dice, the probability of throwing a total of 7 or 11 is ⅖. Thus the *odds for* throwing 7 or 11 would be $\frac{2/9}{1 - 2/9}$, or ²⁄₇. This would be called 2-to-7 odds.

If the computation of odds using the formula given above seems difficult, it is because it involves a complex fraction (a fraction within a fraction). A somewhat easier approach involves calculating odds as the ratio of occurrences to nonoccurrences in a large number of trials.

- In 100 coin tosses, the odds of (or *for*) getting a tail would be the ratio of the number of tails thrown (which should be 50) to the number of heads thrown (which should also be 50). The odds would be 50 to 50 (usually referred to as *fifty-fifty*), which is the same as 1 to 1. This is also called even odds.

**3.** If the *odds for* an event are given as *a* to *b*, then the probability of that event would be $\frac{a}{a + b}$.

• If a bookie lays odds of 3 to 5 for a horse to win, he is assuming the horse's probability of winning is $\frac{3}{3+5}$, or ⅜. In this case, if the horse wins, a $3 bet would return $5 in winnings plus the return of the original $3; the payoff would therefore be $8.

**4.** The *odds against* an event are the reverse of the odds for the event. Odds of 3 to 5 *for* an event translate into odds *against* of 5 to 3. In gambling, the standard practice is to list the odds *against* a wager rather than the odds *for* it.

• A gambler places a $5 bet on a wager that carries odds of 20 to 1. In betting parlance, this is called a *20-to-1 shot*. These are the odds *against* a successful wager. They convert to a probability of ²⁰⁄₂₁ *against*, or ¹⁄₂₁ *for* a win. With these odds, a $1 bet would result in a $20 profit (plus the return of the $1 stake). A $5 bet would reap a $100 profit.

**5. True Odds and House Odds** In most betting situations, the person or establishment setting the payoffs on bets seeks an advantage. This is done by making the payoff less than the actual (or true) odds would dictate. The simplest example is a coin toss. The probability of success with a fair coin is ½, which is the same as 1-to-1 odds. Thus a successful $1 bet should earn $1 in winnings. If the house will only pay 95 cents on a $1 bet, it has an advantage of 2.5 cents per bet (since it will win half the time). Thus the *house odds* would be 95 to 100 against, even though the *true odds* are 1 to 1. Every casino game carries a house advantage, which means that, in the long run, every casino game is a losing proposition for the bettor.

**6. A warning about payoff odds:** The payoffs, or house odds, for casino games are usually displayed on or at the betting table. A win on 20-to-1 odds should return 20 times the amount of the bet, *plus the bet itself.* So winning a $5 bet at 20 to 1 earns $100 in winnings, which, along with the original five dollars, combines for a total payoff of $105.

Some casinos count on the bettor to overlook this and take winnings of only $100. This might be listed as a payoff of 20 *for* 1, but it is technically only 19-to-1 odds. Depending on the house rules, 20 *for* 1 may or may not mean the same as 20 *to* 1. It is worth finding this out before deciding on a betting strategy.

## MATHEMATICAL EXPECTATION

Whenever the outcomes in a game of chance have known probabilities, the average amount a player can expect to win or lose on each play is called the *expected winnings,* or simply the *expectation.* The expected winnings on any bet can be found by multiplying the probability of each possible outcome by its payoff, and then adding these results. In a simple coin toss there are two possible outcomes, each of probability ½. Assume a $1 bet is placed on heads. If heads comes up, the player wins $1; if tails comes up, the player loses $1.

| outcome | heads | tails |
|---------|-------|-------|
| probability | ½ | ½ |
| payoff | $1 | –$1 |

$$expectation = \left(\frac{1}{2}\right) \times (\$1) + \left(\frac{1}{2}\right) \times (-\$1) = 0$$

Any game in which the expectation is 0 is called a *fair game*. In a fair game, the bettor will win as often as he or she loses. There are no fair casino games. In craps, roulette, and blackjack, as well as in lottery games, the expected winnings on all bets are negative. This is the *house advantage* or *house edge*. However, because expectation is a long-run phenomenon, it does not rule out the possibility of winning streaks or a lucky jackpot. This possibility is what gives gambling its appeal. But it is important to remember that the odds are always stacked in favor of the house, the track, and the lottery commission. The soundest betting strategies are those that try to exploit the most favorable expectations.

**1. Lotteries** There are many different lottery games and sweepstakes. What they have in common is that most are required to display the odds of winning and the payoffs on the back of the ticket. From these figures, the mathematical expectation of winnings can be calculated.

• If a 50-cent ticket issued in a number-matching game indicates that 9,000 out of a million tickets sold (on average) will win $5, then the expectation is the probability of winning (9,000 out of 1,000,000, or 0.009) times $5, plus the probability of losing (991,000 out of 1,000,000, or 0.991) times (−$0.50).

$$expectation = (.009) \times (\$5) + (.991) \times (-\$0.50)$$
$$= -\$0.4505$$

Thus a player can expect to lose about 45 cents on the average for each 50-cent ticket bought. In general, the expectation on lotteries is very poor, but it is countered by the size of the jackpots, which offset the odds in most people's minds.

**2. Strategies at the Craps Table** Payoff odds are fairly standard from casino to casino for the game of craps. Table 4.3 shows the basic bets with their

**Table 4.3. Craps Table Odds and Payoffs**

| Bet | Payoff odds | Probability of win | Expectation |
|---|---|---|---|
| pass | 1 to 1 | 0.493 | −0.014 |
| don't pass, bar 12 | 1 to 1 | 0.493 | −0.014 |
| come | 1 to 1 | 0.493 | −0.014 |
| don't come | 1 to 1 | 0.493 | −0.014 |
| field | 1 to 1 or 2 to 1 on 2 and 12 | 0.444 | −0.056 |
| big 6 or big 8 | 1 to 1 | 0.4545 | −0.0909 |
| 6 or 8 the hard way | 9 to 1 | 0.0909 | −0.0909 |
| 4 or 10 the hard way | 7 to 1 | 0.111 | −0.111 |
| seven | 4 to 1 | 0.167 | −0.167 |
| any craps | 7 to 1 | 0.111 | −0.111 |
| 2 or 12 | 29 to 1 | 0.028 | −0.167 |
| 11 | 14 to 1 | 0.0556 | −0.167 |
| 3 | 14 to 1 | 0.0556 | −0.167 |

**Pass** A bet that the roller will win. This bet must be made on the first roll.

**Don't pass, bar 12** A bet that the roller loses, where a first roll of 12 (on which the roller loses) is considered a tie for the bettor.

**Come** Identical to *Pass*, but may be bet after the first roll.

**Don't Come** Identical to *Don't pass* after the first roll.

**Field** A bet that the next roll produces a 2, 3, 4, 9, 10, or 12. The payoff is doubled for a 2 or 12.

**Big 6** A bet that a 6 comes up before a 7 is rolled.

**Big 8** A bet that an 8 comes up before a 7 is rolled.

**The Hard Way** *The hard way* refers to matching dice. Thus, "4 the hard way" means rolling two 2's, "6 the hard way" is two 3's, "8 the hard way" is two 4's, and "10 the hard way" is two 5's. *The easy way* refers to nonmatching dice. A bet on an even number the hard way wins if the number comes up the hard way before it comes up the easy way.

**Seven** A bet that the next roll is a 7.

**Any Craps** A bet that craps (a 2, 3, or 12) comes up.

**Numbers** A bet on the specific outcome of the next roll.

payoffs, probabilities, and expected winnings per play. Note that the expected winnings on each bet is a negative number. For example, on a $1 bet of *pass*, the probability of winning is .493, and the probability of losing is .507. The payoff on a win is $1. Thus the mathematical expectation is

$$(\$1) \times (.493) + (-\$1) \times (.507) = -0.014.$$

This means that a player can expect to lose 1.4 cents per $1 bet, on average. Explanations of the bets are explained below Table 4.3.

Craps is a fast-paced game. While the expected losings per play are not great, the number of bets per hour (up to 130) makes it a difficult game at which to lose slowly. The safest bets are *Pass, Don't pass, Come,* and *Don't come.* The worst bets are "hard way" bets and bets on individual numbers.

**3. Roulette**   In American roulette, the wheel is divided into sections numbered 1 through 36, with two more labeled 0 and 00. The numbers 1 through 36 are split between two colors—red and black—and the 0 and 00 are green. A ball is rolled onto the spinning wheel and has an equal likelihood of landing in any one of the 38 slots.

The probability that the ball will land in any particular slot is 1 in 38, or 37 to 1 against. At the casino table there are a series of designated bets, of which certain combinations are possible. With the house odds listed below, every bet has an expectation of −$0.0526. The expectation, when expressed as a percent, is often called the house edge; thus the house edge on any bet is about 5.3%, or about 5 cents on every dollar bet.

### Table 4.4. Odds at the Roulette Table

| Bet | True odds (probability) | House odds |
|---|---|---|
| Color (red or black) | 20 to 18 (.4737) | 1 to 1 |
| Parity (even or odd) | 20 to 18 (.4737) | 1 to 1 |
| 1–18 | 20 to 18 (.4737) | 1 to 1 |
| 19–36 | 20 to 18 (.4737) | 1 to 1 |
| 1–12 (1st dozen) | 26 to 12 (.3158) | 2 to 1 |
| 13–24 (2nd dozen) | 26 to 12 (.3158) | 2 to 1 |
| 25–36 (3rd dozen) | 26 to 12 (.3158) | 2 to 1 |
| 12 numbers (any column) | 26 to 12 (.3158) | 2 to 1 |
| 6 numbers (any 2 rows) | 32 to 6 (.1579) | 5 to 1 |
| 4 numbers (any 4-number square) | 34 to 4 (.1053) | 8 to 1 |
| 3 numbers (any row) | 35 to 3 (.0789) | 11 to 1 |
| 2 adjacent numbers | 36 to 2 (.0526) | 17 to 1 |
| any single number | 37 to 1 (.0263) | 35 to 1 |

House odds may vary from casino to casino.

As can be seen in Table 4.4, the true odds (or actual probability) of winning on a particular combination contrast with the house odds, which determine the payoffs that the casino makes on any winning bet. The house odds are always less than the true odds, so the casino is guaranteed to win steadily and regularly. This is its edge.

## HORSE RACING

The system of betting used at all tracks in North America for thoroughbred racing, quarter-horse racing, harness racing, and dog racing is called the *pari-mutuel* system. It is also the system used for jai alai. Pari-mutuel is a French term that refers to the idea of shared betting. In this system, the total amount wagered on each race is divided among the winners after a house share (or *take*) has been deducted.

**1.** In the pari-mutuel system, a wager may be placed on any horse to *win* (finish first), *place* (finish first or second), or *show* (finish first, second, or third). The amounts of money wagered in each category are totaled to form three separate pools. A machine called a *totalizer* calculates the odds on each horse to win based on the amounts bet, and also sets payoff odds that reflect a certain percentage (usually 15–20%) taken out of the pool by the track and the state. The amounts bet (to win) and the odds against each horse are displayed on a *tote board*, which is periodically updated while the betting windows are open.

In the pari-mutuel system there are really two sets of odds—the true odds as determined by the bettors themselves, and the less favorable house odds, which are used to determine payoffs. This contrasts with a *bookie system*, in which an individual offers bets by calculating odds for each horse in a race based on such factors as past performance, weather conditions, the jockey, starting position, and perhaps some inside information. A bookie does not pool bets in order to determine odds, and thus has no guaranteed take. He must set odds in a way that best assures his advantage. Both bookies and racetracks list odds as *odds against*.

**2.** A horse that is a "15-to-1 shot" would return a profit of $15 for every dollar bet. Because the cheapest ticket is a $2 ticket, a single ticket at 15 to 1 would earn $30 in profit (plus the original $2). A winning ticket on a horse that won against odds of 2 to 5 would pay $2 on a $5 bet, or $4 on a $10 bet. A $4 profit on a $10 bet is equivalent to an 80 cent profit on a $2 bet.

The amount bet plus the profit is the *extension* or *payoff*—that is, the amount actually paid out when a winning ticket is presented at the ticket window. The extension is, in a sense, the money on the table. All of it goes either to the bettor or to the house.

**3.** If $15,000 is bet on a race, the house take would be 20% of $15,000, or $3,000. This leaves $12,000 to be split among the winners. However, the track automatically rounds the payoff on a $2 bet down to the nearest dime. This further reduces the $12,000 winners' pool by an amount called the *breakage*. The breakage, which adds to the house take, is not listed on the tote board.

# Statistics

Statistics is the science of manipulating raw data into usable information. It is a way of organizing and summarizing the results of experiments conducted with large groups, or with a single experiment repeated many times. The data sets considered in this section are called *distributions*.

## DISTRIBUTIONS

A distribution is essentially a set of measurements. Any list of numbers generated from a single experiment or test constitutes a distribution. Exam scores, per capita incomes, heights, weights, and IQs of a given sample population all constitute distributions.

A distribution may contain a large number of measurements. In fact, the more measurements there are, the more accurately the test summarizes the situation. Political pollsters try to assess the mood of an entire country by polling 1000 people at a time. The Nielsen rating system uses a cross-section of American families to reveal the television viewing habits of the entire country. In either case, the larger the sample, the more representative it will be of the entire population.

When a distribution is a very large list of numbers, it is useful to have some way of summarizing it. What is the range of numbers involved? What is its middle value? How are the numbers spread? Do they cluster around a middle value or are they spread over a wide range with very little clustering? These loosely phrased questions, which will be stated more precisely in this section, generate a set of numbers called *statistics*. These include the *mean, median, mode, spread, standard deviation*, and a few other measures.

This section is about the most basic statistics and how they can be used to convey the essential trends or results contained in a distribution. It begins with a brief overview of distributions and their representations.

**1. Bar Graphs and Pie Charts** The best way to visualize a distribution is to represent it with a bar graph or a pie chart. In a bar graph, the length or height of each bar represents the frequency of a score or measurement in a list of scores or measurements. Thus a bar graph is a graph of a *frequency distribution.*

• Assume a test given to 10 students resulted in the following scores:

  100, 90, 90, 80, 80, 80, 80, 70 , 70, 60

These results can be summarized in a frequency table.

| score | 100 | 90 | 80 | 70 | 60 |
|-------|-----|----|----|----|----|
| frequency | 1 | 2 | 4 | 2 | 1 |

A bar graph for this distribution would consist of a bar for each test score, whose length or height would be proportional to the frequency of that score.

A pie chart is another way of representing the same kind of distribution. To create a pie chart, first change each frequency to a percentage. If 4 out of 10 students scored 80 on an exam, this amounts to 40 percent.

| score | 100 | 90 | 80 | 70 | 60 |
|---|---|---|---|---|---|
| frequency | 1 | 2 | 4 | 2 | 1 |
| percent | 10% | 20% | 40% | 20% | 10% |

The corresponding pie chart represents the frequency of each score as a slice of the pie.

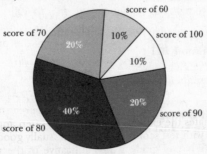

There are other ways to summarize a data set. Graphs and charts have the advantage of immediate visual impact. They can quickly summarize a key idea or trend contained in a data set. But they do not so clearly convey other summary information. The pie chart in particular is useful in showing the proportional size of categories, but not very good at showing how the data looks within categories, or how it looks as a whole. These issues can be addressed by supplementing the chart or graph with a few useful numbers: (1) the *spread*, which describes the difference between the highest and lowest values; (2) the *average*, which describes the "middle value"; and (3) the *standard deviation*, which describes how much the distribution clusters around its middle value.

## THE SPREAD (OR RANGE) OF A DISTRIBUTION

**1.** The **range** of the set of numbers 3, 25, 27, 27, 28, 29, 33, 53 is 3 to 53. This is also called the **spread**. It is a simply the high and low values of the distribution, between which all of the other values fall.

**2.** Whenever the low and high terms of a distribution are out of scale with the middle terms, it may be more informative to define a spread that eliminates the extreme values. This is often appropriate with test scores, where an unusually good or extremely bad grade is not indicative of the performance of the group as a whole.

There are several schemes for showing a spread that eliminates numbers or scores at the low and high end. Most take a certain percentage off the top and the bottom. One way to do this is to use

**percentiles**. This is most appropriate in distributions with a large number of scores or measurements.

**3. Percentiles** As discussed in Chapter 1, a **percentile** is one of 100 equal divisions of a distribution. For example, if 20,000 students take the SAT exam on a given day, and they are all ranked according to their score, the top 1% is called the 99th percentile. The bottom 1% is the zero percentile. In general, a percentile identifies a group or range by the percent of values that fall below it. The 50th percentile is the top half of a set of ordered numbers.

If a group is divided into 10 equal groups in order of rank, each subgroup is called a **decile**. If the same group is divided into 4 subgroups, each subgroup is called a **quartile**.

One method of giving the spread in a distribution is to lop off the top and the bottom decile, and give the spread of the set of numbers that remain. Another scheme is to lop off the top and bottom quartiles. The spread that remains is called the interquartile range. The **interquartile range** represents the "middle" half of the distribution.

## AVERAGES: MEAN, MEDIAN, AND MODE

Within any distribution, there is always a "middle" value that is referred to as an **average**. But there are several types of averages: the middle *value*, or **mean** value; the middle *number*, or **median**; and the most frequently occurring number, or **mode**.

There is also a specialized average known as the **geometric mean**. These are discussed below.

**1.** The most common mathematical average is the **arithmetic average**, or **mean**. It can be thought of as the middle value in a group of values.

Given any set (or list) of numbers, the arithmetic mean is found by summing all of the numbers in the list, and then dividing by the total number of numbers.

- The mean of the set 2, 5, 6, 7, 10, 20, 25, 75 is

$$\frac{2 + 5 + 6 + 7 + 10 + 20 + 25 + 75}{8} = \frac{150}{8} = 18.75$$

**2.** Another type of average, one that can be more meaningful in a list in which some numbers are much larger or smaller than the rest, is called the **median**. In an ordered list of numbers, the median is the middle number—that is, if the numbers were to be listed in order from smallest to largest, the median would fall in the middle of the list. (If the list has an even number of elements, the median would be the arithmetic average of the two middle values.)

- The median of 18, 24, 27, 30, 35, 42, 50 is 30.
- The median of 4, 5, 7, 10, 14, 22, 25, 30 is the average of 10 and 14, which is 12.

**3.** The **mode** is the number that occurs most frequently in a list of numbers. It is not used formally in many settings. It is important in any study that tracks the most popular choice in a vote or poll.

- Given the list of numbers 2, 3, 7, 7, 8, 12, 15, 26:

  The *mean* is given by:

  $(2 + 3 + 7 + 7 + 8 + 12 + 15 + 26)/8 = 10.$

  The *median* is the average of 7 and 8, which is 7.5.

  The *mode* is 7.

**4.** The word *mean* is almost always understood to imply the *arithmetic mean*. This should be distinguished from another type of mean—the **geometric mean**. The arithmetic mean is typically used with sets of numbers that are spread out somewhat evenly. A good example would be a set of test scores. By contrast, the geometric mean applies to a list of numbers which seem to increase rapidly, or in a pattern similar to 1, 2, 4, 8, 16, 32, . . . , where each term is a multiple of the previous term. This is a growth pattern that is commonly seen in population studies or in investments.

**5.** The geometric mean is defined to be the $n^{th}$ root of the product of the $n$ numbers in a list of numbers.

- The geometric sequence 1, 2, 4, 8, 16 has five terms. Its geometric mean is $\sqrt[5]{1 \cdot 2 \cdot 4 \cdot 8 \cdot 16} = \sqrt[5]{1024} = 4$. Notice that this is the same as the middle term of the sequence (the median) in this example. This will not always be the case. The arithmetic mean of this set is $(1 + 2 + 4 + 8 + 16)/5 = 31\frac{1}{5} = 6.2$.

**6.** Assume the population of a city was 55,000 in 1980 and 73,000 in 1990. To estimate the population in 1985, one could find the arithmetic mean of 55,000 and 73,000, which is 64,000. But because populations tend to grow exponentially (that is, they double at fairly regular intervals, and thus tend to follow a geometric progression such as the one used in the above example), a geometric mean would be more appropriate. In this case, with only two numbers, the geometric mean would be:

$$\sqrt{55000 \times 73000}$$

which is about 63,364.

**7.** The arithmetic mean is not appropriate in certain situations because it can be skewed by a single value that is way out of proportion with the other numbers on a list. In the following example, the arithmetic mean could be appropriate, depending upon what it is supposed to be showing.

• The gross annual incomes of families living on a certain street are

$35,000; $37,000; $42,500; and $51,000.

The mean income is

$(35,000 + 37,000 + 42,500 + 51,000)/4 = \$41,375.$

If a millionaire, with a yearly income of $975,000, moves into the vacant estate at the end of the street, the mean gross annual income becomes $285,125. But this is not representative of the group. The median income, by contrast, would be $42,500, which gives a better idea of the prevailing income level, although it disguises the fact that there is a millionaire on the block. Thus it is important to understand what type of average is being used, and what facts it may reveal or disguise.

## WEIGHTED AVERAGES

A **weighted average**, unlike an arithmetic average, assumes that each number in a set of numbers carries a predetermined **weight**, which is given as a percent. The sum of the weights in any set should be 100%.

To calculate a weighted average of a set of numbers, multiply each number in the set by its weight (expressed as a decimal), then sum them up.

- The final average in a college chemistry course is weighted in the following way:

| | |
|---|---|
| midterm exam: | 25% |
| final exam: | 40% |
| labs: | 20% |
| homework: | 15% |
| total | 100% |

A student who scored 75 on the midterm, 80 on the final exam, 85 on the labs, and 90 on the homework would have a weighted average of

$$75\%(.25) + 80\%(.40) + 85\%(.20) + 90\%(.15)$$
$$= 81.25.$$

# STANDARD DEVIATION

A useful description of the spread of a distribution is provided by the **standard deviation**. The standard deviation is best suited for computation by a computer program or a calculator. It can be calculated by hand, but this is reasonable to do only for a small set of numbers, as in the simple example given below.

## 1. Calculation of the Standard Deviation of a Distribution of Numbers

Assume that a distribution consists of the numbers 2, 4, 7, and 11. The standard deviation is calculated as follows:

1. Calculate the mean:

$$\text{mean} = \frac{2+4+7+11}{4} = \frac{24}{4} = 6$$

2. Subtract the mean from each number in the set. The results are the set of deviations from the mean. Square each deviation, and add the resulting squared deviations.

| deviation | squared deviation |
|-----------|-------------------|
| $2 - 6 = -4$ | $(-4)^2 = 16$ |
| $4 - 6 = -2$ | $(-2)^2 = 4$ |
| $7 - 6 = 1$ | $(1)^2 = 1$ |
| $11 - 6 = 5$ | $(5)^2 = \underline{25}$ |

sum of squared deviations = 46

3. Divide the sum of the squared deviations by the number of elements in the set.

$$46 \div 4 = 11.5$$

4. Take the square root: $\sqrt{11.5} \approx 3.39$

The standard deviation of 3.39 is an average of the deviations from the mean. In other words, it measures how the numbers in the set are spread out around the mean value.

**2. Interpreting Standard Deviation** The standard deviation provides a quick summary of the way a distribution of numbers is clustered around its mean. With a sample of four values, as in the example above, the standard deviation is relatively uninteresting. But with a large distribution, such as one representing the population of a city (income levels, age, etc.) or any other large set, the standard deviation is a useful way to summarize a vast quantity of data.

This is done by dividing the distribution into intervals having widths that are multiples of the standard deviation. For example, if an exam is given to 1000 students, and the mean score is 71 with a standard deviation of 5, then the group that is *one standard deviation from the mean* is the group that scored between $71 - 5$ and $71 + 5$, which is the interval from 66 to 76. The range of scores falling *two standard deviations from the mean* falls between $71 - (2 \times 5)$ and $71 + (2 \times 5)$, which is the interval from 61 to 81. *Three standard deviations from the mean* includes scores between 56 and 86.

The general rules for interpreting standard deviation are:

> 68% of the scores fall within one standard deviation from the mean.
>
> 95% fall within two standard deviations from the mean.
>
> 99.7%, or almost all of the scores, fall within three standard deviations of the mean.

## BELL CURVES

The classic bell curve is the shape of a *normal distribution.* A normal distribution is any set of numbers that is distributed evenly and symmetrically around its mean in a shape that looks much like a classic bell.

Most measures of physical characteristics fall into normal distributions—heights, weights, shoe sizes, hat sizes, and so on. The weight of each baby born in a given city in one year is a distribution of numbers which, if graphed in a bar graph, would look like a bell-shaped curve.

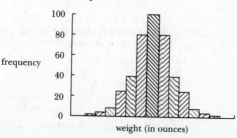

The peak of the bell falls at the mean. In fact, in any normal distribution, the mean, median, and mode coincide. As many scores or measures fall above the mean as below. Because the normal distribution is the most useful distribution, it has been tabulated in Table 4.5 in a way that allows probabilities to be calculated easily.

**1. The Standard Normal Distribution** A *standard normal distribution* is a distribution that is adequately modeled by a bell-shaped curve with a mean value of 0 and a standard deviation of 1. This means that the distribution (and its bar graph) are centered at the value 0 on the horizontal axis, and the bell shape is neither too wide nor too narrow. (A standard deviation greater than 1 means that the distribution is relatively "spread out," and thus looks like a gently sloping bell

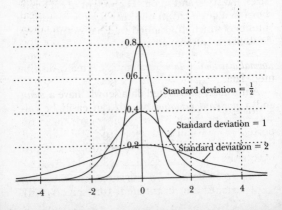

curve; standard deviation less than 1 implies relatively little deviation from the mean, and thus a steep, high-peaked bell curve.)

**2. Normally Distributed Data Sets** A *standard normal density table* is a table of proportional values that describe normally distributed data sets. Its interest to the consumer, or to the student of everyday mathematics, lies mostly in its use in the field of intelligence testing, product testing, and other demographic studies. Because bell curves are used to summarize a wide variety of test results concerning physical attributes or cognitive skills, some understanding of the accompanying vocabulary is indispensable.

Any distribution of test scores or measurements is said to be *normally distributed* if its frequency bar graph can be accurately modeled by a bell-shaped curve. Such a bell-shaped curve can be converted to a *standard normal distribution* by a mathematical transformation. The details of this transformation are not crucial. What is more important for the consumer is to understand how to use a *standard normal distribution table* to analyze normally distributed data.

A normally distributed data set will have a *mean* and a *standard deviation*, which can easily be calculated by machine. These numbers are always reported in any statistical summary. The standard normal density table is used to perform one of two basic tasks:

    i. To examine how the scores or measurements are distributed (or spread out) around the mean. (Do they all cluster right around the mean, or are they spread out over a wide range of values?)

ii. To make predictions about how similar experiments will come out in the future. (That is, determine the probability that in future studies, or even in individual instances, a certain result will be obtained.)

## 3. Standard Deviations from the Mean: How to Convert Normal to Standard Normal

The spread of values in a normal distribution is measured by using the mean as a point of reference. From there, ranges of data values are stepped off in "standard deviations from the mean."

*In a standard normal distribution, the mean is 0 and the standard deviation is 1.*

This means that the range of numbers between $-1$ and 1 falls within one standard deviation of the mean. The range between $-2$ and 2 falls within two standard deviations of the mean. And the range of numbers from $-3$ to 3 falls within three standard deviations of the mean.

In a standard normal distribution:

*68.26% of all values fall within one standard deviation of the mean.*

*95.44% of all values fall within two standard deviations of the mean.*

*99.73% of all values fall within three standard deviations of the mean.*

To convert a range of values in a normally distributed data set to the equivalent range in a standard normal distribution:

> *Subtract the mean and divide the result by standard deviation.*

• If a set of exam scores is normally distributed with a mean score of 72 and a standard deviation of 6, then:

The range of scores that lies one standard deviation from the mean is 66 to 78.

The range of scores that lies two standard deviations from the mean is 60 to 84.

The range of scores that lies three standard deviations from the mean is 54 to 90.

To change these to standard normal ranges, subtract the mean from each range boundary value, and divide by the standard deviation.

66 to 78 becomes $\dfrac{66 - 72}{6}$ to $\dfrac{78 - 72}{6}$, or the range from $-1$ to 1.

60 to 84 becomes $\dfrac{60 - 72}{6}$ to $\dfrac{84 - 72}{6}$, or the range from $-2$ to 2.

54 to 90 becomes $\dfrac{54 - 72}{6}$ to $\dfrac{90 - 72}{6}$, or the range from $-3$ to 3.

Thus 68.26% of all values fell between 66 and 78, 95.44% of all values fell between 60 and 84, and 99.73% of all values fell between 54 and 90.

## 4. Reading a Standard Normal Density Table   Table 4.5 shows what percent of a standard normal data set (or one that has been converted to standard normal) falls within certain ranges. The range boundaries are technically referred to as *z-values* or *z-scores*. Because the graph is the same shape to the right of 0 as to the left, only z-values between 0 and 3 are given.

For a standard normal distribution:

Column 1 gives the proportion of the distribution that falls above the value specified by z.

Column 2 gives the proportion of the distribution that falls below the given z-value.

Column 3 gives the proportion of the distribution that falls within a range to the right or left of the mean by the amount specified by the value of z.

• The Stanford-Binet IQ test has a mean score of 100 and a standard deviation of 15. The proportion of those who score above 118 would be calculated as follows:

$$z = \frac{118 - 100}{15} = 1.2$$

Using Table 4.5, read column 1 at z = 1.2. It shows that .1151, or about 11½%, score above 118. This is the same as the percent that score below 82 (which is 18 points *below* the mean). Column 3 at z = 1.2 shows that .7698, or almost 77% of the group, fall within 18 points of the mean score (that is, between 82 and 118).

## Table 4.5. z-scores (Normal Distribution)

| z | greater than z | less than z | between −z and z |
|-----|------|------|------|
| 0.0 | .5000 | .5000 | .0000 |
| 0.1 | .4602 | .5398 | .0796 |
| 0.2 | .4207 | .5793 | .1586 |
| 0.3 | .3821 | .6179 | .2358 |
| 0.4 | .3446 | .6554 | .3108 |
| 0.5 | .3085 | .6915 | .3830 |
| 0.6 | .2743 | .7257 | .4514 |
| 0.7 | .2420 | .7580 | .5160 |
| 0.8 | .2119 | .7881 | .5762 |
| 0.9 | .1841 | .8159 | .6318 |
| 1.0 | .1587 | .8413 | .6826 |
| 1.1 | .1357 | .8643 | .7286 |
| 1.2 | .1151 | .8849 | .7698 |
| 1.3 | .0968 | .9032 | .8064 |
| 1.4 | .0808 | .9192 | .8384 |
| 1.5 | .0668 | .9332 | .8664 |
| 1.6 | .0548 | .9452 | .8904 |
| 1.7 | .0446 | .9554 | .9108 |
| 1.8 | .0359 | .9641 | .9282 |
| 1.9 | .0287 | .9713 | .9426 |
| 2.0 | .0228 | .9772 | .9544 |
| 2.1 | .0179 | .9821 | .9642 |
| 2.2 | .0139 | .9861 | .9722 |
| 2.3 | .0107 | .9893 | .9786 |
| 2.4 | .0082 | .9918 | .9836 |
| 2.5 | .0062 | .9938 | .9876 |
| 2.6 | .0047 | .9953 | .9906 |
| 2.7 | .0035 | .9965 | .9930 |
| 2.8 | .0026 | .9974 | .9948 |
| 2.9 | .0019 | .9981 | .9962 |
| 3.0 | .0014 | .9986 | .9973 |
| 3.1 | .0010 | .9990 | .9980 |

# Statistical Likelihood in Everyday Life

Any almanac contains page after page of statistical tables, as does the annual *Statistical Abstract of the United States*. These kinds of publications are pored over by newspaper editors, talk-show hosts, lobbyists, and political aides, who try to use statistics to bolster an argument or sway public opinion. In this sense, statistics is perhaps the most misused of all the sciences. When cleverly crafted bar graphs, pie charts, bell curves, and statistical averages can be used to demonstrate a trend where none exists, or to grossly overstate the extent of a social problem—be it crime, poverty, or reports of missing children—the public's attention can be diverted from more serious issues and solvable problems.

When statistics are reported in the media, it is wise to be skeptical. Given the results of a poll, it is essential to know how many people were polled and what biases they might have. Given the results of a "scientific" study, it is worth asking who conducted the study, whether the results are reliable, and whether the results could be attributed to factors other than those cited. Statistics can be a very powerful tool for both revealing and concealing the truth; therefore, they should be interpreted with care.

Both of the following tables are good examples of meaningful statistics. Table 4.6 gives current life

## Table 4.6. Life Expectancy

| | | *Remaining Life Expectancy* | | | |
|---|---|---|---|---|---|
| | *All* | *White* | | *Black* | |
| *Age in 1990* | *groups* | *Male* | *Female* | *Male* | *Female* |
| at birth | 75.4 | 72.7 | 79.4 | 64.5 | 73.6 |
| 1 | 75.1 | 72.3 | 78.9 | 64.8 | 73.8 |
| 2 | 74.1 | 71.4 | 78.0 | 63.9 | 72.9 |
| 3 | 73.1 | 70.4 | 77.0 | 62.9 | 71.9 |
| 4 | 72.1 | 69.4 | 76.0 | 62.0 | 71.0 |
| 5 | 71.1 | 68.5 | 75.0 | 61.0 | 70.0 |
| 10 | 66.3 | 63.5 | 70.1 | 56.1 | 65.1 |
| 15 | 61.3 | 58.6 | 65.2 | 51.3 | 60.2 |
| 20 | 56.5 | 54.0 | 60.3 | 46.7 | 55.3 |
| 25 | 51.9 | 49.3 | 55.4 | 42.4 | 50.6 |
| 30 | 47.2 | 44.7 | 50.6 | 38.2 | 45.9 |
| 35 | 42.6 | 40.1 | 45.8 | 34.1 | 41.3 |
| 40 | 38.0 | 35.6 | 41.0 | 30.1 | 36.8 |
| 45 | 33.4 | 31.1 | 36.2 | 26.2 | 32.4 |
| 50 | 29.0 | 26.7 | 31.6 | 22.5 | 28.2 |
| 55 | 24.8 | 22.5 | 27.2 | 19.0 | 24.2 |
| 60 | 20.8 | 18.7 | 23.0 | 15.9 | 20.5 |
| 65 | 17.9 | 15.2 | 19.1 | 13.3 | 17.2 |
| 70 | 13.9 | 12.1 | 15.4 | 10.7 | 14.1 |
| 75 | 10.9 | 9.4 | 12.0 | 8.6 | 11.2 |
| 80 | 8.3 | 7.1 | 9.0 | 6.7 | 8.6 |
| 85 and over | 6.1 | 5.2 | 6.4 | 5.0 | 6.3 |

[Source: *Statistical Abstract of the United States, 1995*]

expectancies over a range of ages for black and white males and females. It shows that life expectancy differs between age groups, between racial groups, and between males and females. The table is predictive, although it is clearly based on past data. It also shows that probabilities can change as events unfold. The life expectancy of a newborn white female baby is close to 80 years. Yet an 80-year-old white female can expect to live another 9 years. This is because, statistically, those who formed the left side of the bell curve (to the left of the original mean of 80) have died. The new life expectancy represents an average. It guarantees nothing more than that the entire group of 80 year old white women will average 9 more years.

Table 4.7 lists causes of death. It should be interpreted carefully. It does not say that any particular person, chosen at random, has a 23.5% chance of dying of cancer. It simply says that, of all deaths recorded in the United States (over an unspecified period), 23.5% resulted from cancer. Many of those deaths occurred within high-risk groups. Yet not everyone falls into a high-risk group, so the frequency should not automatically be converted to a probability. A more detailed study, taking into account many other lifestyle and hereditary factors (other than mere membership in a demographic group) would have to be done if an individual wanted to know his or her risk of death from cancer.

**Table 4.7. Causes of Death in the United States**

**Natural Causes**

| | |
|---|---|
| Heart disease | 34.0% |
| Cancer | 23.5% |
| Cerebrovascular disease | 6.7% |
| Influenza and pneumonia | 3.7% |
| Diabetes | 2.2% |
| Diseases of arteries | 2.0% |
| Chronic liver disease, cirrhosis | 1.2% |
| Other diseases | 19.7% |
| **Total** | **93.0%** |

**External Causes**

| | |
|---|---|
| Motor-vehicle accidents | 2.2% |
| Other accidents | 2.2% |
| Suicide | 1.4% |
| Homicide | 1.2% |
| **Total** | **7.0%** |

[Source: *Life Insurance Fact Book*, American Council of Life Insurance]

# Baseball Statistics

No sport is more invested in statistics than baseball, and no fans are more obsessed with statistics than baseball fans. This obsession has produced encyclopedias containing every imaginable baseball stat. Although television commentators often delve into the most obscure statistical facts ("he doesn't hit well from the left side in the late innings of afternoon games"), there are a few essential stats that measure the effectiveness of a batter or pitcher. These so-called "averages" are simply relative frequencies, or ratios.

**1.** An *at-bat* is a turn at the plate that results in a hit or an out. It does not include walks, hit batsmen, a base awarded because of obstruction or interference, or sacrifices to advance a baserunner.

**2.** A player's *batting average* is the ratio of hits to at-bats. It is expressed as a decimal number between 0 and 1 carried out to three (or sometimes four) decimal places. In speaking of batting averages, the decimal point is ignored; thus a "300 hitter" is someone whose batting average is .300.

$$batting\ average = \frac{number\ of\ hits}{number\ of\ at\text{-}bats}$$

• In the 1941 season, Ted Williams of the Boston Red Sox led the American League in hitting with a batting average of exactly .400 (179 hits in 448 at-bats). Given the option to sit out the last day of the season to preserve a mark that had not been equaled in over a decade, Williams did not hesitate to risk his average in a doubleheader against the Philadelphia Athletics. In the two games, he got 6 hits in 8 at-bats, and finished with a .406 average (185 hits in 456 at-bats).

**3.** *On-base average* is the number of times a batter reaches base divided by the number of plate appearances. Unlike at-bats, plate appearances include walks, hit by a pitch, sacrifice flies, and dropped third strikes.

**4.** *Slugging average* is a measure of a batter's ability to hit for extra bases. A decimal number that theoretically ranges between 0 and 4 carried to three decimal places, it is obtained by dividing the total number of bases reached safely on hits by the number of official at-bats.

• The record for slugging average is held by Babe Ruth, who slugged .847 for the New York Yankees in the 1920 season. Here is how his average was calculated:

| At-Bats | Singles | Doubles | Triples | Home runs |
|---------|---------|---------|---------|-----------|
| 458 | 73 | 36 | 9 | 54 |

Total bases: $73 + (36 \times 2) + (9 \times 3)$
$+ (54 \times 4) = 388$
Total bases/At-bats: $388/458 = .847$

**5.** *Earned run average* is a measure of a pitcher's effectiveness. An *earned run* is a run that scores as a result of an offensive or defensive action where no error is involved. An earned run average is the average number of earned runs scored against a pitcher every nine innings. It is calculated by the following formula:

$$earned\ run\ average = \frac{total\ earned\ runs}{no.\ of\ innings\ pitched} \times 9$$

If a pitcher does not complete a given inning, the fraction of the inning (⅓ or ⅔, determined from the number of outs recorded against the opposing team) is used. The lowest ERA recorded in the modern era is that of Bob Gibson of the St. Louis Cardinals in 1968: 1.12.

6. A pitcher's *on-base percentage* is another measure of his effectiveness. It is the ratio of the number of hits and walks given up, divided by the number of outs plus hits and walks. It does not include intentional walks.

7. A fielder's competence is measured by his *fielding average*. This is the ratio of putouts and assists to the total number of fielding chances. It is expressed as a number between 0 and 1 carried to three decimal places.

# Chapter 5

# Business and Personal Finance

The mathematics of business and personal finance is mostly concerned with the time value of money— with the difference between the face value of money and its buying power today or in the future. A ten-dollar bill, for example, maintains a constant face value. But if it is not invested, the amount of goods it can buy diminishes over time. If it is invested wisely, its buying power may increase over time.

Moreover, a $10 bill can play a small part in a wide variety of activities: it can be earned, paid out, spent, gambled, invested, inherited, borrowed against, loaned out, taxed, stashed away, or given away. In each of these transactions, a value can be assigned to it, and that value will change over time.

This chapter shows how a sum of money gets paid, invested, loaned, taxed, and accounted for. It describes the mechanisms behind routine procedures that people conduct each day—paying bills, charging purchases, depositing checks, and paying taxes. Many of these procedures involve complicated formulas which are usually carried out by experts using computers, tables, and business calculators. The result is a sometimes discouraging abundance of fine print on monthly statements, contracts, and application forms. In a financial world that grows more complicated every day, this is unavoidable.

Short of wading into the mathematical intricacies of investing and borrowing, the consumer may still seek an advantage in learning some generalities. That is the purpose of this chapter. The information contained here should be supplemented by asking bankers, accountants, stockbrokers, and investment analysts to clearly explain how they derive the numbers they use. As in the world of gambling, there is a great deal of obfuscation that goes with every type of monetary transaction. But each transaction can be clearly explained.

The fundamental concept behind all of the investment decisions discussed here is interest. This provides a good starting point. Once the idea of interest is understood, everything else follows.

# Interest

Interest earned on investments or paid on loans can be thought of as rent charged (or paid) for the use of money over a period of time. When someone opens a savings account they are loaning their money to a bank in return for compensation in the form of interest, which is calculated as a percentage of the total amount. When someone borrows money from any type of lender, they are expected to pay a fee for it.

In this section, types of interest payments and ways to calculate them are examined in the context of different types of investments.

## INTEREST RATES

**1.** *Interest* is a fee paid for the use of money. The amount loaned (or borrowed) is referred to as the *principal amount*, or simply as the *principal*. The interest on the principal can be expressed either as a percent or as the actual dollar amount of fees paid. Depending on the type of loan or investment involved, a percent interest rate might be referred to as a *finance charge, discount rate, current yield,* or *annual percentage rate*.

**2.** As a percent, the *rate of interest* on an investment or a loan must refer to a time interval. Almost all interest rates, unless otherwise indicated, are based on a full year. Thus interest can be thought of as a yearly payment. This is usually specified as an *annual interest rate*, which is a ratio of the amount of interest paid (or earned) in one year to the principal amount invested (or borrowed) over that time.

• When $100 invested for one year earns $8 in interest, the annual interest rate is $8/100$, or 8% per year.

• If a bank lends $500 for one year and charges $40 in interest, the annual interest rate is $40/500$, or $8/100$, or 8%.

**3.** On installment loans, a monthly statement will often refer to a *daily interest rate*—the interest charge for one day's use of money. This is the annual rate divided by 365. The *monthly rate* is the annual rate divided by 12, the *weekly rate* is the annual rate divided by 52, and so on.

## THE DISCOUNT RATE, T-BILL RATE, AND PRIME LENDING RATES

**1.** The *discount rate* is the rate at which commercial banks may borrow short-term funds from the Federal Reserve Bank (the nation's central bank). It is, essentially, the interest rate that commercial banks have to pay for money. It is set by the Federal Reserve Board, a presidentially appointed board of directors who govern the country's monetary policies. The Fed's discount rate is a key economic indicator. It is one of the principal determinants of the prime lending rates set by the country's leading banks.

**2.** The *prime lending rate* (also known simply as the *prime*) is the interest rate banks use when lending to their most creditworthy customers. Although technically each bank sets its own prime rate, in effect most commercial banks follow the rates set by the major banks. The prime rate published daily by the *Wall Street Journal* is an average based on the rates of corporate loans issued by 30 of the nation's largest banks. In addition, prime lending rates are calculated for individual countries. The *London Interbank Offered Rate* (*LIBOR*) is another interbank loan rate, which is based on five European banks. It is a kind of international prime rate.

Banks set their mortgage, equity loans, and personal loan rates using simple formulas based on the prime rate. Equity loans, for example, are often set at two points above the prime. (In general, a *point* refers to a percentage point, or to 1% of some principal amount.)

**3.** There are several other interest rates that act as key economic indicators by setting the cost of money. The *federal funds rate* is an interest rate for cash reserves held at Federal Reserve district banks. When one bank has excess reserves, it may lend funds to a bank that has a deficit. Although the rate they can charge is determined by the market, it is influenced by the Federal Reserve Board, which sets the amount of reserves banks must maintain. The federal funds rate is considered the most sensitive indicator of the direction that bank interest rates will go. Changes in the discount rate and the prime rate usually follow the federal funds rate.

**4.** The *T-bill rate* is the interest rate that the government pays on short-term debt obligations known as *Treasury bills.* There are several types of T-bills that can be distinguished by their terms of maturity—three months (13 weeks), six months (26 weeks), and one year (52 weeks). Interest rates for each type of T-bill are set every Monday. They are calculated from the discount price at which each type of bill is sold at auction.

# Calculating Interest Payments

Banks are required by law to post their interest rates on investments and loans. In such a listing, the first figure given is the *annual interest rate.* The second figure is the *effective rate* or *effective yield,* which is higher. This discrepancy exists because interest, while stated as an annual payment, is often paid (or collected) several times in a single year. As a result, interest that has been added to the principal begins to earn interest, which *compounds* the total interest payment. This suggests that there are several ways of calculating interest. They are:

*simple interest,* which is a fee paid at the end of a contract.

*discount interest,* in which a fee is paid at the beginning of the contract.

*compound interest,* in which a fee is broken into a series of payments made at regular intervals during the contract.

It should be noted that, in practice, interest payments are calculated using computers, business calculators, or interest tables. These in turn are based on the mathematical formulas given below.

## SIMPLE INTEREST

*Simple interest* refers to a one-time calculation of a percent of a principal. It is paid at the end of a time period specified by a lending agreement or contract. In a simple scenario, a person who borrows $100 for one year with simple interest of 6% per year would have to repay the $100 principal plus an interest charge amounting to 6% of $100, which is $6.

All simple interest is calculated using the formula

$$I = P \times r \times t$$

where $P$ is the principal amount, $r$ is the annual interest rate (expressed as a decimal), and $t$ is the time in years. Although most investments and loans are not calculated using simple interest, certain types of bonds do pay simple interest annually or semiannually on the face value of the bond.

• A 12½% bond has a face value of $1000. If simple interest is paid as a dividend each year, the annual payment would be 12½% of $1000, or $125. After five years the total interest earned would be

$$I = \$1000 \times 0.125 \times 5 = \$625.$$

## DISCOUNT INTEREST

A *discount* is an interest charge that is collected at the beginning of the term of a loan. Typically, the amount of the discount is subtracted from the loan amount. A $5000 student loan with a 10% discount, for example, puts $4500 in the student's hands at the outset of the contract. The $500 discount (10% of $5000) is the interest charge. When the student finishes school, the $5000 becomes due in full after six months. If not paid in full at that time, the debt converts to an installment debt which entails additional interest charges paid at regular intervals over a given number of years (usually 5 or 10).

Another type of discounted debt is a U.S. Treasury bill. These are issued in denominations that start at $10,000. All T-bills are sold at a *discount*, which means that the purchase price is lower than the face value. They may be redeemed for the face value when they have matured. Three- and six-month T-bills are sold at auction every Monday, and one-year bills are auctioned once a month. T-bills may also be sold on secondary markets without a great loss of value through commissions. The difference between what brokers charge for T-bills and what they will pay for them is usually in the range of 2 to 4 *basis points* (which means 2 to 4 *hundredths* of a percent of the face value).

A three-month Treasury bill worth $10,000 upon redemption might sell for $9,800. The discount, or interest earned by the investor, is $200.

For a more detailed discussion of Treasury bills, see page 000.

## COMPOUND INTEREST

**1.** When the interest earned on an investment is paid at regular intervals (rather than as a single payment at the beginning or end of a contract), it can be added onto the principal amount. When this is done, all subsequent interest payments are based on the principal and the accumulated interest. That is, the accumulated interest earns interest. This is called *compounding* the interest.

For example, an investment of $100 earns 10% per year compounded yearly. Table 5.1 shows how this investment grows if the interest is automatically added onto the principal.

**Table 5.1. Compound Interest on $100**

| year | starting balance | interest earned | new balance |
|------|------------------|-----------------|-------------|
| 1 | 100 | $100 \times 0.10 = 10$ | 110.00 |
| 2 | 110 | $110 \times 0.10 = 11$ | 121.00 |
| 3 | 121 | $121 \times 0.10 = 12.1$ | 133.10 |
| 4 | 133.10 | $133.10 \times 0.10 = 13.31$ | 146.41 |
| 5 | 146.41 | $146.41 \times 0.10 = 14.64$ | 161.05 |

After five years the interest amounts to $61.05. If simple interest had been paid instead of compound interest, the interest payments would have totaled $50.

$$I = P \times r \times t = \$100 \times 0.10 \times 5 = \$50$$

Because of compounding, an extra $11.50 was earned.

**2.** Interest may be compounded yearly (once a year), semiannually (every six months), quarterly (four times a year, or every three months), monthly, biweekly, weekly, or daily. In theory, interest can be compounded any number of times at regular intervals during a year. The number of compoundings is a crucial consideration in calculating the total amount of interest earned. The more frequently interest is compounded, the faster the investment grows.

**3.** Adding an interest payment onto a principal amount is the same as calculating a *markup* (see p. 16). Assume a percent increase is given in decimal form as $r$ (see p. 7 for how to change percents to decimals). To increase or *mark up* an amount by a rate $r$, multiply the amount by $(1 + r)$.

- If a salary of $20,000 is increased by 5%, the new salary is $20,000 \times (1 + 0.05)$, which equals $21,000.

If interest is automatically added onto the principal amount, it acts like a markup.

• A 5% interest payment on $20,000, added directly to the principal, results in a new principal amount of $20,000 × (1 + 0.05), which equals $21,000.

Just as the calculation of an initial interest payment involves multiplying the principal by $(1 + r)$, each subsequent compounding of interest can be calculated by multiplying the initial principal by the same factor.

• The second compounding of the principal of $20,000 is calculated by multiplying the result of the first compounding (which is $21,000) by (1 + 0.05). In this calculation, $20,000 is written as $20,000 (1 + 0.05) in order to show a pattern. The principal after the second compounding would be

$$[20,000 \times (1 + 0.05)] \times (1 + 0.05).$$

This can be written as $20,000 \times (1 + 0.05)^2$.

After three compoundings, the principal amount would be

$$20,000 \times (1 + 0.05)^3.$$

After $n$ compoundings, the principal would be

$$20,000 \times (1 + 0.05)^n.$$

**4.** The process of compounding involves multiplying a principal amount by an *interest accumulation factor* of the form $(1 + i)$, where $i$ is the interest rate paid *for that compounding period*.

If interest is compounded annually, and $r$ is the annual interest rate, then the interest accumulation factor is $(1 + r)$. If interest is compounded monthly, then the interest rate used in the interest accumulation factor has to be converted to a monthly rate. The monthly rate is the annual rate divided by 12. Thus $(1 + i)$ would take the form $(1 + r/12)$.

In general, if the annual interest rate is $r$ and interest is compounded $m$ times per year, then the interest accumulation factor used for each compounding is $(1 + r/m)$. In compounding the interest on an investment of P dollars, multiply P by the interest accumulation factor *one time for each compounding*. This leads to a general formula for accumulated compound interest known as the *future value formula*.

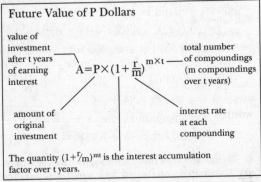

Future Value of P Dollars

value of investment after t years of earning interest

$$A = P \times \left(1 + \frac{r}{m}\right)^{m \times t}$$

total number of compoundings (m compoundings over t years)

amount of original investment

interest rate at each compounding

The quantity $(1 + r/m)^{mt}$ is the interest accumulation factor over t years.

• Assume $750 is invested at 8% per year for five years with monthly compounding. Then $P = 750$, $r = .08$, $m = 12$, and $t = 5$. At the end of five years, the investment would be worth

$$A = 750 \times \left(1 + \frac{.08}{12}\right)^{12 \times 5} = \$1117.38.$$

This calculation can be done on a scientific calculator by using the key marked $x^y$. First compute the value of $(1 + .08 \div 12)$. Then press $x^y$ followed by 60 (which is $12 \times 5$). The result (about 1.4898) is the total interest accumulation factor over five years of compounding. Multiply it by \$750 to get the final answer of \$1117.38.

## FUTURE VALUE AND PRESENT VALUE

**1.** Once invested, a sum of money will increase in value over time (assuming it is invested wisely). If left under a mattress, it retains its face value but diminishes in buying power because of the effects of inflation (see p. 17). Consequently, \$500 in cash today is worth more than a promise to pay \$500 five years from now. Assuming an annual interest rate of 5% and monthly compounding, \$500 invested *now* would in five years turn out to be worth

$$500 \times (1 + {}^{.05}\!/_{12})^{12 \times 5} = \$641.68.$$

**2.** In the last calculation, \$500 is referred to as the *present value* of the money, and \$641.68 is the *future value* of the money. The formula that relates the present and future value of money is the compound interest formula

$$A = P \times \left(1 + \frac{r}{m}\right)^{m \times t}$$

where P represents the present value and A represents the future value.

**3.** The above formula, when solved for the present value P, looks like this:

$$P = A \div \left(1 + \frac{r}{m}\right)^{m \times t}$$

In comparing this to the previous formula, notice that a division symbol has replaced the multiplication symbol on the right-hand side, and A and P have been reversed.

**4.** Together, these two formulas can be used to solve two types of compound interest problems:

   i. *The future value problem:* How much is *P* dollars worth in *t* years if it earns an interest rate *r* and is compounded *m* times per year?

   ii. *The present value problem:* How much money should be invested *today* if it is to be worth A dollars *t* years from now?

The first type of problem was solved above. An example of the second is given below.

   • In order to have $1000 in a bank account eight years from now, the amount that should be invested *now* at 6% per year with weekly compounding would be

$$1000 \div \left(1 + \frac{.08}{52}\right)^{52 \times 8} = \$618.95.$$

Using a scientific calculator, first calculate the value of $(1 + .08 \div 52)$. Then press $x^y$ followed by 416 (which is $52 \times 8$). The result should be put into the memory (usually marked M+). Enter 1000 followed by the division key, and then recall the figure from memory (using a key marked MR, or its equivalent). The result given above should appear.

**5.** When a loan is *discounted* using compound interest, the present value of the loan amount can be calculated using the formula in paragraph 3 above, but it can also be discounted using simple discount interest (see page 230).

• If a $10,000 loan is discounted at 6% and comes due in six months, the borrower would receive the present value of $10,000, which is

$$P = 10,000 \div \left(1 + \frac{.06}{2}\right)^{2 \times 1/2} = \$9708.74.$$

If the same note were discounted using simple interest, the borrower would receive

$$\$10,000 - (10,000) \times (0.06) \times (\tfrac{1}{2}) =$$
$$10,000 - 300 = \$9700.$$

**6.** The first method of discounting shown above is called a *true discount*. The second method is called a *bank discount*. The first method is more favorable to the borrower because it puts more money in his or her hands, and thus entails a smaller interest payment. The second method, however, is the more standard practice.

## EFFECTIVE YIELD AND ANNUAL PERCENTAGE RATES (APR)

Table 5.2 compares the interest earned on $100 invested for one year at 10% per year, where different compounding schemes are followed. The formula used to compute the values is

$$A = P \times \left(1 + \frac{r}{m}\right)^{m \times t}$$

where P = $100, r = 10% = 0.1, and t = 1 year. With these substitutions, the formula simplifies to

$$A = 100 \times \left(1 + \frac{0.1}{m}\right)^{m}$$

In this table there are two patterns worth noting. First, the amount of interest earned increases

**Table 5.2. Effective Yield for Various Compounding Periods**

| m<br>No. of<br>compoundings | A<br>Value of $100<br>after 1 year | Interest<br>earned | Effective<br>interest rate |
|---|---|---|---|
| 1 | 110 | 10 | 10% |
| 2 | 110.25 | 10.25 | 10.25% |
| 4 | 110.38 | 10.38 | 10.38% |
| 12 | 110.47 | 10.47 | 10.47% |
| 52 | 110.51 | 10.51 | 10.51% |
| 365 | 110.52 | 10.52 | 10.52% |

with the frequency of compounding. Thus the stated annual interest rate is increased through the process of compounding into a higher interest rate. This higher rate, calculated over one year, is called the *effective annual interest rate*, or simply the *effective yield*.

Secondly, the effective yield does not increase indefinitely as the number of compoundings increases. There is an upper limit on the effective yield. In this example, the limit is precisely $(e^{0.1} - 1)$, where $e^{0.1}$ is calculated on a calculator using the key marked $e^x$.

**1.** The **effective yield** of any investment depends on the stated annual interest rate and the number of compoundings per year. It represents the actual amount of interest that is earned (or paid) in one year when the effect of compounding is taken into account. The formula for effective yield is:

$$effective\ yield = \left(1 + \frac{r}{m}\right)^m - 1$$

The greatest possible yield (assuming an infinite number of compoundings per year) is $e^r - 1$.

- A passbook savings account that is earning 5% per year with daily compounding has an effective yield of

$$\left(1 + \frac{.05}{365}\right)^{365} - 1 = 0.0512675,\ \text{or about}\ 5\tfrac{1}{8}\%.$$

**2.** While the term *effective yield* applies to interest earned on invested money, the term *APR*, or *an-*

*nual percentage rate* applies to interest owed on loans. The idea is essentially the same. When a debt is being paid off in installments, interest charges accumulate. In time, interest is owed on unpaid interest. This compounding causes the effective rate of interest to be higher than the stated rate. If a loan contains no charges other than compound interest, the APR is the same as the effective yield. But most loans include extra charges that technically constitute interest. These may take the form of application fees, points (which are a form of prepaid interest in the amount of 1% of the borrowed amount), maintenance fees, and so on. The APR is calculated by adding these charges into the cost of the loan as interest. Thus the APR is always greater than the stated annual interest rate used for compounding purposes, and it is usually greater than the effective yield. By law, every lender must disclose the APR in large bold type.

• A variable rate mortgage is advertised at 6.75% per year for the first five years, after which it adjusts to 2 percentage points over the T-bill rate (see p. 286). Because of loan origination fees, interest compounding, and monthly private mortgage insurance, the bank lists an APR of 7.85%. It is possible that another bank offering a rate higher than 6.75% may have a lower APR than this because they are willing to pick up some of the application fees and closing costs. Therefore it is advisable to shop for mortgages and other loans by com-

**Table 5.3. Summary of Compound Interest Formulas**

P = present value (or principal amount)
A = future value of P
r = annual interest rate (in decimal form)
m = number of compoundings per year
t = number of years

$$\text{Future Value: } A = P \times \left(1 + \frac{r}{m}\right)^{m \times t}$$

$$\text{Present Value: } P = A \div \left(1 + \frac{r}{m}\right)^{m \times t}$$

$$\text{Effective Interest Rate} = \left(1 + \frac{r}{m}\right)^{m} - 1$$

$$\text{Greatest Possible Effective Yield} = e^{r} - 1$$

paring APR, and not the listed annual interest rate.

## DOUBLING TIME—THE LAW OF 70

**1.** If an investment pays interest at an annual rate of $i$ percent with $m$ compoundings per year, it will double in size over a certain number of years. This does not depend on how much is invested. It will double a second time over the same time interval. The doubling time is given by the formula below.

$$doubling\ time = \ln(2) \times \frac{1}{m} \div \ln\left(1 + \frac{r}{m}\right)$$

where $r$ is the decimal form of the annual interest rate.

• Suppose \$5,000 is invested at 6% per year compounded monthly.

$$doubling\ time = \ln(2) \times \frac{1}{12} \div \ln\left(1 + \frac{.06}{12}\right)$$
$$= 11.58\ years$$

**2.** A much simpler doubling-time formula assumes that interest is compounded continuously (meaning at every instant of time). This formula provides a good-enough approximation to use for any compounding situation.

$$doubling\ time = \frac{\ln(2)}{r}$$

where $r$ is the decimal form of the annual interest rate.

• In the example above, the annual rate of 6% gives a doubling time of $\ln(2)/.06$, which equals 11.55 years. This differs from the exact answer by about 11 days.

**3.** The simplified doubling-time formula leads to similar formulas for tripling time, quadrupling time, and so on.

$$doubling\ time = \frac{\ln(2)}{r}$$
$$tripling\ time = \frac{\ln(3)}{r}$$
$$quadrupling\ time = \frac{\ln(4)}{r}$$
$$quintupling\ time = \frac{\ln(5)}{r}$$

Although it is not obvious from these formulas, the quadrupling time is twice the doubling time.

**Table 5.4. Doubling, Tripling, Quadrupling, and Quintupling Times**

| Annual interest rate | Doubling time | Tripling time | Quadrupling time | Quintupling time |
|---|---|---|---|---|
| 4% | 17.32 | 27.47 | 34.66 | 40.24 |
| 5% | 13.86 | 21.97 | 27.73 | 32.18 |
| 6% | 11.55 | 18.31 | 21.1 | 26.82 |
| 7% | 9.9 | 15.7 | 19.8 | 23 |
| 8% | 8.66 | 13.73 | 17.33 | 20.12 |
| 9% | 7.7 | 12.21 | 15.4 | 17.88 |
| 10% | 6.93 | 10.99 | 13.86 | 16.09 |
| 11% | 6.3 | 9.99 | 12.6 | 14.63 |
| 12% | 5.78 | 9.16 | 11.55 | 13.41 |
| 13% | 5.33 | 8.45 | 10.66 | 12.38 |
| 14% | 4.95 | 7.85 | 9.9 | 11.5 |
| 15% | 4.62 | 7.32 | 9.24 | 10.73 |
| 16% | 4.33 | 6.87 | 8.66 | 10.06 |
| 17% | 4.08 | 6.46 | 8.15 | 9.47 |
| 18% | 3.85 | 6.1 | 7.7 | 8.94 |
| 19% | 3.65 | 5.78 | 7.3 | 8.47 |
| 20% | 3.47 | 5.49 | 6.93 | 8.04 |

**4. The Law of 70** A convenient rule of thumb for calculating doubling time is to divide the percent annual interest rate into 70.

$$doubling\ time = \frac{70}{i}$$

• An investment earning 7% per year will double in about $70/7 = 10$ years. At 14%, it will double in about $70/14 = 5$ years. Comparing these to the values in the table shows that the Law of 70 is adequate for most purposes.

# Annuities and Rents

**1.** An *annuity* is a sequence of equal payments made at regular intervals. This includes anything that entails fixed weekly, monthly, or yearly payments. Salary, insurance premiums, rent, and mortgage payments are all forms of annuities. An annuity is also a form of investment. Insurance companies offer policies that not only provide life insurance, but also accumulate cash value with each payment made.

Because annuity payments are spread out over time, their total future value is greater than the sum of the individual payments. Moreover, because the payments are made *periodically*, each payment accumulates interest over a time interval different from that of other payments. A simple example will serve to illustrate this.

• If a payment of $100 is made each month into an account that earns 6% interest compounded monthly, the total amount deposited over a year will be $1200. However, the first $100 deposit will earn interest over the entire 12 months, the second $100 over 11 months, the third over 10 months, and so on. These principal and interest amounts can be calculated individually using the future value formula for compound interest as follows:

payment 1: $A = 100 \times (1 + {}^{0.06}\!/_{12})^{12}$
$= 100 \times (1.005)^{12} = \$106.17$

payment 2: $A = 100 \times (1 + {}^{0.06}\!/_{12})^{11}$
$= 100 \times (1.005)^{11} = 105.64$

payment 3: $A = 100 \times (1 + {}^{0.06}\!/_{12})^{10}$
$= 100 \times (1.005)^{10} = 105.11$

$\cdots$

payment 10: $A = 100 \times (1 + {}^{0.06}\!/_{12})^{3}$
$= 100 \times (1.005)^{3} = 101.51$

payment 11: $A = 100 \times (1 + {}^{0.06}\!/_{12})^{2}$
$= 100 \times (1.005)^{2} = 101.00$

payment 12: $A = 100 \times (1 + {}^{0.06}\!/_{12})^{1}$
$= 100 \times (1.005)^{1} = 100.50$

The total value of the year's worth of payments is:

$$S = 100(1.005)^{1} + 100(1.005)^{2} + 100(1.005)^{3}$$
$$+ \cdots + 100(1.005)^{11} + 100(1.005)^{12}$$
$$= \$1239.72.$$

Fortunately, the calculation of the future value of an annuity can be summarized in a single formula. Assume a regular payment of P dollars is made $n$ times per year into an account in which interest is compounded at the end of each payment period. The total future value of these $n$ payments is given by the formula

$$FV = P \times [(1 + i)^{n} - 1] \div i$$

where

$\quad$ FV = total future value of the annuity

$\quad$ P = amount of periodic payment

$\quad$ $n$ = total number of payments

$\quad$ $i = r/m$ = interest rate per compounding period, where $r$ = annual interest rate, and $m$ = number of compoundings.

Note that for this formula to work, $m$, the number of *compoundings* per year, must equal the number of *payments* made per year. To use a different compounding period requires a more complex formula. In practice, the task of calculating annuity sums and payments is entrusted to computers or annuity tables.

- If a father deposits $100 each month into a 5% savings account for his son, 18 years later the account will be worth

$$100 \times [(1 + .05/12)^{12 \times 18} - 1] \div (.05/12) = \$34,920.20.$$

**2. Sinking Funds** Instead of calculating the future value of a series of regular payments, it may be more useful to calculate the installment payment that must be made if an annuity is to grow to a certain amount over a fixed interval of time. This situation—meeting an investment goal through a series of regular payments—is called a *sinking fund.*

If the formula for the future value of an annuity is rearranged, it can be used to solve for the installment payment in a sinking fund.

$$P = FV \times i \div [(1 + i)^n - 1]$$

where P is the payment size, FV is the future value of the annuity, $i$ is the interest rate per compounding period (which coincides with the installment period), and $n$ is the total number of installment payments.

- A father who wishes to set aside $50,000 for his daughter's college tuition sets up a monthly payment plan over 15 years. Assuming a rate of growth of 8% per year (using monthly compounding), the monthly payment should be

$$50,000 \times (.08/12) \div [(1 + .08/12)^{12 \times 15} - 1] = \$144.49.$$

## 3. Present Value of an Annuity

Because the promise to pay a sum of money sometime in the future is worth less than the same amount of cash in hand, a promise to pay a fixed sum over a series of regular intervals is worth less than the total value of the payments. A promise to pay $100 a month over the next year, for example, is worth less than $1200. How much less is determined by the present value of each of the $100 payments. The first payment needs to be discounted over a month, the second over two months, the third over three months, and so on.

- Assume that $100 is to be paid on the last day of the month over an entire year. The present value of each payment, assuming 6% interest compounded monthly, is:

payment 1: $P = 100(1 + {}^{0.06}\!/_{12})^{-1}$
$= 100(1.005)^{-1} = \$99.50$

payment 2: $P = 100(1 + {}^{0.06}\!/_{12})^{-2}$
$= 100(1.005)^{-2} = 99.01$

. . .

payment 11: $P = 100(1 + {}^{0.06}\!/_{12})^{-11}$
$= 100(1.005)^{-11} = 94.66$

payment 12: $P = 100(1 + {}^{0.06}\!/_{12})^{-12}$
$= 100(1.005)^{-12} = 94.19$

The sum of these 12 present values would be:

$S = 100(1.005)^{-1} + 100(1.005)^{-2} + \cdots$
$+ 100(1.005)^{-11} + 100(1.005)^{-12} = \$1161.89.$

As in the case of the future value of an annuity, there is a formula that can be used to calculate such a sum.

$$PV = P \times \left[1 - \frac{1}{(1 + i)^n}\right] \div i$$

where

$PV$ = the present value of the annuity

$P$ = amount of periodic payment

$n$ = the number of payments

$i = {}^{r}\!/_{m}$ = the interest rate per compounding period, where

$r$ = the annual interest rate

$m$ = the number of compoundings

Using this formula, the example given above is calculated in the following way:

$$present\ value = \$100 \times \left[1 - \frac{1}{(1 + .06/12)^{12}}\right] \div (.06/12)$$

$$= 100 \times \left[1 - \frac{1}{1.005^{12}}\right] \div (.005)$$

$$= \$1161.89$$

In this formula, as in the future value formula given earlier, the compounding period must be the same as the payment period. If it is not, this formula will at least provide a good estimate.

**4. Amortization of Debt** When a loan amount is paid off through a series of regular installments, it is said to be *amortized*, which literally means "killed off." Each payment retires some of the unpaid balance, and the rest constitutes interest on the balance. This is what happens when a mortgage payment is made. The principal owed is reduced with each payment. This contributes to the amount of *equity* the owner has in the property.

This is also the premise of any time payment plan, or installment plan. A borrower is advanced a sum of money or credited with a purchase, and then makes periodic payments in order to retire the debt. The periodic payments consist of principal and interest. That is, with each payment, a part of the debt is retired, and an interest charge is paid. At any time, the principal may be paid off in full (although sometimes there is a prepayment penalty). Loans of this type are the most common loans. They include mortgages and credit-card debt installments. By order of the Truth in Lending Act of 1968, all installment loans are required to disclose their annual percentage rate (or APR).

An *amortization schedule* shows specifically, payment by payment, how a debt is retired. That is, it shows how much of a payment constitutes interest, and how much goes toward retiring the debt. Amortization schedules are based on the annuity formulas given above. An example is given in Table 5.5.

**6. Amortization Schedules** An *amortization schedule* is a table that lists each payment of an installment loan and the resulting unpaid loan balance that remains. It also breaks each payment into interest and principal components, so that the total amount of interest paid can be calculated at any time. Table 5.5 consists of an amortization schedule for a $1000 loan which is paid back in six monthly payments. The interest rate is 1% per month, which is equivalent to 12% per year. The monthly payment is $172.55.

**Table 5.5. An Amortization Schedule**

| Payment number | (Payment | = Interest | + Principal) | Unpaid balance |
|---|---|---|---|---|
| 1 | $172.55 | $10.00 | $162.55 | $837.45 |
| 2 | $172.55 | 8.37 | 164.18 | 673.27 |
| 3 | $172.55 | 6.73 | 165.82 | 507.45 |
| 4 | $172.55 | 5.08 | 167.47 | 339.98 |
| 5 | $172.55 | 3.40 | 169.15 | 170.83 |
| 6 | $172.55 | 1.70 | 170.83 | |
| Totals | 1035.30 | 35.28 | 1000.00 | |

At the end of the first month, a payment of $172.55 is due. This includes interest in the amount of 1% of $1,000, which amounts to $10. Thus the first payment consists of $10 in interest and $162.55 of debt reduction, which reduces the debt to $1000 − 162.55 = $837.45.

At the end of the second month, the interest amounts to 1% of this new balance, which works out to $8.37. The interest payment will always be 1% of the previous unpaid balance. With each payment the unpaid balance diminishes, as does the size of the interest payment.

The last payment usually has to be adjusted by a small amount in order to retire the unpaid balance. This is because each computation involves some round-off error when figures are given to the nearest cent.

# Mortgages

Buying a home is the single largest purchase most people will ever make. It would be beyond the means of most consumers if it were not for *mortgages*, which are installment loans for purchasing real estate. Unlike other types of loans, mortgages carry a considerable tax advantage—all of the interest paid on a home mortgage is tax-deductible. And because real estate is a relatively dependable form of investment, banks, credit unions, and mortgage companies actively compete with each other to offer the most attractive terms.

Over the last 20 years, lending institutions have come up with a confusing array of options. Where once the 30-year fixed rate mortgage reigned supreme, many combinations of repayment schemes are now possible. In addition, the mortgage industry has ridden a wave of refinancing over the last decade as interest rates have fallen. *Second mortgages* or *equity loans* have become increasingly popular. Because the interest on equity loans (money borrowed against the equity an owner has accumulated in a property) is tax-deductible, many homeowners have applied for equity loans instead of personal loans, which are far more expensive.

There are two basic types of mortgage—those with fixed interest rates (and therefore fixed monthly payments) and those with variable interest rates (and potentially varying monthly payments). Either type is offered over time periods ranging from five years to 30 years or more. The debt is amortized over this time, but the possible amortization schedules are numerous. Some mortgages are designed so that the payments are small at the outset. Others involve a sizable jump in payments after an initial grace period. But all mortgages are nothing more than annuities—installment loans that are governed by the same present and future value formulas discussed in the previous section.

## INTEREST RATES AND POINTS

**1.** Mortgages are offered at *annual interest rates*. Rates offered by banks are competitive, and tend to fluctuate in anticipation of changes in such indexes as the Federal Reserve discount rate, the average yield on Treasury securities, and the federal funds rate.

Banks will usually allow a borrower to *lock in* at the rate that is in effect when a mortgage application is filled out. (The *commitment letter*, which is the lender's written statement of the terms of the loan they will offer, refers to this as a *rate lock* or *interest rate commitment*.) This is particularly advantageous during periods of rising interest rates. If the rate falls during the time it takes to close on the house, some banks will automatically offer the lower rate. Others will charge a fee for it.

**2.** Banks maintain a *margin* between the interest rates they pay on bank accounts and the interest rates they charge for mortgages. This is one way they make money. The margin is not a fixed amount. Banks will offer different rates for almost every type of loan they make. Their lowest rates are usually for their shortest-term variable rate mortgages. The highest are for personal loans. With mortgages, it is often possible to buy a rate down by paying fees referred to as *points*.

**3.** A *point* is a fee which is treated as prepaid interest for tax purposes. It is equal to 1% of the amount borrowed. Points may be charged by a bank as a *loan origination fee*. They may also be paid by a buyer who wishes to buy into a lower interest rate. In some instances, the seller may be willing to pay points on behalf of the buyer if it helps the sale go through.

- A married couple buys a $150,000 house with a 20% down payment. The amount borrowed is

$$\$150,000 - (.20 \times 150,000) = \$150,000 - 30,000$$
$$= \$120,000.$$

If the bank is charging 2 points on the mortgage, the closing costs will include a fee in the amount of 2% of $120,000, or $2400.

**4.** The Internal Revenue Service allows mortgage points to be deducted. This includes not only the points a home buyer pays to obtain a mortgage (or to buy down the interest rate of a mortgage), but even the points paid on behalf of the buyer by the seller. The rule is retroactive to the year 1991. Regulations also stipulate that points paid on a loan to remodel a home are deductible in the year they are paid. However, points paid on a refinanced mortgage must be deducted gradually over the life of the loan.

**5.** Most financial advisers recommend against paying points if possible, unless the seller is willing to pay them. The money could be better invested in an IRA or mutual fund. The principal advantage to buying down the mortgage rate is that it allows the buyer to qualify for a larger loan. At the same time, if qualifying is not an issue, and there is a choice between a loan with no points and a lower rate loan *with* points, the tax deduction might be a consideration. The lower rate will entail lower interest payments, and consequently a smaller annual tax deduction. But the points will be deductible in the year they are paid.

**6.** While there is no set formula, it is generally the case that one point of prepaid interest will buy down the mortgage rate by ¼%.

* A $100,000 mortgage at 8¼% per year carries a monthly payment of $751.27. The same loan at 8% costs $733.76 per month. The monthly difference is $17.51, which amounts to $210.12 over a year. This should be weighed against the single point of interest—amounting to $1000—which would be charged up front in order to get the lower rate.

**7.** The *contract interest rate* of a mortgage is the rate stated on the commitment letter and mortgage contract. This figure can be misleading. More useful is the *annual percentage rate* or *APR*, which is the effective rate of interest the borrower will pay each year. This rate is always higher than the contract interest rate because it not only incorporates the effect of compounding (which is usually semiannual), but it also includes costs in the form of points, private mortgage insurance, or other fees. For fixed rate mortgages the APR is calculated over the life of the loan. For adjustable rate mortgages, the APR is calculated over the period leading up to the first adjustment of the rate.

The formula for determining an APR is complicated and beyond the resources of the typical consumer. However, all lenders are required to state the APR of every loan they offer (not just mortgages). All a buyer has to do is remember to compare the APR of the loans that are available, rather than the advertised contract rates.

- A bank offers two fixed-rate loans—one at 8¾% and the other at 8¼%. The APR for the first loan is 9.125% and for the second is 9.3%. Which one is better will depend upon the situation. The buyer might need a lower contract rate in order to qualify for the loan. The seller might be willing to pay the points at the lower rate, which would reduce the APR.

## QUALIFYING FOR A MORTGAGE

In a buyer's market such as the real estate market of the 1990s, banks, credit unions, and mortgage companies actively pursue customers. They try to match their competitors' best rates, and sometimes offer to pay some of the closing costs. They will also engage in some creative accounting so that a customer will qualify for a mortgage. In the past a mortgage applicant had to meet strict cost-to-income ratios. Some banks have relaxed these standards, but the old ratios still provide a good test of what a prospective buyer can afford.

**1.** Many banks, especially large ones, sell their mortgages on the *secondary market*, which consists of investors who buy mortgages in bundles while retaining the issuing bank as the servicer of the loan. This type of transaction is regulated by the Federal National Mortgage Association (or Fannie Mae), which dictates what types of loans may be resold. Their long-standing rule requires that a buyer should have a monthly-cost-to-monthly-income ratio of at most 28%. That is, the monthly cost of the house—which is the sum of the mortgage payment, property tax, and insurance premium—should not exceed 28% of the buyer's gross monthly income. This is called the *housing ratio*.

$$\begin{array}{c} housing \\ ratio \end{array} = \frac{mortgage\ payment + property\ tax + insurance\ premium}{gross\ monthly\ income}$$

The costs listed in the numerator are *monthly* costs. In order to determine how big a mortgage he or she can afford, a buyer can use this formula:

$$\begin{array}{c} lowest\ qualifying \\ monthly\ income \end{array} = \frac{total\ monthly\ housing\ cost}{0.28}$$

Some lenders who do not sell their loans on the secondary market may allow up to a 33% ratio. This considerably reduces the minimum qualifying income.

Table 5.6 shows the annual income level required to qualify for a 30-year mortgage in the amount of $100,000. It compares a 28% qualifying ratio with the 33% ratio some banks allow. The house is assumed to cost $125,000, and the buyer

### Table 5.6. Income Required to Qualify for a Mortgage on a $125,000 Home

| Rate | Cost per month | Lowest qualifying income (28% ratio) | Lowest qualifying income (33% ratio) |
|------|-----|---------|---------|
| 6% | $782 | $33,510 | $28,436 |
| 6.5% | $815 | $34,900 | $29,636 |
| 7% | $848 | $36,325 | $30,836 |
| 7.5% | $882 | $37,780 | $32,073 |
| 8% | $916 | $39,260 | $33,310 |
| 8.5% | $951 | $40,765 | $34,580 |
| 9% | $987 | $42,300 | $35,890 |
| 9.5% | $1023 | $43,840 | $37,200 |
| 10% | $1060 | $45,420 | $38,545 |

is putting 20% down. Property tax is estimated at 1.5% of the selling price, and insurance at 0.25% of the selling price. These are converted to monthly figures (by dividing by 12), and added to the monthly mortgage payment, which is taken from a mortgage table. If the monthly costs are divided by .28 (which is 28%) or .33 (which is 33%), they give the minimum required monthly income at each qualifying ratio. The resulting figure is multiplied by 12 to give the required annual income.

**2.** Another qualifying ratio is the *total obligation ratio*. This is the ratio of *all* monthly obligations—mortgage plus car loan plus personal loans plus alimony, for example—to gross monthly income. The Fannie Mae limit is 36%, although some lenders will allow up to 38%. Like the housing ratio, the total obligation ratio is based on monthly costs.

$$\frac{total}{obligation\ ratio} = \frac{total\ monthly\ housing\ costs\ +\ other\ monthly\ debt}{gross\ monthly\ income}$$

$$\frac{lowest\ qualifying}{monthly\ income} = \frac{total\ monthly\ obligation}{0.36}$$

• A mortgage applicant wishes to buy the $125,000 house referred to in Table 5.6. At a fixed rate of 8½%, the total monthly cost would be $951. If the applicant also has $300 per month in other payments (car loan, credit cards, etc.), her total monthly obligation is $1251. To find the minimum qualifying gross monthly income, divide the total monthly obligation by .36.

$$\$1251 \div .36 = \$3475$$

To find the minimum qualifying annual gross income, multiply this figure by 12.

$$\$3475 \times 12 = \$41,700$$

**3.** Not only does a buyer have to qualify for the mortgage, but the property has to qualify as well. If the bank believes that the property is not worth the selling price, it may reduce the amount of the loan, or simply refuse to offer one. This determination is made based on the *loan-to-value ratio (LTV ratio)*.

$$loan\text{-}to\text{-}value\ ratio = \frac{loan\ amount}{appraised\ value\ of\ property}$$

The maximum LTV ratio for a mortgage on a one to four family, owner occupied residence is 90%. Thus if a buyer makes an offer on a house which is then appraised at a lower value, the bank may ask for additional collateral or require the buyer to purchase private mortgage insurance.

● A house sells for $125,000, but is appraised at $110,000. If the buyer wanted to put down 20%, the loan amount would be 80% of $125,000, which is $100,000. The loan-to-value ratio would be

$$\frac{\$100,000}{\$110,000} = .909 = 90.9\%.$$

Because this exceeds the limit, the bank would ask for a larger down payment. If the buyer put up another $1000, the ratio would be satisfied.

$$\frac{\$99,000}{\$110,000} = .90 = 90\%$$

## FIXED RATE MORTGAGES

Until the 1980s the standard mortgage was a 30-year fixed rate mortgage. But as interest rates rose precipitously in the early 1980s, fixed rates became unattractive and unaffordable. In response, banks came up with variable rate mortgages, which allowed buyers to meet qualification ratios by establishing lower initial rates of interest.

In a fixed rate mortgage, the annual rate remains the same for the life of the loan. Consequently, the monthly payment also remains the same. These payments consist mostly of interest at the outset of the loan, with relatively little of the principal being paid off. But with each payment this balance changes. The portion constituting interest diminishes while the retirement of principle increases. This is described in detail in the section on amortization schedules (page 250).

## VARIABLE RATE MORTGAGES/ ADJUSTABLE RATE MORTGAGES

The advantage of an *adjustable rate mortgage (ARM)* or *variable rate mortgage (VRM)*, is that it offers an initial rate (or teaser rate) that is well below the market rate for fixed rate loans. Therefore buyers can qualify more easily, and enjoy lower payments in the initial period of the loan. The disadvantage of ARMs is their uncertainty. At regular intervals the rate is adjusted to reflect the prevailing interest rates in the securities markets. An adjustable rate can jump as much as 2 to 3 percentage points at once, and the monthly payment can therefore increase considerably. Many buyers of ARMs are surprised to find that their rate has risen over an adjustment period in which national rates have fallen. This results from a misunderstanding of the terms of ARMs.

**1. The Initial Interest Rate** ARMs are offered at tempting rates which entice many buyers who would not qualify for a fixed rate loan. These *initial rates*, or *teaser rates*, can be misleading. When the adjustment period comes up, the discounted teaser rate is readjusted according to an index.

**2. The Index** Banks set interest rates on ARMs according to a formula that is based on some key economic *index*. This is a market index that can be found each week in business newspapers. The most commonly used indexes are:

> The *Contract Rate:* a nationwide average of fixed rate mortgage rates.
>
> The *Cost-of-Funds Index:* a national average of the interest rates that banks and S&Ls pay to borrow money.
>
> *Treasury Yields:* the average rates of returns on U.S. government securities. (A bank may use a specific rate such as the six-month Treasury-bill rate.)
>
> The *Prime Rate:* the rate of interest that the biggest banks charge their best customers.
>
> The *LIBOR:* the London Interbank Offered Rate, a kind of international prime rate.

**3. The Margin** A *margin* is a percentage that is added to the index in order to arrive at the *fully indexed rate.* It is important to ask what each lender's margin is, because this number determines how the rate will be set at each adjustment.

• A one-year ARM is offered at 6½% per year. The margin is 2½% and the index is the six-month Treasury-bill rate. If in the first year the

T-bill rate falls from 5¼% to 4¼%, the ARM rate would still rise to 4¼ + 2½ = 6¾%.

**4. Caps** An *interest rate cap* determines how much the interest rate on an ARM can change at each adjustment period. Most ARMs carry an adjustment cap of around 2%. The mortgage should also have a *life-of-loan cap,* which defines a maximum interest rate that cannot be exceeded. A typical life-of-loan cap is 5-6% over the initial rate.

• A one-year ARM with an initial rate of 6½% per year and a "2 and 5" cap can rise 2 percentage points each year, up to a maximum increase of 5%. The worst-case scenario would be a steady rise in interest rates that results in rates of 6½%, 8½%, 10½%, and finally 11½% through the first four years of the loan.

## ADJUSTABLE RATE, FIXED PAYMENT MORTGAGES

One variation of the adjustable rate mortgage is a loan that establishes a fixed monthly payment. If the interest rate changes at the end of an adjustment period, the amortization schedule changes—that is, the part of the monthly payment that constitutes interest will change. Thus the rate at which the unpaid balance is retired can change from adjustment period to adjustment period.

The danger of a fixed payment loan is that if the interest rate goes too high, the monthly payment will not be enough to cover the monthly interest charge. When this happens, the unpaid interest is charged to the principal, so that the amount owed (the unpaid balance) actually increases with each monthly payment. This is referred to as *negative amortization*.

## BALLOON MORTGAGES

A *balloon mortgage* is a loan which is not fully paid off by the last installment payment. This type of loan offers a low initial rate of interest and low payments. However, after an initial grace period is up, a large payment—often the entire original loan amount—comes due. (A *balloon payment* is a large payment that is owed after a period of relatively modest monthly payments.)

Balloon mortgages work by allowing the borrower to pay only interest (or mostly interest) on the principal for the initial period. The disadvantage is that the borrower builds little or no equity. In one type of balloon mortgage, none of the principal is retired until the balloon payment is due. This type of loan is typically contracted over a three-to-five-year period. The borrower, who faces repaying the entire mortgaged amount, usually refinances the mortgage. In another type of balloon mortgage, part of the loan has been repaid after the initial period, but a significant sum is due at maturity, which might be 15 years.

## REFINANCING

When interest rates fall to record low levels, holders of fixed rate mortgages and ARMs are tempted to refinance their loans at lower rates. But because refinancing incurs most of the closing costs paid at the original settlement, the common wisdom has held that refinancing is only worthwhile when the interest rate differential is at least 2%. That is, it is only worth doing if it will result in a rate reduction of 2% or more.

Some analysts now say that even a 1% reduction justifies the switch, but the decision rests on more factors than a simple formula can accommodate. The decision to refinance should take into account the numbers of years the owner will keep the house, the amount of the tax deduction, and the yield on the owner's other investments. After all, buying a house should be thought of as an investment. As an investment, it ties up money that could earn interest elsewhere. The value of this equity, the tax advantages of a mortgage, and the cost of financing the property should be assessed in the context of the homeowner's entire investment picture.

# Investing Money

The goal of investing is to increase the future spending power of money. People invest in order to earn money that will offset the effects of inflation. Very successful investors earn a living on investments alone.

All investment decisions pit two competing factors against each other: the rate of return and the amount of risk. In the world of investments, as in many areas of life, the greater the risk, the higher the potential return. The most secure monetary investments, considered risk-free, are U.S. government securities—Treasury bills, notes, and savings bonds. Historically, these have paid rates of interest that keep pace with inflation. But when the tax paid on interest earnings is taken into account, these investments in the long run have fallen behind the cost of living. The same can be said for many other guaranteed investments such as passbook savings accounts, money market accounts, and municipal bonds. Consequently, an investor who is looking to beat the inflation rate must take some risks. The risks can be balanced, however, if the money is invested in a variety of ways, some high-risk, some low-risk, and some that are in between. To do this, the investor designs a *portfolio*, which is a plan reflecting an investment philosophy that pits possible gains against acceptable risks. The portfolio might mix stocks, bond, government securities, mutual funds, and other investments in a way that takes advantage of tax deferments, tax deductions, the prospect of steady income, or the possibility of steady growth.

The purpose of this section, and those that follow it, is to provide an introduction to investments, and thereby provide a foothold on an inexact science, but one that clearly favors the prepared mind.

## SECURITIES

When a company reaches a stage of its growth where it wants to raise money (referred to as *capital*), it may *go public* by offering to sell shares of ownership of the company. These shares take the form of *stock,* which is then sold (or *traded*) on the floor of a *stock exchange.* A broker acts as a buyer for an investor, and facilitates the transaction.

Another way for a corporation or government to raise money is to issue *bonds,* which are promissory notes that pay interest in the form of *dividends.* With stock, ownership of the corporation is actually conferred to the stockholders as a group, and they share in the profits (or losses). With bonds there is no controlling interest, and the risk is reduced, although not eliminated. When a company goes bankrupt, any money that remains is first distributed among the bondholders, then the stockholders.

For those who prefer to leave investment decisions to a professional, mutual funds offer a way to invest in a wide selection of bonds or stocks. Mutual funds are offered by investment companies that make owning shares as simple as opening a bank account.

Stocks, bonds, mutual funds, legal notes, certificates of deposit (CD's), and debentures are all forms of *securities*—written documents of ownership or creditorship used to establish an investment in some business enterprise. All securities are ultimately assessed by the amount of money they earn for the investor calculated as a percent of the amount invested. This is usually converted to an annual rate.

$$\begin{array}{c} \textit{annual rate} \\ \textit{of return} \end{array} = \frac{\textit{annual earnings}}{\textit{initial value of investment (on January 1)}}$$

• If a $10,000 portfolio earns $800 over the course of a year, the rate of return is $^{800}/_{10,000}$, or 8%.

## KEY ECONOMIC INDICATORS

An investor's rate of return is always measured against certain indexes that show how the securities market has performed. These indexes are numbers that are constructed by averaging the performance of a selected group of securities. The actual index number has meaning only in reference to index numbers from other periods. That is, index numbers from year to year form ratios that represent the percent growth of the market.

$$\begin{array}{l} percent\ change \\ of\ an\ index \end{array} = \frac{last\ value - initial\ value}{initial\ value} = \frac{change}{initial\ value}$$

**1.** The *Dow Jones Industrial Average* is an index that measures the performance of 30 *blue-chip stocks* that are traded on the New York Stock Exchange. These are stocks issued by well-established companies whose economic stability is thought to reflect the state of the national economy. "The Dow," as it is called for short, is a gauge of the stock market as a whole. To "beat the Dow" is a test of a portfolio's annual performance.

The Dow tends to fluctuate by as much as 10 or 20 points on any given day. Any change near 100 points is considered significant, while anything over 100 would indicate that some serious news shook the market. Because the Dow reached the 5000 level in 1995, a 100-point gain or loss represents only a 2% change. This would occur if the price of each of the 30 stocks upon which the Dow is based were to rise or fall a dollar in value. Thus, as an indicator, the Dow is not precise.

**2.** The *Standard & Poor 500 Index* is similar to the Dow-Jones Average, but it is based on 500 stocks that are spread across a wide range. Like the Dow, it includes industrials, in addition to financials, transportation stocks, and utility companies.

**3.** There are many indexes that go beyond the Dow-Jones or Standard & Poor 500 by focusing upon narrowly defined categories. These work like all indexes: they can be used to chart the percent change—on the average—of a class of investments from day to day, week to week, month to month, or year to year.

**4.** The *Gross National Product (GNP)* and the *Gross Domestic Product (GDP)* are two measures of economic activity in the United States. As such they are seen as indicators of economic growth.

The gross national product is the total cost of all goods produced by labor or property that is supplied or owned by residents of the United States. This includes goods produced in foreign countries by or for American business interests.

The gross domestic product is a similar measure of the cost of goods produced, but it includes only those goods produced *within* the United

States proper, by any U.S. residents. Thus the GNP is a measure of the level of total U.S. production, while the GDP focuses only on domestic production. Consequently, the GDP is currently viewed as a better indicator of the national economy than the GNP. It more accurately reflects the levels of unemployment, of productivity, and industrial activity. The GNP, by contrast, is seen as a better measure of purely economic activity of American businesses, many of which may be producing goods abroad. At this time, the numerical difference in GNP and GDP is small, and thus the difference between the two as economic indicators is slight.

## Stocks

The price of a share of stock is determined by market mechanisms at work on the trading floors of stock exchanges. There are two major stock exchanges in the United States—the New York Stock Exchange (NYSE) and the American Stock Exchange (AMEX). There is also a national market for *over-the-counter* stocks. This is not an actual trading floor as much as a virtual marketplace conducted over telephones, wire services, and computer networks. This trading information is tabulated by the National Association of Securities Dealers. Their computerized quote system is called NASDAQ (National Association of Securities Dealers Automated Quotations). In addition to these, there are regional stock and commodities markets in major cities such as Boston, Chicago, Philadelphia, and Los Angeles, as well as many overseas stock exchanges.

Anyone may purchase stock by getting in touch with a stockbroker, who will arrange to buy or sell stocks in return for a commission. This charge may be a flat fee, a sliding-scale fee, or a percentage of the transaction. Almost all of the information relevant to the performance of a stock can be found in the daily newspaper. Although financial papers such as the *Wall Street Journal* provide the most detailed information, the stock-exchange listings in most daily newspapers are adequate for the average investor.

## READING STOCK-EXCHANGE LISTINGS

Stock tables consist of 10 columns of information that identify a stock and give the most relevant information about its performance. A typical listing for two stocks might look like this:

| 52-week High | 52-week Low | Stock | Div | Yld % | P/E | Sales 100s | High | Low | Close | Change |
|---|---|---|---|---|---|---|---|---|---|---|
| 32¼ | 20⅞ | AbCo | .56 | 2.3 | 10 | 237 | 25⅜ | 23 | 24⅛ | +⅛ |
| 30 | 26½ | AbCo pf | 3.16 | 10.7 | ... | 168 | 30⅛ | 29½ | 29⅝ | +⅛ |

Key:

*High/Low:* 52-week high and low. Stock prices are given as *points,* which are dollar amounts per share. The high and the low prices listed in the first two columns give the highest and lowest prices the stock has been traded for within the last 52-week period. Dollar amounts are broken down no further than eighths. One eighth of a point is equivalent to 12½ cents.

*Stock:* This column identifies an issue of stock by the company name and by the type of stock. It may also give some information about the stock's history or status. The abbreviations of stock names come from the Associated Press market quotations supplied daily to newspapers.

The two types of stock are *common stock* and *preferred stock*. Preferred stock is identified by the letters *pf* next to the company name. Preferred stock pays a *dividend* each year (usually in four installments) at a set percentage rate.

Other identifiers that may appear in this column are:

*n* means that the stock was issued within the last 52 weeks.

*s* means that the stock has split within the last 52 weeks.

*rt* indicates a right to buy at a specified price.

*vj* in front of the company name indicates that the company is in bankruptcy, receivership, or reorganization.

*x* signifies "ex-dividend," or the fact that the previous day was the first day that the stock did not carry a guaranteed dividend.

*g* indicates that figures are given in Canadian dollars.

*Div:* This column indicates the estimated yearly dividend paid based on the dividends that have been paid thus far. For AbCo's common stock, the dividend is 56 cents per share. AbCo preferred is paying $3.16 per share annually.

*Yld%:* The *yield percentage* is the percent return on investment as calculated from the day's closing price. Specifically, it is the ratio (expressed as a percent) of annual earnings to closing price. For AbCo preferred,

$$\text{Yld\%} = \frac{\textit{estimated annual earnings}}{\textit{closing price}} \times 100\%$$

$$= \frac{3.16}{29.625} \times 100\% = 10.667\%.$$

This is rounded to 10.7%.

*P/E:* The *price/earnings (P/E) ratio* expresses the relation of selling price to earnings per share. The earnings per share are found in the company's quarterly reports, and are calculated as the earnings over the last four quarters. P/E ratios are not given for preferred stock.

*Sales 100s:* This is the volume of shares traded in that day given in units of hundreds. On this day, 23,700 shares of AbCo common stock changed hands.

*High:* The highest price at which the stock was traded that day.

*Low:* The lowest price at which the stock was traded that day.

*Close:* The price of the stock at the last sale of the day.

*Change:* The net change in selling price, calculated as the difference in closing prices between the two previous days.

# PRICE/EARNINGS RATIO

The *price/earnings ratio,* also known as the *multiple,* is used by investors to judge the earning potential of a stock. It can be calculated in two ways.

The *trailing P/E* is the ratio of earnings to current price per share, where the earnings are taken from the previous year's financial report.

The *forward P/E* is the same ratio calculated from the projected earnings over the coming year.

Earnings per share are calculated as follows:

$$\frac{earnings}{per\ share} = \frac{profit\ after\ taxes\ on\ most\ recent\ financial\ report}{total\ number\ of\ shares\ outstanding}$$

• A stock selling for $40 with a previous year's earnings of $2 per share has a P/E ratio of 20. If projected earnings for the next year are $4 per share, the forward P/E would be 10.

There is no recommended range of P/E values; each company's P/E ratio must be judged in comparison to those of companies in the same industry. A low P/E indicates a mature, steady-growth company. Blue-chip stocks in particular are noted for paying regular dividends and maintaining good earnings per share. High P/E stocks have lower annual yields and are often fast-growing companies that reinvest most of their profits back into the company. These tend to be riskier, aggressive growth stocks.

P/E ratios are inversely related to interest rates. This means that if interest rates rise, P/E numbers on average fall, and vice versa. When an investor talks about a stock being *undervalued*, this means that its P/E seems low compared to the industry average.

## STOCK SPLITS

As the value of a company's stock grows, the board of directors may decide to *split* the stock. When this occurs, each share converts to two shares and the price is cut in half. Thus shareholders double their number of shares while retaining the same dollar value of stock.

The reason for a split is largely psychological. It is based on the idea that a price of $30 or $40 a share is more attractive and accessible than $60 or $80 a share. Stocks that have climbed rapidly to the $70–90 range are considered ripe for a split.

What experienced investors look for is not the fact of a split, but the effect on the price/earnings ratio. In general, the lower the P/E, the better.

## MARGIN ACCOUNTS

A *margin account* is a way of purchasing stock without paying for it in full up front. The purchaser who buys on margin puts up only a fraction of the purchase price, and a broker lends the remaining amount. The broker then holds the stock as collateral for the loan.

The *margin* is defined as the percentage of the purchase price that has been paid by the purchaser.

$$margin = \frac{market\ value\ of\ stock\ -\ amount\ of\ loan}{market\ value\ of\ stock}$$

This should be expressed as a percent.

• A buyer pays $2500 for 100 shares of stock at $40 per share. The market value of the stock is

$4000. To make up the difference, the buyer takes a $1500 loan from the broker.

$$margin = \frac{4000 - 1500}{4000} = .625 = 62.5\%$$

This figure is called the *initial margin*. The smallest allowable initial margin is 50%. Once established, the margin can change as the value of the stock changes. Any revised value of the margin is called a *maintenance margin*. On the New York Stock Exchange, a maintenance margin is not allowed to fall below 25% (some brokers set an even higher limit). When the margin does threaten to fall below the minimum, the stock is referred to as *under-margined*, and the buyer will be asked to come up with more cash in order to reduce the size of the loan, and thereby increase the maintenance margin. This is a *margin call*. If it is not met, the broker will immediately sell the stock in order to cover his loan.

• If the stock in the example above fell to $20 per share, the market value of 100 shares would fall to $2000, and the margin would fall to

$$\frac{2000 - 1500}{2000} = .25 = 25\%$$

The broker would issue a margin call at this point. If forced to sell, the broker would recoup his $1500 loan plus any commissions or fees that are owed. The remainder would go to the buyer.

## SHORT SELLING

*Short selling* is a way of profiting from the decline in value of a stock. The buyer, anticipating a drop in a stock's price, uses a broker to borrow stock belonging to someone else. The stock is then sold, and the proceeds are held by the broker. At a later time, the borrowed shares must be repurchased and returned. Any dividends the stock earned during the intervening time must be paid to the original owner of the stock. If the price did fall, the short seller can keep the difference between the original selling and final repurchase price, minus any dividends. He must still pay a commission, both when the stock is sold, and again when it is repurchased.

The short seller is usually required to put up a percentage of the value of the borrowed stock—usually 50% of its value. This is called a *margin*.

Short selling carries a high level of risk, and can result in a substantial loss if the price of the stock goes up. Securities regulations also stipulate that a stock cannot be sold short while its price is falling; the price must first rise before the stock can be sold.

# Bonds

A *bond* is a debt security issued by a company, a municipal government, a federal agency, or the federal government itself. As a means of raising money, it is essentially a loan that pays interest in a variety of forms.

A bond has a *face value* (or *par value*) and a maturity date, at which it can be cashed in. The face value for most bonds is $1000, although there exist so-called *baby bonds* that have denominations of $500 or less. The maturity period is usually 15 years, 20 years, or a higher multiple of 10 (up to 100 years, which is known as a *century bond*). Most bonds also have stated rates of interest (called *coupon rates*, because at one time many corporate bonds had tear-off coupons that could be redeemed periodically). The coupon rate does not change over the life of the bond.

Bonds are rarely sold for par value. Instead they are sold at either a *discount* or at a *premium*. A *premium* is the amount above par value at which a bond sells. A *discount* is the amount below par.

Because their dividend rates are fixed, the values of bonds fluctuate with market interest rates. When interest rates go down, bonds increase in value. When interest rates go up, bonds decrease in value. A bond's market value will also change (decrease, usually) as it gets closer to maturity.

## READING BOND LISTINGS

Some financial newspapers list bond prices in the format shown below. These statistics summarize the previous day's trading activity. A fictitious company might have a bond listing that looks like this:

| Bonds | Cur. Yld. | Vol. | High | Low | Close | Net Chg. |
|-------|-----------|------|------|-----|-------|----------|
| AbCo 12½s99 | 12 | 46 | 101¼ | 99¾ | 100⅞ | +¼ |

Key:

*Bonds:* The first column lists the name of the bond (using Associated Press abbreviations), its *coupon interest rate* (here 12½% per year; this is usually paid semiannually), and its *maturity date* (here September 1999). The interest rates are listed in increments of ⅛%.

*Cur. Yld.* The *current yield* is the rate of return that the buyer would earn by buying at the closing price.

$$current\ yield = \frac{annual\ interest\ earned}{cost\ per\ bond\ +\ commission}$$

The annual interest payment is the stated rate (here 12½%) times $1000.

If this column contains the letters **CV**, then the bonds is *convertible* into stock.

*Vol.:* The volume is the total number of bonds traded on the previous day.

*High, Low, Close:* These three columns give the highest, lowest, and last price paid in the previous day's trading. These figures must be multiplied by 10 in order to find the actual dollar value. Here the high price was 101¼ × 10, or $1012.50.

*Net Chg:* This is the *net change* in price from the previous day's closing price. To convert to dollars, convert the figure to a decimal and multiply by $10. A change of +¼ means an increase of 0.25 × $10, or $2.50 per bond from the previous day.

# YIELD-TO-MATURITY

The interest paid on a bond is based on its par value, not its selling price. But its listed interest rate is not the best indicator of the bond's performance. More revealing is the *yield-to-maturity*, which can be compared to prevailing market interest rates to determine the true market value of a bond.

Yield-to-maturity can be calculated for a bond by following these steps:

1. Find the amount of the *discount (D)* or *premium (P)*.

2. Divide D or P by the number of years to maturity. This is called the *annual discount* or *annual premium*.

3. If working with a premium, deduct the annual premium from the annual interest earned.

*or*

If working with a discount, add the annual discount to the annual interest earned. This new figure is the *adjusted annual interest*.

4. Find the average of the original cost of the bond and the anticipated proceeds from its sale using this formula:

$$[(price + sales\ commission) + (face\ value - sales\ commission)] \div 2$$

5. The yield-to-maturity is found by dividing the result of step 3 by the result of step 4.

• A 9% bond maturing in five years is purchased at 108 (which means $1080—the premium is $80). Assuming a $5 commission, the total cost is $1080 + 5 = $1085. The annual interest is 9% of $1000, which is $90 per year. Assume also that the commission will be $6 when the bond is sold. The yield-to-maturity is found by dividing the premium of $80 by 5 and deducting the result from the annual interest of $90 (steps 2 and 3).

$$90 - \frac{80}{5} = 90 - 16 = \$74$$

The cost of purchase was $1085. The selling price will be $1000 minus the $6 commission, or $994. The average of $1085 and $994 is $1039.50. Therefore the yield-to-maturity is

$$\frac{74}{1039.50} \approx .0712, \text{ or } 7.12\%.$$

# U.S. Government Securities

The federal government raises money by issuing securities in the form of *Treasury bonds, Treasury notes,* and *Treasury bills.* The distinction between these three categories is a matter of years to maturity. Treasury bonds are issued for terms from five to 30 years. The most popular is the 30-year bond. Notes are issued in terms from five to seven years. Treasury bills mature in a year or less. The most common maturities are three months, six months, nine months, and one year.

## TREASURY BONDS AND NOTES

**1.** Treasury bonds and notes are issued in denominations of $1000. They pay interest twice a year.

The *face value* of the bond is its value at maturity, and its *coupon rate* is the annual rate of interest that it pays.

**2.** A $1000 bond has a face value of $1000, but this may not be its sale price. Treasury bonds and notes are typically bought at either a *discount*, which means at a price below face value, or at a *premium*, which means at a price above face value. The difference between the purchase price and the face value is referred to either as the discount or premium.

- A $1000 bond purchased at $850 has a discount of $150. It can also be described as "discounted $150."

The market prices of bonds and notes change week by week in response to changes in interest rates and other economic indicators. Thus a bond or note has three prices: a face value, a purchase price, and a current market value. The market value depends on the coupon rate and the years to maturity.

**3.** The semiannual interest payment is calculated using the face value, not the purchase price. It is based on the *coupon rate*, which is specified on the bond. It is calculated as simple interest using a 365-day year.

- A $1000 bond with a coupon rate of 8% earns a semiannual interest payment of

$$\frac{1}{2} \times (\$1000 \times .08) = \$40.$$

**4.** Bond and note purchase prices fluctuate from week to week, but the interest they pay is always calculated on their fixed face value. Consequently it is not immediately apparent what rate of return is being earned on the money invested (which usually does not coincide with the face value). The measure of return on investment is called the *current yield*. It is calculated as follows:

$$current \; yield = \frac{\$1000 \times coupon \; rate}{purchase \; price}$$

• A $1000 bond with a 9% coupon rate purchased for $875 has a current yield of

$$\frac{\$1000 \times .09}{\$875} \approx .1029 = 10.29\%.$$

This percentage represents the interest rate of return on the $875 investment.

**5.** Another measure of the value of a bond is its *yield-to-maturity (YTM)*, earlier discussed with respect to corporate bonds. This is a rate of return that takes into account the number of years until maturity, the interest earned over those years, and the gain or loss when the bond is cashed in at maturity. It is a measurement of how the bond "performs" over the years it takes to mature.

YTM figures for government bonds and notes are given in published tables. The calculation is complex, but it can be approximated with a simple formula:

Let

$$i = interest\ earned\ per\ year = \$1000 \times coupon\ rate$$

$$a = \frac{\$1000 - current\ market\ price}{years\ to\ maturity}$$

$$b = \frac{\$1000 + current\ market\ price}{2}$$

Then

$$yield\text{-}to\text{-}maturity = \frac{i + a}{b}$$

- A \$1000 bond with a 9.5% coupon rate and 20 years remaining to maturity has a market value of \$1150. Its approximate yield-to-maturity is calculated as follows:

$$i = \$1000 \times .095 = \$95$$

$$a = \frac{\$1000 - 1150}{20} = -7.5$$

$$b = \frac{\$1000 + 1150}{2} = \$1075$$

$$YTM = \frac{\$95 - \$7.50}{\$1075} = 0.0814 = 8.14\%$$

## READING TREASURY BOND AND NOTE QUOTATIONS

The business pages of most large daily newspapers list price and yield quotations for U.S. government securities. The listing reprinted from the *New York Times* below is typical.

| Month | Rate | Bid | Ask | Chg | Yld |
|-------|------|-----|-----|-----|-----|
| Apr98 n | 7.875 | 105-10 | 105-14 | +01 | 5.42 |
| Apr98 n | 5.125 | 99-11 | 99-15 | ... | 5.42 |
| May98 n | 6.125 | 101-18 | 101-22 | −01 | 5.43 |

Key:

*Month:* The date gives the month and year of maturity. The letter *n* indicates that it is a note. The absence of a letter indicates a bond.

*Rate:* The rate is the coupon rate of interest. These are listed in increments of one eighth of a percent. This is the percent used to calculate the semiannual interest payment.

*Bid:* The *bid price* is the price at which the note or bond is offered to dealers. All prices are given as a percent of the face value, which is $1000. However, fractions of a percent are given as multiples of $\frac{1}{32}$. Thus 105-10 means $105\frac{10}{32}\%$. The decimal form of $\frac{1}{32}$ is 0.03125, so $\frac{10}{32}$ equals 0.3125, and $105\frac{10}{32}\%$ converts to 105.3125%. Move the decimal point two places to the left and the percent becomes a decimal multiplier. The note sells for $1.053125 \times \$1000 = \$1,053.125$.

*Ask:* The *ask price* is the price at which a dealer will sell to an investor. The price is given as a percentage that is converted in the same way as the bid price. 105-14 means $105\frac{14}{32}\%$ of $1000. This converts to 105.4375% of $1000, or $1.054375 \times \$1000 = \$1,054.375$.

*Chg:* The *change* in price from the previous day's closing price is also in units of $\frac{1}{32}\%$.

*Yld:* This is the *yield-to-maturity* as calculated from the ask price.

## U.S. TREASURY BILLS (T-BILLS)

**1.** *Treasury bills,* as described earlier, are debt obligations which mature in a year or less. The most common T-bills mature in three months, six months, or a year. They are sold in denominations starting at $10,000.

**2.**  Unlike treasury bonds or notes, T-bills pay *discount interest* (see page 230). That is, they are sold at a discounted price, and can be redeemed for their face value at maturity. The discount is calculated as a straight percentage using a 360-day year and a stated rate called the *discount rate*.

• A 91-day (13-week) T-bill is discounted at 9%. The buyer would pay $10,000 minus the discount interest, where

$$\frac{discount}{interest} = \left(\$10,000 \times .09 \times \frac{91}{360}\right) = \$227.50.$$

Thus the buyer pays $10,000 − 227.50 = $9,772.50. The discount is not compounded. It is simple interest which the buyer gets up front through the discounted price, but may not realize until the bill is redeemed for its full value.

**3.** Because interest on T-bills is paid in a fundamentally different way than interest on treasury bonds or notes, some method of comparing their rates of return is needed. This is called the *bond equivalent yield*. It reflects the fact that T-bill interest is calculated over a 360-day year, while notes and bonds use a 365-day year.

$$\frac{bond}{equivalent\ yield} = \frac{365 \times discount\ rate}{360 - (discount\ rate \times days\ to\ maturity)}$$

The T-bill in the previous example has a discount rate of 9% and 91 days to maturity. Its bond equivalent yield is

$$\frac{365 \times .09}{360 - (.09 \times 91)} = 0.0934 = 9.34\%.$$

## READING TREASURY-BILL QUOTATIONS

The *Wall Street Journal* gives daily quotations for government securities. A typical listing for T-bills might look like this:

| Date | Days to Mat. | Bid | Asked | Chg. | Ask Yld. |
|------|------|------|------|------|------|
| Dec21 | 7 | 5.58 | 5.56 | −0.09 | 5.68 |
| Dec28 | 14 | 5.46 | 5.44 | ... | 5.56 |
| Jan 4 | 21 | 5.17 | 5.15 | +0.05 | 5.27 |

Key:

*Date:* The date is the date of maturity.

*Days to Mat.* The *days to maturity* is self-explanatory.

*Bid:* The *bid price* is a percent discount rate at which dealers can buy the bill. The actual dollar price is equal to $10,000 minus the discount, where

$$discount = \left(\begin{array}{c}discount \\ rate\end{array}\right) \times 100 \times \left(\begin{array}{c}days\ to \\ maturity\end{array}\right) \div 360$$

- A listed discount rate of 5.29 on a 91-day T-bill would carry a discount of

$$5.29 \times 100 \times 91 \div 360 = \$133.72.$$

The dollar bid price would be $10,000 − $133.72 = $9,866.28.

*Asked:* The *asked price* is the price at which the dealer will sell to a buyer. The price is given as a percent in the same way as the bid price.

*Chg:* The change in price from the previous day's trading is also given in percent increments. These are easily read as *basis points*. A change of −0.09 is a drop of 9 basis points. A basis point is ¹⁄₁₀₀ of a percent, or .01%.

*Ask Yld:* This column gives the *bond equivalent yield* in percent form.

# Mutual Funds

A *mutual fund* is a diversified investment that pools investors' money into a stock and/or bond portfolio. An investor can buy shares in a fund, and the value of each share fluctuates with the performance of the portfolio. Every fund portfolio has a manager who follows an investment strategy that is laid out in general terms in a prospectus. Some funds spread the money over as few as 20 stocks; others invest in up to 200. A fund may promote itself as aggressive or conservative. The most conservative, low-risk (and steady-yield) funds tend to buy corporate bonds and preferred stock only.

On the other end of the scale, there are speculative funds that invest in progressive start-up firms.

Mutual funds constitute a large share of the investment market. There is a mutual fund for every taste. There is also a basic vocabulary that is necessary to navigate these waters.

**1.** Issuers of mutual funds can be either *open-end investment companies* or *closed-end investment companies*. The term *open-end* refers to the fact that the investment company issues an unlimited number of shares to anyone who wants to buy in. In contrast, a *closed-end company* issues a fixed number of shares, which are listed on a major stock exchange. Once these shares have been issued and the initial sale is complete, a buyer must buy shares from a shareholder through a broker. Unlike an open-end investment fund, which sells directly to the investor, a closed-end company does not issue or redeem shares, and the price per share is determined on the open marketplace.

**2.** Investment companies pool investors' money in funds that are spread over stock and/or bond portfolios in accordance with an investment philosophy. The company may offer several funds, each with its own philosophy and manager. These are described in a publication called a *prospectus*. The fund usually retains from ½% to 1% of the total investment as their annual *management fee.*

**3.** There are too many types of portfolios to list here, but they fall into some general categories.

One way to categorize them is by investment philosophy. Here are the four most basic approaches:

> *income fund* invests in corporate bonds and dividend paying stocks which generate immediate dividend income for the investor, but do not increase in value very fast.
>
> *growth fund* targets stocks which have long-term growth potential, but may not pay dividends or generate immediate revenue.
>
> *balanced fund* seeks to split funds between income (dividend paying, slow growth) and growth.
>
> *performance fund* targets high-risk stocks with the potential for high yields.

Funds may also be classified by the type of securities they target. Here are four basic types (out of many):

> *stock funds* invest the pool solely in common and preferred stock.
>
> *bond funds* target bonds only.
>
> *stock and bond funds* split the pool between stocks and bonds.
>
> *municipal bond funds* concentrate on municipal bonds with tax-exempt interest earnings.
>
> *money market funds* invest in a variety of short-term debt instruments such as Treasury bills.

**4.** Some mutual funds are purchased through securities dealers, brokers, or banks. These funds may carry a sales commission which is referred to as a *load*. The load can be deducted from the investment up front, or when the shares are redeemed. An up-front charge is called a *front-end load*. A *back-end load fund* charges a commission when it is sold. A *no-load fund* is a mutual fund with no sales commission.

A typical commission is between 4¾% and 5¾% of the total investment. Thus when an investor spends $10,000 to buy into a 5% front-end loaded fund, $500 goes to the broker or dealer, leaving $9500 worth of shares. The investor has to earn back $500 just to break even. By contrast, a no-load fund, which is not bought through a middleman, retains its full principal value.

Back-end loaded funds often use a six-year declining load, which charges 5% if the fund is sold in the first year, 4% for the second, 3% for the third, 2% for the fourth, 1% for the fifth, and no load after the sixth. There are also *hybrid funds*, known as *low-load funds*. These charge a commission of about 3%.

**5.** An investor may buy into a mutual fund by purchasing a certain number of shares (where *total investment = number of shares × price per share*). An alternative is to buy into the mutual fund at a lump sum value which may not convert to a whole number of shares.

**6. Dollar Cost Averaging** Some investors follow a policy of investing a fixed sum at regular intervals. One possibility is a monthly lump-sum investment. The practice of purchasing a fixed dollar value of shares is referred to as *dollar cost averaging*.

## READING MUTUAL-FUND QUOTATIONS

Listings of mutual-fund performance in the business pages of newspapers follow a standard format. The price of a share is determined by the *net asset value* (or *NAV*), which is a ratio of the investment fund's assets to the number of shares outstanding. Shares are sold at the NAV, to which sales commissions may be added. They are also redeemed at the NAV, minus any redemption charges.

| Fund Family<br>Fund Name | Type | Rating | NAV | Wkly<br>%Ret | YTD<br>%Ret | 1-Yr<br>%Ret | 3-Yr<br>%Ret |
|---|---|---|---|---|---|---|---|
| **Acme Capital** | | | | | | | |
| AcmeGro | G | 5/2 | 18.75 | −0.2 | +23.6 | +23.0 | +12.1 |

Key:

*Fund Family:* Names of investment companies are given in boldface, followed by the individual funds they maintain. The name given here is fictitious.

*Type:* This listing follows the style of the *New York Times*. The key to their abbreviations of bond types is given in a table they include with the price quotations. In this instance, the *G* indicates that this is a growth fund.

*Rating:* The rating is a measure of risk versus return as judged by Morningstar, Inc., a mutual-fund rating firm. The first number rates the return on investment. As explained by the *Times*, "a

return rating of 5 shows top performance among similar funds over the last 3 years, while a rating of 1 shows poor performance. The ratings are based on overall return after deducting sales charges."

The second number assesses risk. It is based on the fund's downward performance as compared to Treasury bills during market downswings. That is, when interest rates rise, bond prices tend to fall. The benchmark for such downswings is the price of T-bills. Bonds which devalue more rapidly than T-bills are considered higher risk. On the scale of 1 to 5, a 5 is the lowest risk rating, a 1 is the highest risk. Acme's ½ rating shows strong performance but with relatively high risk.

The distribution of the ratings is such that about 10% of all rated funds fall into the extreme categories of 1 or 5.

*NAV:* The *net asset value (NAV)* is the current price per share, not counting sales commissions. It is calculated by the following formula:

$$\text{NAV} = \frac{\textit{total value of fund investments} - \textit{debts}}{\textit{number of shares outstanding}}$$

Closed-end mutual funds are often discounted below net asset value.

*Wkly % Ret:* The total return for one week is a percent change in the net asset value of a share (the price per share). Any dividends earned on the securities in the portfolio are reinvested, therefore dividends show up in the calculation of net asset value.

YTD % Ret: This is the *year-to-date* return on investment.

*1-Yr % Ret:* This is the total percent increase in net asset value over the past year.

*3-Yr % Ret:* This is the total percent increase in net asset value over the last three years.

# Tax-Deferred Investment Plans

A *tax-deferred investment* is a type of tax shelter that at one time was available only to the very rich. Changes in tax laws in the 1970s and 1980s, however, created a wide variety of tax-deferment plans that were available to the average wage earner. Among these, the *IRA* (or *individual retirement account*) is the best-known and most popular. It is offered by almost every financial institution—banks, credit unions, S&Ls, and investment companies.

The basic idea is very simple. The tax laws allow anyone to deposit up to $2000 per year out of their taxable income in an IRA account. For those in the lowest tax brackets, the IRA contribution is not taxed in the year it is earned. Instead, this pretax income is allowed to collect interest in an investment fund, and becomes available to the investor when he or she turns 59½ years of age. Taxes are then paid on the money in the year it is withdrawn. The assumption is that in retirement, most people will be in a lower tax bracket, and their IRA contributions will be taxed at a lower rate than they would have been during the years in

which they were set aside. In the meantime, and more importantly, the untaxed income is allowed to earn interest, and the interest is not taxed until it is withdrawn.

Other tax-deferred plans—*SEP-IRAs*, *Keogh*, and *401(k)*—use the same basic principle. Keoghs and SEPs, or *simplified employee pensions*, are intended for the self-employed or for employees of small firms, and 401(k)s and 403(b)s are available to employees of most public corporations and non-profit organizations such as universities and public schools. In each type of plan, the employee is allowed to set aside a percent of taxable income (which may be partially matched by the employer) before taxes are taken out. These amounts may exceed the $2000 allowable limit for IRAs, and can go as high as 25% of total income. The funds accumulate in an investment portfolio and become available after age 59½.

Assume $1000 is to be set aside in a tax-deferred retirement account. What is the advantage of tax deferral to investing after tax? Tables 5.7 and 5.8 compare the growth of an after-tax and tax-deferred investment over 30 years. The after-tax investment has a lower starting principal, and tax must be paid on the interest earned each year. The tax-deferred investment is not taxed until the money is withdrawn.

The tables assume that both portfolios earn an effective rate of 10% per year. They also assume a 34% tax bracket, which is the national average for total income tax paid.

**Table 5.7. An After-Tax Investment**

| Value after | | Interest earned | Value if withdrawn (after taxes) |
|---|---|---|---|
| 5 years | $1,063 | 403 | $926 |
| 10 years | 1,712 | 1,051 | 1,355 |
| 15 years | 2,757 | 2,097 | 2,044 |
| 20 years | 4,440 | 3,780 | 3,155 |
| 25 years | 7,151 | 6,491 | 4,944 |
| 30 years | 11,517 | 10,857 | 7,826 |

In a 34% tax bracket, the total tax paid on a $1000 after-tax investment would be $340, leaving $660 available to be invested. The figures above show the value of $660 invested over 30 years. With a tax-deferred investment, the entire $1,000 is available to be invested; it grows as shown in Table 5.8 below.

**Table 5.8. A Tax-Deferred Investment**

| Value after | | Interest earned | Value if withdrawn (after taxes) |
|---|---|---|---|
| 5 years | $1,611 | 611 | $1,403 |
| 10 years | 2,594 | 1,594 | 2,052 |
| 15 years | 4,177 | 3,177 | 3,097 |
| 20 years | 6,727 | 5,727 | 4,780 |
| 25 years | 10,835 | 9,835 | 7,491 |
| 30 years | 17,449 | 16,449 | 11,517 |

This example is oversimplified, but it is intended to show that there is a considerable cumulative advantage to investing pretax dollars. The 34% figure used to calculate the tax on the interest earned on the after-tax investment is excessive. But even at a lower rate, the tax-deferred investment earns enough to offset even a 10% early withdrawal penalty.

## IRA'S

There are few restrictions on who may open and contribute to an IRA. But the tax deductibility of the yearly contribution is more complicated, partly because the tax laws covering IRAs have undergone several changes since they were instituted. In particular, in 1986 the qualifications for the full IRA deduction were tightened, and many people pulled back on their investments in these programs. Those with high incomes were hit hardest by the change. Today the deductibility of these pension plans depends on adjusted gross income, marital status, and whether the contributor already participates in a sponsored retirement plan. This means that anyone contemplating one of these plans should carefully check the rules with an accountant. In brief, here is a basic outline of eligibility requirements for IRAs.

**1. Allowable Contributions** Any individual may contribute to an IRA account up to $2000 per year or 100% of earned income, whichever is less. If husband and wife both work, each may contribute up to $2000 per year. A couple with one wage earner, when filing jointly, may contribute up to $2250 per year (the extra $250 would go into a separate IRA).

**2. Allowable Deductions** The full IRA tax deduction of $2000 is allowed if the contributor is not covered by an employer-sponsored pension plan. A contributor who *does* belong to a pension plan may still deduct the full $2000 IRA contribution if:

    i. adjusted gross income is less than $40,000 (on a joint return), or

    ii. adjusted gross income is less than $25,000 (when filing single).

A partial deduction is allowed if:

    i. adjusted gross income is greater than $40,000 but less than $50,000 (on a joint return), or

    ii. adjusted gross income is greater than $25,000 but less than $35,000 (when filing single).

No deduction is allowed above these limits.

**3. Deadlines and Penalties** Money can be contributed to an IRA at any time up until April 15 and still be deducted for the preceding tax year. In addition, a first IRA may be opened by April 15 in order to establish a deduction for the previous calendar year.

Tax-deferred money that is withdrawn before age 59½ is subject to a 10% penalty levied by the IRS, in addition to the tax that must be paid. However, some penalty-free withdrawals are possible if they are part of a regular withdrawal schedule in which withdrawn amounts are based on life expectancy and the expected rate of return of the IRA. Under such a plan, withdrawals must be made for at least five years (or until age 59½), after which withdrawals can be made freely with no penalty.

To calculate the payment schedule for early withdrawals, divide total IRA savings by life expectancy and estimate the expected rate of return. (There is a maximum rate allowed by the IRS.)

**4. Taking Money Out of an IRA** After age 70½, no money may be contributed to an IRA. Furthermore, money must be withdrawn yearly in an amount proportional to the contributor's remaining life expectancy. The IRS mandates this so that taxes will be paid on the tax-deferred income. If the contributor does not withdraw the minimum amount, the IRS levies a 50% penalty tax on the difference.

## SEP-IRA'S

A simplified employee pension plan (SEP-IRA) is an option available to those who earn a substantial part of their income through self-employment. In an SEP-IRA, an individual can make a tax-deductible contribution to an investment program of as much as 15% of self-employment income (to a maximum of $22,500). This option assumes that the individual is not part of any other retirement program.

The advantage of an SEP-IRA is clearly in the amount of allowable contributions. In an ordinary

IRA, $2000 is the annual limit. In an SEP-IRA, the limit is $22,500. Even if $5000 were to be set aside each year in an SEP-IRA, the difference between the two would grow significantly over 20 years.

> IRA: $2000 per year at 10% per year. Total after 20 years: $114,550.
>
> SEP-IRA: $5000 per year at 10% per year. Total after 20 years: $286,375.

## KEOGH PLANS

Keogh plans were designed for employees in small businesses such as accounting, law, architecture, and engineering firms. A Keogh plan requires a lot of effort to set up, but it allows higher yearly contributions than an SEP.

There are three basic types of Keogh plans: profit sharing, money purchase, and paired plan.

> *Profit sharing* Of all Keogh plans, this option has the lowest allowed annual contribution, at just 15% of earned income (up to no more than $30,000 per participant). But profit sharing is the most flexible of the Keogh plans because it allows the contribution to vary from year to year, from as little as nothing to as high as the dollar or percent limit.
>
> *Money Purchase* This plan allows a yearly contribution of up to 25% of earned income, but not more than $30,000. However, it requires the contributor to specify a fixed an-

nual contribution, and this contribution must be met every year until the contributor reaches age 59½.

*Paired Plan* The paired plan stipulates that the contributor invest the maximum allowable amount each year. This may be determined by a percent of salary (25%) or by the $30,000 allowable limit, whichever is lower.

Banks and financial services offer ready-made SEP and Keogh plans featuring many different types of investment portfolios. Like IRAs, these plans defer taxes on a portion of income, allowing that money to earn interest until the contributor reaches age 59½, after which he or she may begin to withdraw the money without penalty. Income tax must be paid on the withdrawal as though it were income in the tax year of the withdrawal.

## 401(k) AND 403(b)

The names 401(k) and 403(b) come from item numbers of the 1978 tax code that created these retirement plans. 401(k) is a tax-deferred income investment plan available to corporate employees. 403(b) is designed for employees of universities, public schools, and other nonprofit organizations.

In these plans, the employee can make pretax contributions of up to 15% of salary (with an upper limit of $9240 in 1995) to an investment fund set up and managed by the employer (with input from the employees). Employers will usually match some percentage of the employee contribution. The pool of 401(k) or 403(b) money can be invested in several ways—stock or bond funds, money market funds, or GIC's (guaranteed income contracts). The tax advantage is similar to that of IRA and Keogh plans. Taxes on income are deferred until the money is withdrawn after retirement. Thus not only will taxes be paid after peak earning years (and thus at a lower rate), but the deferring of taxes allows the fund to earn interest during the years until retirement.

# Guidelines for Investment Decisions

Designing an investment portfolio involves many choices and some degrees of uncertainty. The inflation rate, and thus the value of a dollar in the future, looms as the primary consideration in deciding how much saving is enough, and what return on investment is adequate to meet future expenses. Because of this uncertainty, exact mathematical formulas are not necessary. Instead, an investor needs some guidelines that establish minimum levels of investment and earnings in order to meet future goals.

**1. The Effects of Inflation on Future Costs** This formula shows how much something costing P dollars today will cost several years from now. It is nothing more than a compound interest calculation that shows the rise in price due to inflation.

$$F = P \times (1 + i)^n$$

where P is the cost today, F is the cost $n$ years from now, and $i$ is the estimated annual inflation rate.

• A vacation house is priced at $250,000. Assuming a 3% annual rate of inflation, a comparable house 10 years from now would cost

$$250,000 \times (1 + .03)^{10} \approx \$335,979.$$

## 2. Estimating Investment Rate of Return That Will Maintain Purchasing Power

Because the interest earned on investments will be reduced by taxes, the investment rate of return should exceed the rate of inflation in order to maintain purchasing power. The required before-tax rate of return should be

$$r = \frac{i}{1 - t}$$

where $i$ is the annual inflation rate (in decimal form), and $t$ is the income tax bracket (also a percent used here in decimal form).

• An investor in a 34% tax bracket estimates a 3% rate of inflation. To keep pace with inflation, she must have a before-tax annual yield of

$$r = \frac{.03}{1 - .34} = 0.04545 \approx 4.55\%.$$

The following table shows that someone in the 34% tax bracket who wishes to maintain an after-

**Table 5.9. Annual Return on Investments Required to Offset Taxes**

Tax bracket and corresponding annual pretax yields

| After-tax yield | 28% | 30% | 31% | 32% | 34% | 36% | 37% | 39% |
|---|---|---|---|---|---|---|---|---|
| 5½% | 7.64 | 7.86 | 7.97 | 8.09 | 8.33 | 8.59 | 8.73 | 9.02 |
| 6% | 8.33 | 8.57 | 8.70 | 8.82 | 9.09 | 9.38 | 9.52 | 9.84 |
| 6½% | 9.03 | 9.29 | 9.42 | 9.56 | 9.85 | 10.16 | 10.32 | 10.66 |
| 7% | 9.72 | 10.00 | 10.14 | 10.29 | 10.61 | 10.94 | 11.11 | 11.48 |
| 7½% | 10.42 | 10.71 | 10.87 | 11.03 | 11.36 | 11.72 | 11.90 | 12.30 |
| 8% | 11.11 | 11.42 | 11.59 | 11.76 | 12.12 | 12.50 | 12.70 | 13.11 |
| 8½% | 11.81 | 12.14 | 12.32 | 12.50 | 12.88 | 13.28 | 13.49 | 13.93 |
| 9% | 12.50 | 12.86 | 13.04 | 13.24 | 13.64 | 14.06 | 14.29 | 14.75 |
| 9½% | 13.19 | 13.57 | 13.77 | 13.97 | 14.39 | 14.84 | 15.08 | 15.57 |
| 10% | 13.89 | 14.29 | 14.49 | 14.71 | 15.15 | 15.63 | 15.87 | 16.39 |
| 10½% | 14.58 | 15.00 | 15.22 | 15.44 | 15.91 | 16.41 | 16.67 | 17.21 |
| 11% | 15.28 | 15.71 | 15.94 | 16.18 | 16.67 | 17.19 | 17.47 | 18.02 |

tax annual return on investment of 9% must have a portfolio that earns 13.64%.

**3. Necessary Rate of Return When Funds Are Withdrawn** Assuming an investment portfolio is providing regular payments to meet living expenses, the before-tax rate of return calculated in paragraph 2 above would have to be higher to offset both the taxes paid and the amount withdrawn each year.

In this formula, which is a refinement of the formula in paragraph 2, the annual withdrawal from the portfolio is $w$. The rate of return should be

$$r = \frac{i + w}{1 - t}$$

• Assume that 4% of a portfolio is withdrawn each year. The target rate of return for an investor in the 34% tax bracket would be given by

$$r = \frac{.03 + .04}{1 - .34} = 0.10606 \approx 10.6\%.$$

where the inflation rate is 3% per year.

# Basic Bookkeeping

The object of bookkeeping is to record and summarize all business transactions that take place within a given time period. The same methods apply whether the business is a multinational conglomerate or simply a household. A journal of some type is used to record every transaction involving money or possessions with monetary value. The journal entries are periodically transferred to an account ledger (a process called *posting*) where they are grouped by type. These entries are ultimately transferred to summary statements—a monthly, quarterly, or annual report in the form of a *balance sheet* and an *income statement*.

## ASSETS AND LIABILITIES

An *asset* is some property or resource whose use or value is available to the owner. A *liability* is an obligation or debt representing someone else's advantage. A *balance sheet* is a listing of assets and liabilities. It is designed to show how possessions and debts are balanced against each other. The difference between assets and liabilities is what a company or individual actually owns—their *net worth.*

Assets take the form of cash, checks, and other cashable notes, accounts receivable, supplies, inventory, prepaid items, land, buildings, vehicles, equipment, and so on. Essentially, an asset is anything that has a cash value, or that could be converted to cash if necessary.

Liabilities are broken into two categories—short-term and long-term liabilities. Both categories represent types of debt or bills that will have to be paid. In the short term, they consist of monthly utility bills, payroll, and any short-term loans that are coming due. Long-term debts include mortgages, as well as the money that has been raised from (and is therefore owed to) stock and bond holders by a stock-issuing corporation.

*Equity* is defined as what would be left over if a company or individual paid off all debts.

## THE BALANCE SHEET

**1. The Balance Sheet Equation** The purpose of a balance sheet is to show the breakdown of assets, liabilities, and equity. These quantities are related by a simple equation:

$$assets = liabilities + owner's\ equity$$

The equation may apply to an entire business, to a household budget, or to a specific investment such as a house.

• A \$120,000 house purchased with a 20% down payment is a capital asset. The value of the asset (the house) can be broken down into the liability (the mortgage) plus the owner's equity (the down payment).

$$\$120,000 = \$96,000 + \$24,000$$

$$asset = mortgage + equity$$

As the mortgage is paid off, this equation changes. The owner gradually accumulates more equity as the principal is reduced. This process is called *amortization* (see p. 249).

Table 5.10 shows a standard form of balance sheet. It is standard practice to use a single underline for the last figure in a column of numbers that is to be added, or under a number that is subtracted. That is, a single underline is used for every subtotal or last figure in a calculation. A double underline is used for final totals.

A dollar sign should be placed before any figure at the top of a column containing figures that represent sums of money. A dollar sign should also be placed before any dollar figure that is the result of a computation involving figures above it—that is, before any total or subtotal.

## THE INCOME STATEMENT

*Net income* is the difference between the amount of money taken in and the amount of money paid out in a given period of time. This is expressed by

**Table 5.10. A Typical Balance Sheet**

## The Baxter Company
## Balance Sheet
## Dec 31 19___

| Assets | | | Liabilities | | |
|---|---|---|---|---|---|
| **CURRENT ASSETS** | | | **CURRENT LIABILITIES** | | |
| Cash | $30,000 | | Accounts payable | $ 7,000 | |
| Inventory | 15,000 | | Wages payable | 10,000 | |
| Prepaid insurance | 3,000 | | Note payable | 5,000 | |
| Prepaid services | 1,000 | | | | |
| Total current assets | | $49,000 | Total current liabilities | | $22,000 |
| **LONG-TERM ASSETS** | | | **LONG-TERM LIABILITIES** | | |
| Computers | $10,000 | | Mortgage payable | $35,000 | |
| Office furniture | 4,000 | | Total long-term liabilities | | $35,000 |
| Machinery | 3,000 | | | | |
| Total long-term assets | | $17,000 | Total liabilities | | $57,000 |
| | | | Owner's equity | | 9,000 |
| TOTAL ASSETS | | $66,000 | TOTAL LIABILITIES AND EQUITY | | $66,000 |

the statement "profit equals revenue minus cost." The purpose of an income statement is to record revenues and costs in order to state the *bottom line*—the profit or loss for that period—which is literally the last line of the statement.

Income statements cover specific periods of time—a month, a quarter, six months, or a year. For businesses, the annual income statement corresponds to the calendar year of January 1 to December 31, which is also the tax year.

A typical income statement is shown in Table 5.11. It itemizes revenues and costs relevant to a particular company. The variety of costs and revenues is not limited to those listed here. They can vary widely in type. The essential structure and purpose of an income statement, however, remain consistent, whether it applies to a household, a small business, or a large corporation.

## DOUBLE-ENTRY BOOKKEEPING

Every business transaction is recorded in a journal, which serves as a chronological record of transactions. Journal entries correspond to receipts—invoices, shipping receipts, payments stubs, and sales slips. In a double-entry system, each transaction is recorded twice—once as a credit to one account, and again as a debit to another account.

From the journal, debits and credits are transferred to a ledger, in which they are grouped by type (instead of date); that is, cash transactions, individual customer accounts, and other specific classes of records are isolated so that, for example,

**Table 5.11. A Typical Income Statement**

## ACME APPLIANCE COMPANY
### Income Statement
### for the year ending Dec 31, 19___

REVENUES

| | | |
|---|---|---|
| Sales | $150,000 | |
| Service | 75,000 | |
| Total revenues | | $225,000 |

EXPENSES

| | | |
|---|---|---|
| Wages | $110,000 | |
| Rent | 60,000 | |
| Insurance | 10,000 | |
| Taxes | 15,000 | |
| Advertising | 5,000 | |
| Utilities | 4,000 | |
| Total Expenses | | $204,000 |
| NET INCOME | | 21,000 |

an individual customer's account can be examined.

The purpose of double-entry bookkeeping is to maintain a reliable record of transactions. Because each transaction is recorded twice—once as a debit and once as a credit—the sum of the debits must ultimately match the sum of the credits. This is known as *balancing the books*.

A useful rule of thumb for balancing the books is that *all transposition errors create discrepancies that are multiples of 9*. If two digits are transposed (reversed) when entered into the journal, or a cash resister, or checkbook, the mistake will be noticed when debits do not match credits. If the discrepancy is divisible by 9, it is probably a transposition error. This is a common rule observed by all cashiers when they cash out.

## DEPRECIATION

Because assets in the form of durable goods suffer wear and tear, they do not retain their value over time. With use, they depreciate in value. This is true not only in fact (when trying to resell, for example) but for accounting purposes. The assets that are listed on a balance sheet will change in value as they wear out.

A car, for example, has a *book value* that is largely determined by its age. Most of the depreciation in the value of a car or any other heavily used piece of equipment occurs in the first few years of use. It is not uncommon, in fact, for cars, computers, office equipment, and machinery to have no more than five or six years of useful life. Consequently, accounting methods have been developed to allow owners to accurately state the true value of assets. The methods all work from three figures: the *original cost* (or initial value) of the asset, its expected *useful lifetime*, and its *salvage value*. How the initial value of the asset is depreciated depends on how it is used. In accounting, there are four principal methods that can be followed: *straight-line depreciation, sum-of-the-years-digits, double-declining balance,* and *units of production.*

The first method is the simplest because it involves depreciating the same amount each year. The second and third methods depreciate the greatest amount in the first year, with lesser percentages in succeeding years. These are called *accelerated depreciation* methods. The last method is one that depreciates based on the amount of usage, and not the time of ownership.

For tax purposes, the IRS outlines several acceptable methods of straight-line and accelerated depreciation. These are described in IRS Form 4562.

**1. Straight-Line Depreciation** The straight-line method calculates equal depreciation amounts for each year of useful life. The value that remains after the useful life has elapsed is called the *salvage value*.

$$yearly\ depreciation = \frac{initial\ cost - salvage\ value}{estimated\ life}$$

• A company car cost $16,500 new. It has an estimated useful life of six years, after which it will be sold for $4500. Using straight-line depreciation, the yearly depreciation would be

$$\frac{\$16500 - 4500}{6} = \frac{12000}{6} = \$2,000.$$

If the company needs to keep track of *monthly depreciation*, it would divide this figure by 12.

$$monthly\ depreciation = \frac{yearly\ depreciation}{12}$$

**2. Sum-of-the-Years-Digits Method** Unlike straight-line depreciation, which depreciates the same fraction of the useful value of an asset each year, the sum-of-the-digits method employs a sequence of decreasing fractions. These are based on the expected lifetime of the asset. For example, if an asset is allotted a useful lifetime of five years, the method calls for summing 5 + 4 + 3 + 2 + 1 to get 15. This sum of the digits is then used as the denominator of a sequence of five fractions—$5/15$, $4/15$, $3/15$, $2/15$, and $1/15$— that represent the portion of the asset's value that is depreciated each year. The example below depreciates an asset over six years.

• Assume the car in the example above is depreciated over six years using the sum-of-the-digits method.

$$6 + 5 + 4 + 3 + 2 + 1 = 21$$

Thus the fractions are: $6/21$, $5/21$, $4/21$, $3/21$, $2/21$, and $1/21$.

The usable value is

$$initial\ cost - salvage\ value = \$16500 - 4500$$
$$= \$12,000.$$

| | |
|---|---|
| 1st-year depreciation: $6/21 \times \$12,000 =$ | $3428.57 |
| 2nd-year depreciation: $5/21 \times \$12,000 =$ | 2857.14 |
| 3rd-year depreciation: $4/21 \times \$12,000 =$ | 2285.71 |
| 4th-year depreciation: $3/21 \times \$12,000 =$ | 1714.29 |
| 5th-year depreciation: $2/21 \times \$12,000 =$ | 1142.86 |
| 6th-year depreciation: $1/21 \times \$12,000 =$ | 571.43 |
| total depreciation: | $12,000.00 |

**3. Double Declining Balance Method**  This method begins by calculating the percent used in straight-line depreciation and doubling it. Each year's depreciation is the same percent of the *remaining* value of the asset. Salvage value is ignored until the last year's depreciation has been found.

- If a $40,000 machine is depreciated over five years, the straight-line depreciation over one year (ignoring salvage value) would be ⅕ (or 20%) of the value each year. In the double declining balance method, this percentage is doubled and used to find the depreciation in the first year. In the second year, depreciation is the same percentage of the remaining value, and so on.

| Year | Initial value | Depreciation (40% of initial value) |
|------|---------------|-------------------------------------|
| 1 | $40,000 | 0.4 × 40,000 = $16,000.00 |
| 2 | 24,000 | 0.4 × 24,000 = 9,600.00 |
| 3 | 14,400 | 0.4 × 14,400 = 5,760.00 |
| 4 | 8,640 | 0.4 × 8,640 = 3,456.00 |
| 5 | 5,184 | 0.4 × 5,184 = 2,073.60 |
| total depreciation | | $36,889.60 |

$$\text{salvage value} = \text{initial value} - \text{total depreciation}$$
$$= \$40,000 - 36,889.60$$
$$= \$3110.60$$

**4. Units-of-Production Method**  This method is based on usage rather than on the time an asset has been owned. It is primarily used for machinery that has an expected operational lifetime that can be measured in units of service. A car, for example, might be depreciated based on the number of miles it has been driven, rather than how old it is. A stamping machine might be rated for 50,000 stampings before it wears out. The units-of-production method depreciates according to the percent of useful service that has been used up.

The method consists of three steps:

i. Find the asset's usable value by subtracting salvage value from original cost.

ii. Divide the usable value by the number of units of useful service (in miles, hours of operation, individual uses).

iii. Multiply the initial value by the ratio of units used to total units.

• A robot welder with an initial value of $240,000 is built to perform 400,000 welds before it wears out. If it performs 100,000 welds in its first year of use, it has used up $^{100,000}/_{400,000}$, or one quarter of its value. Thus, by the units-of-production method, a fourth of $240,000, or $60,000 can be deducted in the first year.

## PAYROLL

A company's payroll breaks down into two components: salary and wages. *Salary* is compensation that is paid to employees who are hired on contract for specified periods of time. Some employees may be hired for a relatively short period—a few weeks or a month. But the majority of salaried employees have renewable contracts that provide a measure of job security.

*Wages* constitute the money paid to hourly workers—usually long-term, non-management employees or short-term, outside contractors. These workers must keep a record of their hours worked, either by punching a time clock or by submitting accurate accounts. Hourly compensation is set at a predetermined level. Thus a wage earner's weekly salary is found by multiplying the number of hours worked by the hourly pay rate. The standard work week in the United States is a 40-hour week. These hours—the normal working hours from 9 to 5 Monday through Friday—are referred to as *straight time*. If an employee works more than 40 hours in a given week, he may be eligible for a higher hourly rate on the extra hours. The extra hours and the extra money are referred to as *overtime*.

The hourly wage for overtime is given as a multiple of the regular hourly wage. It can vary with the type of overtime. The following overtime schedule is typical:

> Extra weekday work beyond 40 hours: *time-and-a-half*
>
> Sundays and holidays: *double time*
>
> Evening or emergency shifts: variable up to *triple time*

• An $8.40/hour wage earner works 15 hours of overtime one week. The overtime pay is time-and-a-half, or

$$1\frac{1}{2} \times \$8.40 = \$12.60/\text{hour}.$$

Her gross pay for the week will be:

regular pay: $40 \times \$8.40 = \quad \$336.00$

overtime pay: $15 \times \$12.60 = \quad \underline{189.00}$

gross pay: $\qquad\qquad\qquad \$525.00$

## PAYROLL DEDUCTIONS

By law, all businesses must deduct state and federal taxes from paychecks. These withholdings are paid directly to the government. Other deductions may also be made for the employee's contribution to a health care program, unemployment compensation, social security, elective tax-deferred retirement program, day care, insurance, or additional prepaid taxes.

The pay statement lists the total pay before deductions. This is the *gross income*. The amount of pay after deductions is the *net income*. Although the deductions are itemized on a pay statement, their designations can be cryptic. *FICA*, for example, refers to *Social Security* payments. By law, the employer must match the employee contribution. Although the exact percentage can vary year by year, it has recently been 7%. Thus the employer must contribute 7% of the employee's gross pay in addition to the 7% employee contribution. The total contribution is 14%.

*Workers compensation* is a fund maintained by contributions from employers. The contribution for any employer is usually a percentage of total payroll, and may be paid to the state or to a private insurance provider, depending on the local laws.

An employer must file a quarterly report of federal tax withheld on paychecks. At the end of the fiscal year, the employer must also provide each employee with a W-2 form, which states the total wages or salary earned, the total deductions for federal, state, and local taxes, and the total for other deductions that might be tax-deferred.

# Individual Income Tax

Individual income tax is calculated according to one basic formula:

*taxable income = adjusted gross income − deductions − exemptions − credits*

The tax-return form is divided into sections in which totals for each of these categories are computed. When the taxable income is found, the tax payment can be found in a *tax table*, which is a tabulation (at length) involving a sliding scale formula. The formula varies in percent amounts with different categories of taxpayer, but the idea is consistent in all tax brackets: income up to the limit of the lowest tax bracket is calculated at the lowest tax rate; income that falls into the next tax bracket is calculated at the next tax rate, and so on.

Table 5.12 and the example that follows it show how the tax in the tax table is derived. The tax

**Table 5.12. Tax brackets—1995. Taxable Income**

| single | joint | rate |
|---|---|---|
| 0–23,350 | 0–39,000 | 15% |
| 23,351–56,550 | 39,001–94,250 | 28% |
| 56,551–117,950 | 94,251–143,600 | 31% |
| 117,951–256,500 | 143,601–256,500 | 36% |
| 256,500 and up | 256,500 and up | 39.6% |

table itself shows that tax payments increase incrementally with taxable income. Thus it is impossible to reduce net income when moving up into the next tax bracket.

• A joint tax return that shows a taxable income of $110,000 would owe a tax that is calculated as follows:

$$\$39,000 \times 0.15 = \$\ 5,850.00$$
$$(\$94,250 - 39,000) \times 0.28 = 15,470.00$$
$$(\$110,000 - 94,250) \times 0.31 = 4,882.50$$

| total tax | $26,202.50 |
|---|---|

(This calculation is spelled out in more detail in schedules X, Y, and Z of the IRS instruction book.)

## THE 1040 FORM

A taxpayer may file a return using a 1040, 1040A, or 1040EZ form, depending on the complexity of his or her situation. Each of the forms has the same basic format, with the 1040 being the longest and most detailed. They are all designed to arrive at a figure for taxable income. This is based on the adjusted gross income minus certain allowable deductions, exemptions, and credits. These terms are briefly explained below.

**1. Adjusted gross income** The first part of a tax return covers all sources of income. When income that is not subject to tax (welfare payments, interest on municipal bonds, etc.) is deducted from the total income, the result is called adjusted gross income.

*Adjusted gross income* is the total of all wages, salary, unemployment compensation, tips, gratuities, interest and dividend earnings, annuities, royalties, rents, Social Security income, and some other sources of income. It excludes income that is not subject to tax. Thus payments such as public assistance (welfare) and interest on tax-exempt bonds are subtracted from total income to arrive at adjusted gross income. Also subtracted are any amounts on which tax will be paid at a future date or by another party. This includes alimony payments, penalties on early withdrawal of savings, and any payments to tax-deferred retirement plans (IRAs, Keogh plans, etc.).

**2. Deductions** Adjusted gross income is further reduced by certain deductions that are sanctioned by the tax laws. Everyone is entitled to take a *standard deduction*. In 1995, the standard deductions were:

> *single:* $3900
>
> *head of household:* $5750

*married, filing jointly:* $6550

*married, filing separately:* $3275

*over 65 or blind:* additional $950 (single)
additional $750 (married)

Individual items that can be deducted from taxable income include:

> state and local property taxes
>
> mortgage interest payments
>
> charitable contributions
>
> moving expenses related to job relocation
>
> medical expenses (when in excess of 7.5% of adjusted gross income)
>
> casualty losses

When the sum of these deductions exceeds the standard deduction, the taxpayer may opt to *itemize deductions.* This involves adding up all of the allowable deductions and using the sum as a deduction from adjusted gross income.

**3. Exemptions** In addition to deductions, every taxpayer is allowed to take a personal *exemption* (in the amount of $2500 in 1995), and an exemption of the same amount for a spouse and for each dependent not claimed on another taxpayer's return.

**4. Tax Credits** Taxable income can also be reduced if the taxpayer is eligible for a *tax credit.* This is a deduction available to the poor, the elderly, and to those who bear expenses related to the care of a dependent. Schedules for each type of tax credit are part of the tax booklet.

## TAX FREEDOM DAY

*Tax Freedom Day* is the day of the year on which the average taxpayer has earned enough to cover his or her annual taxes (state, local, and federal). In essence, it is a calendar method of expressing the percentage of gross income that goes to pay taxes. For the average American, taxes account for about 34% of income. In 1994, Tax Freedom Day fell on May 5.

The same idea is often applied to an eight-hour workday. By this reckoning, Americans in 1994 began working for themselves 2 hours and 45 minutes into their workday. Everything up to that point was for the government.

# Appendix

# Tables and Formulas

## Mathematical Symbols

**ROMAN NUMERALS**

In the system of Roman numerals, repeating a symbol indicates a repeated value. Thus XXX is three 10s, which equals 30. A symbol preceded by a symbol of lower value is reduced by the lower value. Thus CM is 100 less than 1000, which equals 900. A symbol followed by a symbol of lesser value is increased by the lesser value. Thus MCM is 1000 followed by 900, which is 1900. A symbol that has an overline is multiplied in value by 1000. Thus $\overline{X}$ is 10 × 1000, which equals 10,000.

| | | | |
|---|---|---|---|
| 1 | I | 150 | CL |
| 2 | II | 200 | CC |
| 3 | III | 300 | CCC |
| 4 | IV | 400 | CD |
| 5 | V | 500 | D |
| 6 | VI | 600 | DC |
| 7 | VII | 700 | DCC |
| 8 | VIII | 800 | DCCC |
| 9 | IX | 900 | CM |
| 10 | X | 1000 | M |
| 11 | XI | 1500 | MD |
| 12 | XII | 1600 | MDC |
| 13 | XIII | 1650 | MDCL |
| 14 | XIV | 1700 | MDCC |
| 15 | XV | 1750 | MDCCL |
| 16 | XVI | 1800 | MDCCC |
| 17 | XVII | 1850 | MDCCCL |
| 18 | XVIII | 1860 | MDCCCLX |
| 19 | XIX | 1870 | MDCCCLXX |
| 20 | XX | 1880 | MDCCCLXXX |
| 25 | XXV | 1890 | MDCCCXC |
| 30 | XXX | 1900 | MCM or MDCCCC |
| 40 | XL | 2000 | MM |
| 50 | L | 3000 | MMM |
| 60 | LX | 4000 | MMMM or $M\overline{V}$ |
| 70 | LXX | 5000 | $\overline{V}$ |
| 80 | LXXX | 10,000 | $\overline{X}$ |
| 90 | XC | 100,000 | $\overline{C}$ |
| 100 | C | 1,000,000 | $\overline{M}$ |

# MATHEMATICAL SYMBOLS

| | |
|---|---|
| $+$ | plus or positive |
| $-$ | minus or negative |
| $\times$ | times; multiplied by |
| $\div$ | divided by |
| $=$ | is equal to |
| $>$ | is greater than |
| $<$ | is less than |
| $\geq$ | is greater than or equal to |
| $\leq$ | is less than or equal to |
| $\neq$ | is not equal to |
| $\equiv$ | is equivalent to; is defined as; is identical with |
| $\approx$ | is approximately equal to |
| $\pm$ | plus or minus |
| $\sqrt{\phantom{x}}$ | square root of |
| $\Sigma$ | sum of a series |
| $\angle$ | angle |
| $\cup$ | union (of sets) |
| $\cap$ | intersection (of sets) |
| $\varnothing$ | empty set or null set |
| $\propto$ | is directly proportional to |
| $\infty$ | infinity |
| $\pi$ | pi (approximately 3.14159) |
| $\therefore$ | therefore (used in proofs) |

Q.E.D.   *quod erat demonstrandum* ("which was to be proved") the final statement of a proof

≅   approximately equal to; congruent to

%   percent

# Units of Measurement

## Units of Time

| | |
|---|---|
| 1 minute | 60 seconds |
| 1 hour | 60 minutes |
| 1 day | 24 hours |
| 1 week | 7 days |
| 1 fortnight | 2 weeks |
| 1 month | 28–31 days |
| 1 year | 12 months; 365 days |
| 1 decade | 10 years |
| 1 century | 100 years |
| 1 millennium | 1000 years |

## Units of Length

1 foot = 12 inches

1 yard = 3 feet

1 rod = 5½ yards = 16½ feet

1 furlong = 40 rods = 660 feet

1 mile = 8 furlongs = 1760 yards = 5280 feet

1 league = 3 miles

72 points = 1 inch

1 palm = 3 inches

1 hand = 4 inches (used for heights of horses)

1 span = 9 inches (thumb to little finger of outstretched hand)

1 cubit ≈ 18 inches (based on length of a hand and forearm)

## Units of Area

1 square foot = 144 square inches

1 square yard = 9 square feet

1 square rod = 30¼ square yards

1 acre = 160 square rods = 4840 square yards = 43,560 square feet

1 square mile = 640 acres

## Units Used by Surveyors

1 link = 7.92 inches

1 rod = 25 links = 16.5 feet

1 chain = 4 rods = 100 links = 66 feet

1 mile = 80 chains

1 square rod = 625 square links

1 acre = 160 square rods = 10 square chains

1 square mile = 640 acres

1 township = 36 square miles (6 mi. × 6 mi. of area)

## Units of Volume

1 cubic foot = 1728 cubic inches
(12 × 12 × 12 cubic in.)
1 cubic yard = 27 cubic feet
1 board foot = 144 cubic inches
1 cord foot = 16 cubic feet
1 cord = 8 cord feet = 128 cubic feet

## Units of Dry Measure

1 quart = 2 pints
1 peck = 8 quarts = 16 pints
1 bushel = 4 pecks

## Units of (Avoirdupois) Weight

1 pound = 16 ounces
1 stone = 14 pounds
1 short hundredweight = 100 pounds
1 long hundredweight = 112 pounds
1 short ton = 2000 pounds
1 long ton = 2240 pounds

## Units of Liquid Measure

1 gill = 4 fluid ounces
1 pint = 16 fluid ounces = 4 gills
1 quart = 2 pints = 32 fluid ounces
1 gallon = 4 quarts = 128 fluid ounces
1 barrel (ordinary liquid) = 31.5 gallons

1 pipe = 2 hogsheads
1 tun = 2 pipes
1 barrel (oil) = 42 gallons
1 barrel (beer) = 43.25 gallons

## Nautical Measures

1 fathom = 6 feet
1 cable length = 100 or 120 fathoms or 608 feet
1 nautical mile = 1.1516 statute miles
1 league = 3 nautical miles
1 knot = 1 nautical mile per hour

## Astronomical Distances

1 astronomical unit (AU) ≈ 93 million miles
1 light year ≈ 5.9 trillion miles
1 parsec = 3.26 light years ≈ 19.2 trillion miles

## Units of Power

1 horsepower ≈ 0.75 kilowatt
1 kilowatt ≈ 1.3 horsepower

## Angle Measures

60 seconds = 1 minute

60 minutes = 1 degree = $\frac{1}{360}$ of a full revolution

60 degrees = 1 sextant (a sixth of a full revolution)

90 degrees = 1 quadrant (a quarter revolution)

180 degrees = half revolution

360 degrees = 1 full revolution

1 radian = $\frac{180}{\pi}$ degrees $\approx$ 57.29578 degrees

1 degree = $\frac{\pi}{180}$ radians $\approx$ 0.0174533 radians

$2\pi$ radians = 1 full revolution = 360°

$\pi$ radians = half revolution = 180°

$\frac{\pi}{2}$ radians = quarter revolution = 90°

$\frac{\pi}{4}$ radians = 45°

## Household Measures (recipes, etc.)

1 teaspoon = $\frac{1}{3}$ tablespoon (or $\frac{1}{6}$ fl. oz.) $\approx$ 5 milliliters

1 tablespoon = 3 teaspoons (or $\frac{1}{2}$ fl. oz.) $\approx$ 15 milliliters

1 cup = $\frac{1}{2}$ pint = $\frac{1}{4}$ quart $\approx$ $\frac{1}{4}$ liter

1 pint = 2 cups = ½ quart ≈ ½ liter

1 quart = 4 cups = 2 pints = ¼ gallon = 0.945 liter

1 gallon = 16 cups = 8 pints = 4 quarts = 3.785 liters

1 peck = 8 (dry) quarts

1 bushel = 4 pecks

# The Metric System

The metric system is a system of weights and measures based on powers of 10. It is the basis of the worldwide scientific standard of measurement called the International System (or SI), but it has not been adopted and implemented by all countries. The U.S. system, for example, is not a decimal system, and thus conversions to metric units are not obvious or straightforward.

The metric system was devised by the French during the French Revolution. The U.S. system of measurement (the current name for the old British system) is its predecessor. The basic metric unit of length is the meter, from which the basic units of weight (the gram) and capacity (the liter) can be derived. Because of the difficulty of establishing the exact dimension of a meter, the system did not work out as flawlessly as intended, but grams and liters may still be informally understood as measures based on meters.

Originally, the meter was supposed to be based on a fraction of the circumference of the earth as measured through the poles; however, the actual dimension turned out to be somewhat arbitrary. A gram is the mass of one cubic centimeter of water at 4°C, the temperature at water's greatest density. A liter is the volume of one kilogram of water, and thus is equivalent to 1000 cubic centimeters.

Other units based on meters, grams, and liters are formed by adding Greek prefixes for decimal multiples and Latin prefixes for decimal subdivisions. These are listed below.

## Base units of measurement

| Type of measurement | Unit | Abbreviation |
|---|---|---|
| length | meter | m |
| mass | kilogram | kg |
| temperature | kelvin | K |
| time | second | s |
| electric current | ampere | A |
| light intensity | candela | cd |
| quantity of a chemical substance | mole | mol |

## Metric prefixes

*deka*—ten times

*hecto*—hundred times

*kilo*—thousand times

*mega*—million times

*giga*—billion times

*tera*—trillion times

*deci*—tenth of

*centi*—hundredth of

*milli*—thousandth of

*micro*—millionth of

*nano*—billionth of

*pico*—trillionth part

*femto*—quadrillionth part

## Derived Units of Measurement

newton (force): the force required to accelerate a mass of 1 kilogram 1 meter per second per second

pascal (pressure): 1 newton per square meter

## Linear Measures

|  | No. of meters | U.S. equivalent (approx.) |
|---|---|---|
| kilometer (km) | 1000 | 0.62 miles |
| hectometer (hm) | 100 | 328.08 feet |
| decameter (dam) | 10 | 32.81 feet |
| meter (m) |  | 3.28 feet or 39.37 inches |
| decimeter (dm) | 0.1 | 3.94 inches |
| centimeter (cm) | 0.01 | 0.39 inches |
| millimeter (mm) | 0.001 | 0.039 inches |
| micrometer (μm) | 0.000001 | 0.000039 inches |

## Area Measures

|  | No. of square meters | U.S. equivalent |
|---|---|---|
| square kilometer (km²) | 1,000,000 | 0.3861 square miles |
| hectare (ha) | 10,000 | 2.47 acres |
| are (a) | 100 | 119.6 square yards |
| square meter (m²) |  | 1.196 square yards |
| square centimeter (cm²) | 0.0001 | 0.155 square inches |

## Capacity

|  | No. of liters | U.S. equivalent |
|---|---|---|
| kiloliter (kl) | 1000 | 264 gallons |
| hectoliter (hl) | 100 | 26.4 gallons |
| dekaliter (dkl) | 10 | 2.64 gallons |
| liter (l) |  | 1.057 quarts |
| deciliter (dl) | 0.1 | 3.4 fluid ounces |
| centiliter (cl) | 0.01 | 0.34 fluid ounces |
| milliliter (ml) | 0.001 | 0.034 fluid ounce |
| microliter (µl) | 0.000001 |  |

## Mass and Weight

|  | No. of grams | U.S. equivalent |
|---|---|---|
| metric ton (t) | 1,000,000 (1000 kg) | 1.102 short tons |
| kilogram (kg) | 1000 | 2.2046 pounds |
| hectogram (hg) | 100 | 3.527 ounces |
| dekagram (dkg) | 10 | 0.353 ounces |
| gram (g) |  | 0.035 ounces |

| decigram (dg) | 0.1 | 0.0035 ounces |
| centigram (cg) | 0.01 | 0.00035 ounces |
| microgram (μg) | 0.000001 | |

# Conversion Tables

## LENGTH

| To convert | multiply by |
| --- | --- |
| inches to millimeters | 25.4 |
| inches to centimeters | 2.54 |
| feet to meters | 0.3048 |
| yards to meters | 0.9144 |
| miles to kilometers | 1.61 |
| millimeters to inches | .03937 |
| centimeters to inches | 0.3937 |
| meters to feet | 3.28 |
| meters to yards | 1.0936 |
| kilometers to miles | 0.621 |

## WEIGHT

| To convert | multiply by |
| --- | --- |
| ounces to grams | 28.35 |
| pounds to kilograms | 0.4536 |
| grams to ounces | 0.03527 |
| kilograms to pounds | 2.2046 |

# AREA

| To convert | multiply by |
|---|---|
| square inches to square centimeters | 6.4516 |
| square feet to square meters | 0.0929 |
| square yards to square meters | 0.836 |
| square miles to square kilometers | 2.5887 |
| acres to hectares | 0.4047 |
| square centimeters to square inches | 0.155 |
| square meters to square feet | 10.764 |
| square meters to square yards | 1.196 |
| square kilometers to square miles | 0.3863 |
| hectares to acres | 2.471 |

# VOLUME

| To convert | multiply by |
|---|---|
| cubic inches to cubic centimeters | 16.387 |
| cubic inches to liters | 0.016387 |
| cubic feet to cubic meters | 0.0283 |
| cubic yards to cubic meters | 0.7646 |
| cubic centimeters to cubic inches | 0.061 |
| liters to cubic inches | 61.024 |
| cubic meters to cubic feet | 35.3357 |
| cubic meters to cubic yards | 1.3079 |

# CAPACITY

| To convert | multiply by |
| --- | --- |
| quarts to liters | 0.946 |
| gallons to liters | 3.784 |
| gallons to cubic meters | 0.003785 |
| liters to quarts | 1.0565 |
| liters to gallons | 0.26412 |
| cubic meters to gallons | 264.172 |

# MASS AND WEIGHT

| To convert | multiply by |
| --- | --- |
| ounces to grams | 28.3495 |
| pounds to kilograms | 0.4536 |
| grams to ounces | 0.03527 |
| kilograms to pounds | 2.205 |

# POWER

| To convert | multiply by |
| --- | --- |
| horsepower to kilowatts | 0.7457 |
| kilowatts to horsepower | 1.341 |

# GAS MILEAGE

| To convert | multiply by |
| --- | --- |
| miles per gallon to kilometers per liter | 0.425 |
| kilometers per liter to miles per gallon | 2.353 |

## VELOCITY

| To convert | multiply by |
|---|---|
| miles per hour to kilometers per hour | 1.61 |
| kilometers per hour to miles per hour | 0.621 |

# Trigonometric Functions and Right Triangles

## RIGHT-TRIANGLE TRIGONOMETRY

$$\text{sine} A \ (\sin A) = a/c$$
$$\text{cosine} A \ (\cos A) = b/c$$
$$\text{tangent} A \ (\tan A) = a/b$$
$$\text{cosecant} A \ (\csc A) = 1/\sin A = c/a$$
$$\text{secant} A \ (\sec A) = 1/\cos A = c/b$$
$$\text{cotangent} A \ (\cot A) = 1/\tan A = b/a$$

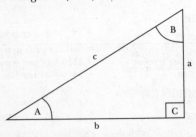

*Pythagorean Theorem:* $a^2 + b^2 = c^2$

*Law of Sines:* $\dfrac{a}{\sin A} = \dfrac{b}{\sin B} = \dfrac{c}{\sin C}$

*Law of Cosines:* $a^2 = b^2 + c^2 - 2 \times b \times c \times \cos A$
$b^2 = a^2 + c^2 - 2 \times a \times c \times \cos B$
$c^2 = a^2 + b^2 - 2 \times a \times b \times \cos C$

**Identities**

$$\sin^2\theta + \cos^2\theta = 1$$
$$1 + \tan^2\theta = \sec^2\theta$$
$$1 + \cot^2\theta = \csc^2\theta$$

$$\sin\theta = \cos(90° - \theta)$$
$$\cos\theta = \sin(90° - \theta)$$
$$\tan\theta = \cot(90° - \theta)$$
$$\cot\theta = \tan(90° - \theta)$$

# Physical Constants

| | |
|---|---|
| Velocity of light in a vacuum | $\approx$ 300,000 km/sec or 186,000 mi/sec |
| Velocity of sound at sea level at 0°C (called Mach 1) | = 331.5 meters per second<br>= 1087 feet per second<br>= 741 miles per hour |
| Velocity of sound at sea level at 60°C | = 340.3 meters per second<br>= 1116 feet per second<br>= 761 miles per hour |
| Velocity of sound through water at 60°C | = 1450 meters per second<br>= 4750 feet per second<br>= 3240 miles per hour |
| Equatorial radius of the earth | = 3963.34 statute miles or 6378.338 km |
| Circumference of the equator | $\approx$ 24,900 miles |

# Rules of Thumb for Measuring and Calculating

A dollar bill is 6⅛ inches long and 2⅝ inches wide.

A standard business card is 3½ inches long and 2 inches wide.

A standard credit card is 3⅜ inches long and 2⅛ inches wide.

A dime has a diameter of ⁹⁄₁₆ inch, which is also the thickness of a stack of 100 sheets of ordinary paper.

A penny has a diameter of ¾ inch.

A quarter has a diameter of ¹⁵⁄₁₆ inch.

A gallon of water weighs about 8.5 pounds.

A gallon of gasoline weighs about 5.8 pounds.

# Index